ALSO BY
ROBERT NOZICK

Anarchy, State, and Utopia

Philosophical Explanations

THE
Examined Life
PHILOSOPHICAL MEDITATIONS

Robert Nozick

A TOUCHSTONE BOOK

Published by Simon & Schuster

New York London Toronto Sydney Tokyo Singapore

Touchstone
Simon & Schuster Building
Rockefeller Center
1230 Avenue of the Americas
New York, New York 10020

Designed by Irving Perkins Associates
Manufactured in the United States of America

3   5   7   9   10   8   6   4

3   5   7   9   10   8   6   4   Pbk.

Library of Congress Cataloging in Publication Data

Nozick, Robert.
The examined life: philosophical meditations/Robert Nozick.
p.   cm.
Includes bibliographical references.
1. Life. 2. Conduct of life. I. Title.
BD431.N65   1989
191—dc20   89-37720
                          CIP

ISBN 0-671-47218-6

ISBN 0-671-72501-7 Pbk.

ACKNOWLEDGMENTS

THIS book underwent many rewritings and I am extremely grateful to friends and family for their comments and encouragement. Eugene Goodheart, Bill Puka, and Stephen Phillips read several versions of the manuscript and offered extensive and very helpful comments and advice; Emily and David Nozick stayed interested and curious; Hilary Putnam, Sissela Bok, Harold Davidson, and Robert Asahina interjected helpful comments or cautions at various times. My wife, Gjertrud Schnackenberg, nurtured the book and me.

The writing took four years and began with a month's stay at Yaddo in 1984–85, a sabbatical year from Harvard for me; it was completed during another year's leave, 1987–88, spent in Rome under the hospitality of the American Academy in Rome. I had been mulling this project over since 1981. An early stage of thinking was supported by a grant from the John M. Olin Foundation, the middle stages by a grant from the Sarah Scaife Foundation, the last stage of writing by a Fellowship from the National Endowment for the Humanities. I revised the manuscript very extensively during a stay at the Villa Serbelloni, the Rockefeller Foundation Study Center at Bellagio. I am grateful to these institutions for their help.

CONTENTS

CONTENTS

THE

Examined Life

1

Introduction

I WANT TO THINK about living and what is important in life, to
clarify my thinking—and also my life. Mostly we tend—I do too—to
live on automatic pilot, following through the views of ourselves and
the aims we acquired early, with only minor adjustments. No doubt
there is some benefit—a gain in ambition or efficiency—in somewhat
unthinkingly pursuing early aims in their relatively unmodified form,
but there is a loss, too, when we are directed through life by the not
fully mature picture of the world we formed in adolescence or young
adulthood. Freud tellingly depicted the strong and lingering effects
of an even younger age, how the child's passionate desires, inadequate understanding, restricted emotional environment, constricted
opportunities, and limited coping devices become fixed upon his
own adult emotional life and reactions and continue to affect them.
This situation is (to say the least) unseemly—would *you* design an
intelligent species so continuingly shaped by its childhood, one
whose emotions had no half-life and where statutes of limitations
could be invoked only with great difficulty? A similar point applies

to early adulthood. It is no disparagement of young adults to think that they *could* not then know enough to set or understand a whole life's course. It would be sad if nothing important about life were learned along the way.

Life or living is not the kind of topic whose investigation philosophers find especially rewarding. Give us specific problems to solve or paradoxes to resolve, sharp questions with enough angle or spin, an elaborate intellectual structure to move within or modify, and we can sharply etch a theory, press intuitive principles to surprising consequences, and perform intellectual figure eights, all the while meeting clear standards of success. However, thinking about life is more like mulling it over, and the more complete understanding this brings does not feel like crossing a finishing line while still managing to hold onto the baton; it feels like growing up more.

Philosophical meditations about life present a *portrait,* not a theory. This portrait may be made up of theoretical pieces—questions, distinctions, explanations. Why isn't happiness the only thing that matters? What would immortality be like and what would be its point? Should inherited wealth be passed on through many generations? Are Eastern doctrines of enlightenment valid? What is creativity and why do people postpone embarking upon promising projects? What would be lost if we never felt any emotions yet could have pleasurable feelings? How has the Holocaust changed humanity? What is askew when a person cares mainly about personal wealth and power? Can a religious person explain why God allows evil to exist? What is especially valuable in the way romantic love alters a person? What is wisdom and why do philosophers love it so? What shall we make of the gap between ideals and actuality? Are some existing things more real than others, and can we ourselves too become more real? Yet the concatenation of these bits of theory constitutes a portrait nonetheless. Think of what it is like to dwell before a painted portrait—one by Raphael or Rembrandt or Holbein, for example—and to let it then dwell within you. Think also of the ways this differs from reading a clinical description of a particular person, or a general psychological theory.

The understanding gained in examining a life itself comes to permeate that life and direct its course. To live an examined life is to make a self-portrait. Staring out at us from his later self-portraits,

Rembrandt is not simply someone who looks like that but one who also sees and knows himself *as* that, with the courage this requires. We see him knowing himself. And he unflinchingly looks out at us too who are seeing him look so unflinchingly at himself, and that look of his not only shows himself to us so knowing, it patiently waits for us too to become with equal honesty knowing of ourselves.

Why is it that no photograph of a person has the depth a painted portrait can have? The two embody different quantities of time. A photograph is a "snapshot," whether or not it was posed; it shows one particular moment of time and what the person looked like right then, what his surface showed. During the extended hours a painting is sat for, though, its subject shows a range of traits, emotions, and thoughts, all revealed in differing lights. Combining different glimpses of the person, choosing an aspect here, a tightening of muscle there, a glint of light, a deepening of line, the painter interweaves these different portions of surface, never before simultaneously exhibited, to produce a fuller portrait and a deeper one. The portraitist can select one tiny aspect of everything shown at a moment to incorporate into the final painting. A photographer might attempt to replicate this, isolating and layering and interweaving aspects of many photographs of the face at different times; could these many minute choices then result in a final printed photograph that achieved the full depth of a painting? (The experiment is worth trying, if only to isolate what is *special* to painting in contrast to even a highly manipulated photographic process, what is contributed, for example, by the special tonalities of oil paint and by the tactile resonance of different ways of applying and building the paint.) However, during the hours he spends with his subject, a painter can come to know things the visible surface did not show—what the person said, the manner of his behavior toward others—and hence add or emphasize details to bring to the surface what resides underneath.

The painter concentrates a person over an extended time into a presence at one moment that, however, cannot be taken in fully in a moment. Because so much more time is concentrated in a painting than a photograph, we need—and want—to spend more time before it, letting the person unfold. In our own memory, too, perhaps we recall people in a way that is more like paintings than snapshot photographs, creating composite images that include details we have culled over many hours of seeing; a painter then would be doing with greater skill and more control what our memory does naturally.

Concentratedness too underlies the richness, depth, and sharpness of focus a novel can achieve, in comparison to a film. A salient aspect of demeanor can be described verbally to the exclusion of others—the pictorial eye takes in all aspects that are simultaneous—and the writer can interweave these selected salient aspects to form a rich texture. Not only is there concentration of detail, thought itself becomes concentrated as the novelist in draft after draft reshapes his sentences into a work more highly wrought and controlled. The editing of film, however, snaps together different already existing bits of footage—yet film too can achieve concentration, as many have emphasized, by interweaving closeups and shots from different angles at different times.

It is likely, though, that more years of thought are devoted to fashioning the contents of a novel, making its texture—think here of the great nineteenth-century novels—more dense than a film's. Thought, too, and painful effort can be devoted to paring language—as with Beckett—and this very bareness serves an unmatched intensity of focus. I do not mean to suggest an intellectual-labor theory of value that focuses upon "thoughtful production time" but ignores differences in talent or inspiration. Nor do I deny the existence of densely textured films whose makers have mulled them over for years; Kurosawa's *Ran* and Bergman's *Fanny and Alexander* are two recent examples. Still, when all other things are equal, the more concentrated thought goes into making something, the more it is shaped, enriched, and laden with significance. So too with living a life.

The activities of a life are infused by examination, not just affected by it, and their character is different when permeated by the results of concentrated reflection. They are interpreted differently—so too are the alternatives forgone—within the hierarchy of reasons and purposes examination has yielded. Moreover, since we can see the components of our life, including its activities and strivings, as fitting together in a pattern, when an additional and distinctive component such as reflection is added—like adding new scientific data to be fit to a curve—a new overall pattern then results. The old components too then get seen and understood differently, just as previous scientific data points now are seen as fitting a new curve or equation. Therefore, examination and reflection are not just *about* the other components of life; they are added *within* a life, alongside the rest, and by their presence call for a new overall pattern that alters how each part of life is understood.

There are very few books that set out what a mature person can believe—someone fully grown up, I mean. Aristotle's *Ethics,* Marcus Aurelius's *Meditations,* Montaigne's *Essays,* and the essays of Samuel Johnson come to mind. Even with these, we do not simply accept everything that is said. The author's voice is never our own, exactly; the author's life is never our own. It would be disconcerting, anyway, to find that another person holds precisely our views, responds with our particular sensibility, and thinks exactly the same things important. Still, we can gain from these books, weighing and pondering ourselves in their light. These books—and also some less evidently grown-up ones, Thoreau's *Walden* and Nietzsche's writings, for example—invite or urge us to think along with them, branching in our own directions. We are not identical with the books we read, but neither would we be the same without them.

Nietzsche has his Zarathustra say, "This is *my* way, where is yours? . . . *The* way—that does not exist." I do not claim, with Nietzsche, that *the* way does not exist—I just don't know—though I do wonder why we crave it so. Still, all this book tries to present, as openly and honestly and thoughtfully as I can, is my version of our lives. Yet I also ask, not just here but throughout, what way is yours? Perhaps this question could sound belligerent, like a challenge to propose a more adequate view than mine if you disagree, in essence taking back my claim to be presenting just one way. But I ask it as a fellow human being, limited in what I know and value, in the meanings I am able to discern and delineate, who wants to learn from another. My thoughts do not aim for your assent—just place them alongside your own reflections for a while.

I do not say with Socrates that the unexamined life is not worth living—that is unnecessarily harsh. However, when we guide our lives by our own pondered thoughts, it then is *our* life that we are living, not someone else's. In this sense, the unexamined life is not lived as fully.

An examination of life utilizes whatever you can bring to bear and shapes you fully. It is difficult for us to grasp precisely what another's conclusions about life come to, without seeing what that person is like who fits these conclusions and who reaches them. Hence, we need to encounter the person—the *figure* of Socrates in the early dialogues of Plato, the figure of Jesus in the Gospels, Montaigne in his own voice, Thoreau in an autobiographical mode, Buddha in his actions and speech. In order to assess and weigh what they tell us, we have to assess and weigh what they are.

The philosophical tradition since Plato has sought to ground ethics by showing that our own well-being is served or enhanced by behaving ethically. To substantiate this, one would first have to understand what is important in life, and afterward depict the role and importance of ethical behavior in those terms. My meditations too begin some distance from ethical considerations; abstracting from ethics facilitates seeing beyond the remedial to what our lives would be occupied with in a time when people no longer desperately needed help. When ethics comes on the scene only later, however, it holds a disproportionately small place and the discussion until then is affected by its absence. It might be more appropriate if a book on life were like a perspectival painting with the important topics looming large in the foreground, each thing having a size or saliency proportionate to its importance. The reader reaching the end of this book will have to cast her mind back over what has come before, seeing it anew in the light of the ethics that ensues, rather as if she has wandered through a painting into the background and now has turned around to see her earlier sights from this new and very marked perspective.

As I reflect now about what is important in life, all I have is my current understanding, in part derived from what I can make of what others have understood, and this no doubt will change. Before adding to what others have written, in decency shouldn't one wait for one's most mature thinking or even intend publication only posthumously? However, such thoughts might diminish in other ways—in energy or vividness, for example. We can be impelled to think by another's interim expression, by thoughts that are still happening.

We do not want to get committed to any one particular understanding or locked into it. This danger looms large for writers; in the public's mind or in their own they easily can become identified with a particular "position." Having myself written earlier a book of political philosophy that marked out a distinctive view, one that now seems seriously inadequate to me—I will say some words about this later on—I am especially aware of the difficulty of living down an intellectual past or escaping it. Other people in conversation often want me to continue to maintain that young man's "libertarian" position, even though they themselves reject it and probably would prefer that no one had ever maintained it at all. In part, this may be due to people's psychological economy—I speak of my own here too. Once having pigeonholed people and figured out what they are saying, we do not welcome new information that would require us to re-understand and reclassify them, and we resent their forcing us to devote fresh energy to this when we have expended more than enough in their direction already! I would do well to recognize, somewhat ruefully, that these meditations too may exert their own retarding gravitational force.

However, it is not quite *positions* I wish to present here. I used to think it important, when I was younger, to have an opinion on just about every topic: euthanasia, minimum-wage legislation, who would win the next American League pennant, whether Sacco and/or Vanzetti were guilty, whether there were any synthetic necessary truths—you name it. When I met someone who had an opinion on a topic I hadn't yet even heard of, I felt a need to form one too. Now I find it very easy to say I don't have an opinion on something and don't need one either, even when the topic elicits active public controversy, so I am somewhat bemused by my earlier stance. It is not that I was opinionated, exactly; I was quite open to reasons for changing an opinion, and I did not try to press mine upon others. I just had to have some opinion or other—I was "opinionful." Perhaps opinions are especially useful to the young. Philosophy too is a subject that seems to invite opinions, "positions" on free will, the nature of knowledge, the status of logic, etc. In these meditations, however, it is enough, it might be better even, simply to mull topics through.

My concern in writing here is the whole of our being; I would like to speak to your whole being, and to write from mine. What can this mean: what are the parts of our being; what is the whole? Plato distinguished three parts of the soul: the rational part, the courageous part, and the appetites or passions. Ranking these parts in that order, he held that the harmonious life, also the best life, was one where the rational part ruled the other two parts. (We might seek relations even more harmonious than one part *ruling* the others.) Freud, it is well known, presented two divisions of uncertain relation to each other: one of the self into ego, id, and superego; the other of modes of consciousness into conscious and unconscious (and also preconscious)—alternative categorizations have been provided by more recent psychologists. Some writers have held that there is an imaginative part of the self, not easily placed in a linear ranking with the rational. Eastern views speak of layered centers of energy and levels of consciousness. Even the self might turn out to be only one particular structure, a part or aspect of our entire being. Some have held that there is a spiritual part, higher than all the rest.

What happens in philosophy now is that the same part speaks and listens, the rational mind speaks to the rational mind. It is not limited to speaking only about itself; the subject matter can include other parts of our being, other parts of the cosmos, as well. Nevertheless, what speaks and to whom, speaker and audience both, is the mind's rational part.

The history of philosophy exhibits a more varied texture, though. Plato argued and developed abstract theories, but he also spoke evocative myths that linger in memory—about people in a cave, about separated half-souls. Descartes rooted his most powerful writing in what was then Catholic meditative practice; Kant expressed his awe of two things, "the starry heavens above and the moral law within." Nietzsche and Kierkegaard, Pascal and Plotinus: the list could continue. Yet the predominant current perspective on philosophy has been "cleansed" to leave a tradition in which the rational mind speaks (only) to the rational mind.

That purified activity has a value that is real and abiding—I expect that my next work will aim at this more austere virtue. Yet there is no overwhelming reason to limit all of philosophy to that. We come to philosophy originally as people who want to think about things, and philosophy is just one way to do that; it need not exclude the modes of essayists, poets, novelists, or makers of other symbolic structures, modes aiming at truth in different ways and at things in addition to truth.*

Would such a philosophy have each different part of our being speak to its corresponding part, or does each one get spoken to by all; does this occur simultaneously or in sequence? Wouldn't such a book have to be a hodgepodge of genres and voices? Are we not best served through a division of labor where each genre does what it does best, with works of philosophy containing only reasoning, argument, theory, explanations, and speculation, and so being clearly distinct from aphorisms, opera, stories, mathematical models, autobiography, fables, therapy, created symbols, and hypnotic trances? Yet the different parts of our being are not themselves similarly separated. Something needs to speak to them together, to provide a model of how they are to be wed. Even an attempt that fails ultimately can evoke our latent need and thereby serve it.

Once upon a time, philosophy promised more than simply contents of thought. "Citizens of Athens," Socrates asked, "aren't you ashamed to care so much about making all the money you can and advancing your reputation and prestige, while for truth and wisdom and the improvement of your souls you have no thought or care?" He spoke of the state of our souls, and he showed us the state of his own.

---

* Do philosophical thought and questioning, by their very nature, though, eventuate not in novels by James or Proust but in something more like the intelligent Martian's primer of human life?

2

Dying

THEY SAY NO ONE is able to take seriously the possibility of his or her own death, but this does not get it exactly right. (Does everyone take seriously the possibility of his or her own life?) A person's own death does become real to him after the death of both parents. Until then, there was someone else who was "supposed to" die before him; now that no one stands between him and death, it becomes his "turn." (Is it presumed that death will honor a queue?)

Details may be hazy, however. An only child, I don't know if older siblings are supposed to go first. Admetus went so far as to *ask* his parents to die in his place—but, then, he asked his wife, Alcestis, too. My eighty-two-year-old father now is ailing, my mother gone for more than a decade. Mingled with concern for my father is the thought that he is blazing a trail for me; I now suspect I will reach my eighties too and—less welcome—perhaps encounter similar woes. People who commit suicide also mark a path for their children by giving them a parent's permission to end life. Identification then finishes what genes may begin.

How unwilling someone is to die should depend, I think, upon what he has left undone, and also upon his remaining capacity to do things. The more what he considered important has been done, and the less the capacity that remains, the more willing he should be to face death. Deaths are called "untimely" when they end lives where much still was possible that went unfulfilled. But when you no longer have the capacity to do what is undone, or when you have done all that you considered important, then—I want to say—you should not be so very unwilling to die. (Yet if nothing important is possible or left, mightn't being someone who continues even so be one of the important ways to be? And having done everything you considered important, mightn't you set yourself a *new* goal?) In principle, a person's regrets when death approaches should be affected by *all* of the important actions left undone. However, some particularly salient hopes or accomplishments might stand as surrogate for the rest; "I never managed to do *that*," he might think, or "Since *this* was included in my life, I can die content."

Might formulas bring more precision to these matters? We can see a person's *regret* over the way he has lived as being due to the ratio of the important things he has left undone (that once he could have done) to the important things he has done. (It follows from this formula that his regret is greater the more he has left undone, or the less he has done.) His degree of *satisfaction* with his life might be fixed by just the opposite ratio, so that his satisfaction is greater the more he has done, or the less he has left undone. And his regret at dying right then—which is different from his regret over the way he has lived—might be seen as being due to the extent to which death cuts short his doing things—that is, the percent of important things he hasn't yet done that he now still has the capacity to do. Although we cannot make such measurements precise, it is illuminating to notice what structure these ratios bring.

The processes of aging, by reducing the capacity to do things, thereby reduce the amount of regret at dying right then. Here the relevant capacities are those someone thinks he possesses, and a gradual process of aging alters his conception of this. However, it would not be a good strategy in life to attempt to reduce your regret at dying by reducing your capacities as much as possible all along. That would reduce the amount you do in life, thereby increasing your regret over the way you have lived. Nor will it do simply to reduce your wanting to do important things; while that might influence the psychological degree of your regret, it would not affect how regrettable such a life is, as fixed by the ratios involving what you've done in life and what you've left undone. The general moral is reasonably clear and unsurprising: We should do what it is important to do, be the way it is important to be.

A major purpose of these meditations is to investigate what the important things are—not in preparation for dying but to advance living. It is undeniably important to avoid the worst fates—*not* to be paralyzed and comatose for the preponderance of one's life, *not* to be forced to witness those you love being tortured, and so on—but I mean to refer to things, activities, and ways of being that are positive and good. As for what typically goes on psychologists' lists of what constitutes "positive mental health"—things such as being healthy and confident, having self-esteem, being adaptable, caring—we might specify our subject by supposing such traits already are present. The question then becomes: How should someone live who has reached the ample launching pad these traits provide? (This supposition that the traits are present is introduced simply as an intellectual device to direct our attention to other questions; we can pursue and attain the things that are important without first fully possessing all those traits.)

Some undergo much torment before dying: weak, unable to walk or turn in bed unaided, constantly in pain, frightened, demoralized. After we have done all we can to help, we can share with them the *fact of* their suffering. They need not suffer alone; whether or not this makes the suffering less painful, it makes it more bearable. We also can share the fact of someone's dying, reducing temporarily the way death cuts off connection to others. Sharing someone's dying, we realize that someday we may share with others the fact of *our* dying—someday our children will comfort us—and those with whom our dying is shared will in their turn share theirs. Superimposing the current and future situation, we can feel at each end of the relation, simultaneously giver and receiver of comfort. Is what matters our sharing the fact of a death, not the particular position we occupy this time?

I find I don't like to think I'm much more than halfway to the end of the major thing I am engaged in. There is leeway to decide what this is, though, and so I adjust boundaries accordingly to create new midpoints. "Not yet halfway through *life*"—that served until the late thirties or the age of forty; "halfway through work life after college" got me to the age of forty-five, "halfway after college to the very end" gets me approximately to now. I next need to find still another midpoint not to be much beyond, and I hope to continue making these adjustments at least until old age, which too for a while I will be no more than halfway through. All this is so that I will be able to think there is as much ahead as behind, as much of something good. The strange fact is that even as I smile at my shifting the boundaries to create a new salient midpoint and a different second half, still it works!

Death does not always mark the boundary of a person's life as an end that stands outside it; sometimes it is a *part* of that life, continuing its narrative story in some significant way. Socrates, Abraham Lincoln, Joan of Arc, Jesus, and Julius Caesar all had deaths that were further episodes of their lives, not simply endings, and we are able to see their lives as *heading* toward those immortal deaths. Not every death of an extraordinary person inflicted for his or her beliefs or mode of life becomes a vivid part of that person's life— Gandhi's death did not, for example. When death does constitute a life's completion, would it be any the more welcome for being that?

We are reluctant to believe that all of what we are gets erased in death; we seem to ourselves deeper than the mere stoppage of life can reach. Yet the writings on "survival" and the evidence for it seem jejune. Perhaps whatever continues is unable to communicate with us, or has more important things to do, or thinks we'll find out soon enough anyway—how much energy, after all, do *we* devote to sig-naling to fetuses that there is a realm to follow?

If death were not extinction—*if*—what then would it be like? (Even if we think nonextinction is extremely unlikely, we can spec-ulate about what, given or supposing this unlikelihood will occur, then would ensue.) My guess—no better than anyone else's— is that it would have a character rather like meditative states in the Hindu or Buddhist traditions, involving conscious states, perhaps including imagery (but not physical perceptions), a state resembling *samadhi,* nirvana, or enlightenment.

Or perhaps each person, in death, permanently is in the highest and most real state she reliably reached during her lifetime, unaided by chemicals, etc. Is realizing this the reason meditative masters (are said to) face death with calmness and equanimity? Or perhaps survival is not a permanent immortality but more like a temporary echo of the life it follows, one that fades away unless further steps are taken then to organize and develop it.

Nonextinction is not unalloyedly cheerful in this view; a person can die before reaching the highest consciousness he is capable of or can sentence himself permanently through his own choices to a lower state. Permanently dwelling in the *highest* state you managed reliably to reach is a more cheerful prospect, though, than permanently occupying the lowest or the average of these. Under any alternative, no doubt, we would welcome an additional chance—it would be ironic if we did get one, but, not realizing it was a second chance, squandered it just like the first.

It might be nice to believe such a theory, but isn't the truth starker? This life is the only existence there is; afterward there is nothing. Even in thinking about death, I find it more congenial to speculate about a bright alternative, and I tend to one-quarter think that things are that way or that in any case we should live on that basis. Even on the starker view, I am reluctant simply to call it *finis;* I want to say, at least, that it will *always* be that we were what we were, and lived the life we did; also that our lives can become a permanent possibility for others to relate to.

I sometimes wonder if not having a taste for a dark or tragic view isn't a mark of superficiality. Yet cannot very different temperaments be equally valid? The great composers each have unique value; we do not wish any one of them had composed in another's style. There is a legitimate latitude for the rest of us too.

Nonsurvival is somber, but immortality too fits darker visions. Here is one that at present sounds like science fiction. One day, computer programs will be able to capture a person's intellectual mode, personality pattern, and character structure so that later generations can retrieve these. Thus would be realized one of immortality's two facets: continuing to exist as a coherent pattern of individual personality that another can experience. And the other facet, continuing to experience things and act, might be gained in part if the program encapsulating a person were made to govern a computer that acted in the world. Such immortality need not be wholly a blessing, however. Just as a person's ideas can be misused or vulgarized, so too could later civilizations exploit or misuse someone's individual personality, calling it up to serve projects and purposes the person never would have chosen to cooperate with when alive in the flesh. And it may not be simply your "individual personality" that is involved. If "your" programs were implanted into an organism, and experiences then induced in it, wouldn't it be *you* who had those experiences? Future civilizations then might be the eventual creators of heaven and hell, parceling out just deserts.

Does the desire somehow to survive physical death stem from the desire to have a larger purpose than we can find for ourselves on earth, another task we are to perform in another realm? We might think we each have the task here of making a soul for ourselves—souls might not be things we are born with—a task made more difficult by not knowing exactly what that soul is for. Perhaps it is more than our own individual souls we are to make, more even than a mosaic of souls together. In responding to the full reality of the world, its processes in their complex interrelations, its beauty, its deepest laws, in knowing the place of our full being, at all its levels, within this, we seem brought to see reality as a profound and wonderous creation. Whether or not it actually was produced through a creative activity, we are moved to delineate and feel those aspects that bespeak such a creation, and the search for them is rewarded amply. It would be exhilarating (and sobering) to think that someday and somewhere, alone or together, we too will have our chance at a creation, and that here we are discovering *one* way it can be done. Our task then would be to know as much of reality as possible and to become as able as possible to do a pleasing work of creation when our own turn comes—perhaps one that even would delight and surprise *our* maker. (Is our relation that of apprentice?)

One very recent speculative theory in cosmology holds that black holes might be newly created universes, which technology also might be able to create. Perhaps in time it also would be possible to shape the particular character of such a created universe nonhaphazardly. Here is a more extreme speculation, that in death a person's organized energy—some might say spirit—becomes the governing structure of a new universe that bubbles out orthogonally right there and then from the event of her death. The nature of the new universe created then will be determined by the level of reality, stability, serenity, etc., that she has managed to reach in her lifetime. And perhaps she then continues eternally as that kind of God of that universe. This immortality, at least, unlike that usually described, would not be *boring*. However, since many quite horrific universes would thereby be created, we would hope that at death only *some* kinds of organized energy can blossom into constituting another universe. (Should we be grateful to our God, then, for having a nature that led to a universe with stable scientific laws and processes and physical beauty on a vast scale?) The ultimate maxim of human life would then be to live as if a universe will be created in your image. (Are these exhilarating speculations or sad indications of how close to megalomania one must sail now to salvage hope?)

When I speculated first that immortality involves the highest state of consciousness and being we are able reliably to reach, no doubt I was willing to project this upon immortality because I care greatly about our present being and consciousness. We might run the projection in the other direction, though. First see what conception of immortality would be best—immortality lasts for a *very* long time—and then (to the extent this is possible) live right now in that mode. Whether or not there is to be a further immortality, live now as if immortality will *continue* and *repeat,* and not merely depend upon, some aspect of yourself and your life.

However, some particular things are desirable only in small finite doses; if there were no immortality to come, mightn't it be best to strive for some such limited thing—there then would be no worries about its *eventually* becoming monotonous or unsatisfactory—instead of for whatever would be best (but) only on the supposition that it and all its alternatives were going to continue endlessly? We should live, I want to say, as though some aspect of our life and being were eternal. It is all the more important to do this if we are wholly finite—as I three-quarters think—for thereby we attach to ourselves the dignity of eternity, if not the fact.

I am not sure, however, whether we should be so attached to *existing*. Why do we want to be told that we continue in time, that death is somehow unreal, a pause rather than an ending? Do we really *want* to continue always to exist? Do we want to travel with our rickety identity forever? Do we want to continue in some sense as an "I," a (changed) center of consciousness, or to be merged into a wider already existing one in order not to miss any of the show? Yet how greedy are we? Is there no point when we will have had *enough*?

I understand the urge to cling to life until the very end, yet I find another course more appealing. After an ample life, a person who still possesses energy, acuity, and decisiveness might choose to seriously risk his life or lay it down for another person or for some noble and decent cause. Not that this should be done lightly or too soon, but some time before the natural end—current health levels might suggest an age between seventy and seventy-five—a person might direct his or her mind and energy toward helping others in a more dramatic and risky fashion than younger, more prudent folk would venture. These activities might involve great health risks in order to serve the sick, risks of physical harm in interposing oneself between oppressors and their victims—I have in mind the kinds of peaceful activities and nonviolent resistance that Gandhi and Martin Luther King engaged in, not a vigilante pursuit of wrongdoers—or in aiding people within violence-ridden areas. Utilizing the freedom of action that is gained by the willingness to run serious risks, people's ingenuity will devise new modes and patterns of effective action which others can emulate, individually or jointly. Such a path will not be for everyone, but some might seriously weigh spending their penultimate years in a brave and noble endeavor to benefit others, an adventure to advance the cause of truth, goodness, beauty, or holiness—not going gentle into that good night or raging against the dying of the light but, near the end, shining their light most brightly.

3

Parents and Children

THERE IS NO bond I know stronger than being a parent. Having children and raising them gives one's life substance. To have done so is at least to have done that. The children themselves form part of one's substance. Without remaining subordinate or serving your purposes, they yet are organs of you. Parents reside within their children's unconscious, children in their parents' bodies. (A romantic mate lodges in the soul.) The connection to a child certainly involves the deepest love, sometimes annoyance or anger or hurt, but it does not exist solely at the level of emotion. It is not accurate or illuminating to say that I love my . . . hand.

In delineating the value and meaning of things I know—I write now of children in one's life, later of sexuality and heterosexual love—I recognize that value and meaning also can be found along other routes. Others I hope will evoke and examine the special (and common) value and meaning of what *they* saliently know.

Children form part of a wider identity you have. It is inappropriate to place upon them the burden of fulfilling your own ambitions, or for them to feel any such burden. Yet you still can feel that their qualities also are somehow your own, and that in your wider identity's division of labor they are taking care of some tasks. The accomplishments of parents might perhaps constitute a burden for their children but, in an asymmetry that seems unfair, those of the children redound to their parents too.

Being a parent helps one become a better child, a more forgiving grown-up child of one's parents, whom one now must act the parent to. One part of the transition to becoming a parent to one's parents is obvious: taking care of them when they are no longer able to cope fully for themselves. Another part is taking responsibility for the state of the relationship. When children are young, it is the task of parents to manage the relationship, to monitor it and keep it continuing on a somewhat even keel. During some brief period, perhaps, that responsibility becomes more equal, and then, before one has had time to notice it, it becomes the now-grown-up child's task to maintain the relationship, sometimes to pamper parents, to humor them, to avoid subjects that upset them, and to comfort the surviving one. If adolescence is sometimes marked by rebelling against one's parents and adulthood by becoming independent of them, what marks maturity is becoming a parent to them.

During *King Lear,* Cordelia comes to maturity. At the beginning she is the paragon of the most absolute and pure honesty, taking no pains to spare Lear's feelings or save him from public embarrassment, refusing to exaggerate her love, offering it "according to my bond, neither more nor less." Love's expression should be unbounded, but Cordelia wonders why her sisters marry if they love Lear all and she announces she will love him half. Especially should Cordelia, who lives with him, know how to handle and humor Lear, know how to manage the relationship and keep it going. She painfully learns. When Lear later says she has cause to hate him, she replies, "No cause, no cause." Yet Lear was right to say she has been given more cause than her sisters. The Cordelia of the first scene would have announced that she did have cause to such and such a degree, because she had suffered precisely to such and such an extent, insisting on stating the precise truth as she meticulously saw it. But after her own sufferings, and Lear's, Cordelia is able to express her love; she speaks of his living with her without announcing she loves him half. She has learned to say—and to feel—that, for hating her parent, she has "no cause, no cause."

Being grown-up is a way of no longer being a child, hence a way of relating to one's parents, not just by acting as their parent but by stopping needing or expecting them to act as yours; and this includes stopping expecting the world to be a symbolic parent, too. The task of trying now to get something from the world that symbolically represents our parents' adequate love is an impossible one. What is possible is to find a *substitute* for that love, something else that performs some of the same or analogous functions for us now as adults. The difference between a substitute for something, and that which must be it symbolically, is intricate and complex. Yet growing up and reaching maturity depends upon mastering that difference and turning, however wistfully, toward a substitute fit for an adult. You may then discover how very loving your parents had been, after all.

Bequeathing something to others is an expression of caring about them, and it intensifies those bonds. It also marks, and perhaps sometimes creates, an extended identity. The receivers—children, grandchildren, friends, or whoever—need not have earned what they receive. Although to some extent they may have earned the continuing affection of the bequeather, it is the donor who has earned the right to mark and serve her relational bonds by bequeathal.

Yet bequests that are received sometimes then are passed on for generations to persons unknown to the original earner and donor, producing continuing inequalities of wealth and position. Their receiving is no expression or outgrowth of *her* intimate bonds. If it seems appropriate for her to pass on what she has earned to those she cherishes and chooses, we are far less certain it is appropriate when these others do the same. The resulting inequalities seem unfair.

One possible solution would be to restructure an institution of inheritance so that taxes will subtract from the possessions people can bequeath the value of what they themselves have received through bequests. People then could leave to others only the amount they themselves have added to (the amount of) their own inheritance. Someone could bequeath to anyone she chose—mate, children, grandchildren, friends, etc. (We might add the further limitation that these all be existing people—or gestating ones—to whom there already can be actual ties and relations.) However, those who receive will not similarly be allowed to pass *that* on, although they will be able to pass on to whomever they choose what they themselves have earned and added. An inheritance could not cascade down the generations.

The simple subtraction rule does not perfectly disentangle what the next generation has managed itself to contribute—inheriting wealth may make it easier to amass more—but it is a serviceable rule of thumb.* To allow a person to make many bequests, yet limit these to one passing which cannot then be repeated or iterated, respects the importance and reality of bonds of caring, affection, and identification, without limiting these to one generation—grandchildren may be given to directly—but does not get extended to include the husk of continued inheritance without the personal substance.

One may ask, if the concern is for the reality and value of personal bonds, why shouldn't an inheritor be allowed to pass that inheritance on too, without first having his estate diminished by what he had inherited? After all, a person who has inherited certainly may have bonds to his own children, friends, and mate as strong as those had by the person who bequeathed the wealth to him. However, many philosophers—Hegel, for one—have commented on the ways in which property earned or created is an expression of the self and a component of it, so that one's identity or personality can become embued or extended in such a creation. When the original creator or earner passes something on, a considerable portion of his self participates in and constitutes this act, far more so than when a non-earner passes on something he has received but not created. If property is a bundle of rights to something (to consume, alter, transfer, spend, and bequeath it) then in bequest not all of these rights

---

* To determine what amount is first to be subtracted in tax, the monetary value of what one had received in inheritance would be calculated in contemporaneous dollars, corrected for inflation or deflation but not including actual or imputed interest earned. Placing an inheritance in a position to earn interest does count, I think, as an earning that may be passed on, after the amount of the original bequest is subtracted from the total. Harder questions are these: Would certain sorts or amounts of gifts be included also? How would the proposal avoid providing an incentive for squandering to those whose wealth near the end of their lives is not far above the amount taxes would subtract?

get transferred, and in particular the right to bequeath that item does not—this adheres to the original earner or creator.

In order to bar an exceedingly wealthy individual from enriching his complete lineal descent, we can add as a further specification to the institution of inheritance that a designated individual recipient must already exist. This further restriction might be objectionable even when the first is not. Consider the following objection, suggested to me by David Nozick. Mightn't a dying childless man donate sperm to a sperm bank and legitimately want to leave an inheritance to whatever future child or children of his might result? And if we permit this case, wouldn't we want to allow a person who leaves money directly to existing grandchildren also to make provision to leave it to whatever grandchildren will be born only years after he dies? Is there some principled way to allow these yet to block the extended concerns creators of wealth might have for the continuing wealth and power of their family through many generations? (I do not think this last evidences any actual relational tie of a weight that need be catered to.) Perhaps the following weaker restriction will suffice: A person may not bequeath to two unborn persons who are in different generations of descent from some last already existing node of a family tree. The first condition continues to hold, of course: Subtracted from the estate someone is able to bequeath will be the amount that person has inherited himself.

Notice that the power to bequeath may also bring a power to dominate, through the threat, explicit or implicit, *not* to bequeath if the potential receivers do not behave to one's satisfaction. We might conjecture that it is this power and continuing control that many wealthy people care about, rather than the ability to enhance and express the bonds of personal relations, and that their compliant children or associates would have been better off without any institution of inheritance at all.

Wealthy people devote their time to amassing money and spending it; they are able to pass this money on to their children. How may the rest of us leave what we have been concerned with? I have spent time thinking about things, reading, talking to people and listening to them, learning some subjects, traveling, looking. I too would like to leave to my children what I have amassed—some knowledge and understanding. It is pleasing to imagine a pill that would encapsulate a person's knowledge and could be given to his children. But then wouldn't the wealthy manage to purchase this too for their own? Perhaps bearers of scientific knowledge and research skills could develop a procedure to transmit adult knowledge that depended upon the recipient's neurons genetically overlapping the donor's; only those sharing half the donor's genes could be at the receiving end. (Unfortunately, this would not serve adoptive children.) Children would not thereby become clones of their parents— they would absorb and utilize and build upon this knowledge in their own ways, just as they do with books. How a society might be transformed over generations if this were possible is a theme for science fiction.

This scheme is undesirable, of course. With the truly worthwhile things we all start roughly evenly—I have written elsewhere that we all are immigrants to the world of thought. It would be oppressive if inequalities of understanding and knowledge were to pile up over generations. And given the ways in which some knowledge builds and depends upon other, it does not make any sense to contemplate a system analogous to the one we suggested for material wealth, whereby someone would pass on whatever knowledge he himself had gained, first subtracting that passed on to him. In any case, with truly worthwhile things such as knowledge and understanding—and curiosity and energy, kindness, love, and enthusiasm—we do not want to hoard these for ourselves or our own children only. What we can transmit directly, though, is a prizing of what is worthwhile, and an example.

4

Creating

CREATIVE ACTIVITY extends beyond the artistic and intellectual realms; it also can occur in everyday life. Its more rarefied instances help provide a lucid model for the rest. Yet to speak about the topic often bespeaks either vanity or yearning. Quoting Boris Pasternak's statement, "The aim of creating is the giving of oneself," Nadezhda Mandelstam writes, "With us, I remember, the word 'create' in this sense was taboo. What would you think of an artist who at the end of his day's work said to you: 'I have created a lot today,' or 'It is good to have a rest after creating.' 'Giving oneself'—in other words, expressing oneself—cannot be made into an end in itself without indulging in a secret desire to assert and promote oneself. Though why secret? It is absolutely blatant!"* No sooner had the notion of creativity emerged in the Italian Renaissance than it became impossible, in any case, for any person later—after Michelangelo, Brunelleschi, Leonardo, and the *host* of others—to take seriously their own.

* Nadezhda Mandelstam, *Hope Abandoned* (New York: Atheneum, 1974), p. 331.

Here, we can try to gain clarity about the phenomenon in its lesser instances.

To be creative is to make or do something novel—so far, so good—but to say specifically what creativity is, more details must be added. It won't count as creative if it simply happens by accident. It must occur through the exercise of an ability to make or do such novel things that also could be exercised on other occasions. Since some things are novel yet quite without value or use, one is tempted to add that a creative act must make something that also is valuable. However, it might be possible to be creative at doing or producing evil. While our concern here is with the creation of something desirable or valuable, we can specify the more general notion of creative activity as an activity that produces something (or is itself something) that is somehow novel along some dimension that is evaluative, even if that novelty be in a negative direction.

Whether or not there really is anything new under the sun, a creative act produces something new or novel in comparison to what the creator had encountered and known previously. If unbeknown to the creator someone else had produced something similar or identical—thinking up and proving a particular mathematical theorem, for example—still the creator's act would have been an act of creation. All that matters is that the effects of this earlier discovery have not seeped through and become known to the new discoverer in a way that makes his act less novel. Calling an act "creative" characterizes it only in relation to the materials it actually arose from, the earlier experiences and knowledge of the creator, not in relation to everything that has preceded it in the history of the universe.*

Creativeness is not an all or none affair. How creative something is depends both upon how novel it is and upon how valuable it is; and each of these has its degrees. A formula that shows how these two factors combine to determine the amount of creativity might be possible, but we need not provide it here.

Whether we call an act or product "novel," different from what went before, will depend upon which similarities and differences

---

* See John Hospers, "Artistic Creativity," *Journal of Aesthetics and Art Criticism,* 1985, pp. 243–255. Within science, though, there is the desire to be the *very first* discoverer; the role and function of this has been treated illuminatingly by Robert Merton in *The Sociology of Science* (Chicago: University of Chicago Press, 1983).

count as salient and important. It is trite to say that everything is like everything else in some respects, perhaps highly artificial ones, and different in others. Whether we call something new and different will depend in part on what pigeonholes of classification we actually have. Does it fall into the same category as previously known things or require a new category of its own? Also, it depends upon how different the new category is from the old. What seems like a sparkling new theorem to me might to a skilled mathematician seem like the drawing of an obvious corollary from an already known result. When we encounter beings from other stars or galaxies, if we and they differ in our classifications or in our sense of what counts as an obvious and natural next step to take—as seems likely—we also will differ in what we term creative.

One way a next step can be made obvious is by following directly from previous material, by mechanically applying an already known rule. For example, an existing multicolored geometrical shape is changed by replacing all its colors with their opposites on a color wheel. Unless applying that rule in this particular case counts as a creative leap, the new product will not count as creative, however much it differs in appearance and nature from whatever came before. Perhaps for a product to be creative it must not only differ from what came before but also stand in no specific obvious relation to its predecessors. (Being derivable from what came before through mechanical application of a clear rule counts as being obviously related.) Or perhaps the resulting product will not be termed creative, although it may have novel characteristics, because the act of producing it was not itself novel and creative, simply another application of that rule. In any case, we won't call something "creative," despite its having new and valuable characteristics in comparison to what came before, if it did not arise through a creative *process*.

A creative process need not actually produce a creative product every time. If Picasso had died while working on a painting, he would have been in the midst of a creative process then even if no valuable product had resulted yet. Rather, we might want to say that a creative process is one that *would* produce a creative product, but this definition still is too strong. Its subjunctive form is an improvement; it allows us to say a process is creative even if it is interrupted and has no result. But a creative process needn't be one that *always* would produce a valuable result, or even be one that would produce it more than 50 percent of the time. It is enough for the process to be good at producing such results, as compared to other processes or people, even if its absolute success rate is low. Einstein was gifted at thinking up new and valuable theories in physics, and when he worked at that task in the same way he did when he previously came up with his theory of Brownian motion or special relativity or general relativity, he was engaged in a creative process. Even if that process actually yielded valuable results only a small percentage of the times Einstein used it, still that was a much higher percentage than the rest of us would achieve at physics. One can lead the major leagues in hitting without batting over .500. (Of course, the "process" here includes the person doing it; the leading batter might be engaged in the same procedure as others, only he does it better.)

If someone in our own or another culture has standards of value that differ from ours, still we might call that person creative even if we can find no value in his novel products. For these might have been produced by a kind of process we want to term creative, namely one that *would* have produced valuable products unusually often, if only that process had been directed differently, by a more adequate conception of what was valuable.

Could there be mechanical and straightforward rules which will guarantee genuine creation and which we would have no trouble following? Making the unlikely supposition that such rules are possible, there would now be a dilemma. The rules guarantee producing things that are valuable and that appear new to others, but if what we produce comes by the conscious application of these (mechanical) rules, it will not count as being creative. (If earlier creative people were *unconsciously* applying such rules, would this call their creativity into question?)* Some writers also have emphasized other themes that would militate against creation through the mechanical application of rules—for example, the continuing critical control exerted by the artist in an attempt to get the product right according to

---

* We might wonder, though, about someone who devises or discovers such rules for herself and thereupon applies them. The act of discovery of the rules itself was creative. What about her application of these rules, then, supposing (implausibly) that these applications are merely mechanical? Here we might say that the sundry applications of these rules were not creative but that the resulting products were, because their origins trace back to her own original creative act of formulating the rules.

standards, standards he may modify somewhat in the course of discovering what his work is turning out to be.

Do we actually care about creativity, though, or are we only concerned about the resulting (apparently) new and valuable products? With regard to others, it may seem that only their products can matter to us; think of our attitude toward consumer goods. Yet our experience of Beethoven's string quartets would be diminished if we discovered he had stumbled upon someone else's rules for musical composition, which he then applied mechanically. We would no longer have the sense that something was being communicated to us, something he knew and felt profoundly. No longer could we marvel at the act of composition, or see the works as evidencing a human ability to transcend circumstances.

Presumably, Beethoven's natural gifts and creative spark were not created by him either. How then do they differ significantly from external rules for composition that he might stumble upon? It is not simply the internality of his talent that makes the difference; if he had come upon a little machine for musical composition and swallowed it, enabling himself to compose music as a player-piano performs it, we would not then admire his work as we now actually do. What if he swallowed a machine that could generate ideas for musical themes and structures, and then evaluated, altered, and tinkered with these ideas before incorporating them into the final work? His own contribution would be no different than that of a partner in a collaborative team; one generates the raw ideas, the other evaluates, refines, and elaborates them. Yet, even though the brain of a single creator in a partnership might be compared to a machine, there is a difference when one of the "partners" actually *is* one. (Even the comparison, however, would have to downplay the extent to which someone *cultivates* his talent, sets himself to exercise it, hones and refines it, etc.) For when it is a person's brain that generates ideas, however "mechanical" the explanation of how it does so turns out to be, we see those ideas as expressive and revelatory of something about the person. The resulting creative product is seen as an act of human communication, as the exercise of a *human* capacity for producing novelty.

For the person creating, there is something more. An important part of the work of artistic creation—also of those theoretical creations where there is great leeway—is work on the creator herself.

The creative work and product comes to stand, sometimes unconsciously, for herself or for a missing piece or part, or for a defective one, or for part of a better self. The work is a surrogate for the creator, an analog of her, a little voodoo doll to tinker with and transform and remake in something analogous to the way she herself, or a part, needs to be transformed, remade, or healed. The process of shaping and crafting an artistic work has, as an important part of its impulse, the reshaping and integration of parts of the self. Important and needed work on the self is modeled in the process of artistic creation, and symbolized there. (Might that work on the self also actually be advanced through the creative work that models it?) The artist herself can represent in her audience's mind a way and possibility of articulating and transforming a life and self.

Creativity itself is important, not simply the new and novel product, I conjecture, because the personal meaning of such creative activity is self-transformation in the fullest sense, transformation of the self and also transformation *by* the self. The process of artistic creation stands for our own autonomous recuperative and transformative powers. Perhaps an artistic product that was the result of mechanically applying rules could somehow stand for a new us, but it is no comfort if "you can't get there from here." When it is done creatively, the artistic product represents a more whole self we can get to under our own powers of enlargement and repair.

Not that artistic creation is *only* about the self; it also is about—perhaps it primarily is about—its themes, techniques, material, subject matter, and formal relationships. Yet creation does have the personal meaning we have described as well, and this helps to explain another somewhat puzzling phenomenon. Despite creative periods' being awaited, anticipated, intensely wanted, and thrilling, nevertheless they are frequently avoided and postponed. Days, weeks, or months of dedicated stalling can take place. To be sure, the blank canvas or blank first page usually will be a hurdle, not a pleasure. Still, other activities with pleasurable middles but difficult beginnings are not similarly postponed; we set out on vacations even when the initial process of travel or packing is stressful or boring. Perhaps in the case of beginning creative activity, there is the worry that no "inspiration" will come. Yet people with skill and experience may delay too, even when they already have promising or exciting ideas about what to do next. So this phenomenon of delay still requires some explanation.

Part of the answer, no doubt, lies in the very intensity and single-mindedness of creative activity. Other claims that will be pushed aside or neglected may be staging their protest. But creative work also is, symbolically, work upon the self, and the result of this is somewhat unpredictable because even works that are planned alter significantly during their execution. The self may be anxious about what artistic work will result and what new mode of self-formation this new work will represent. To be sure, the creating is controlled as it happens. Things can be altered in process; creation is not simply getting on a roller coaster. Yet even changes that are anticipated and desired can be unwelcome to those parts of the self that will be thereby altered or *demoted* in importance. Ambivalence about the changes involved in symbolic work on the self issues in postponement and stalling. (During this delay, do some parts exact better terms for themselves?)*

Writers on economics speak of "entrepreneurial alertness," the mind-set of being ready to notice and seize upon new profitable opportunities, devising new ways to make things or new things to make, imagining possibilities consumers would welcome, seeing opportunities for new economic combinations.† Such people, I imagine, have entrepreneurial antennae constantly directed to profitable opportunities. What someone sets herself to be alert to reveals that personality and shapes it. Creative people too are on the alert—but for something different: new projects, ideas that will aid them in their current projects, new combinations, elements, techniques, or material they can utilize in ongoing work. They scan the environment too quickly, often unconsciously, check the relevance of everything

---

* The demotion of a part may be in its absolute amount of fulfillment or in its relative position, for instance, from third most important to nineteenth. And a part might resist the latter, even if the total change would increase its absolute amount of fulfillment. The apparently paradoxical phenomenon of resistance to spiritual development may involve similar processes.

Not all delay has the same cause; when the explicitly planned artistic structure is inadequate for the material it is to receive, delay can aid the devising of a more adequate and fruitful structure. Also *ripening* can occur wherein within its basic structure a work matures, gains interconnection, acquires weight, and comes to its full maturity.

† See Israel Kirzner, *Competition and Entrepreneurship* (Chicago: University of Chicago Press, 1973).

they encounter to a current task or new project; if creativity too is a goal, they are alert for things suggesting new possibilities. By and large, this scanning and assessment takes place nonconsciously; few things are promising enough to be brought to conscious evaluation—most can be assessed and rejected automatically.

There is a famous story about Friedrich Kekulé, the chemist who discovered the structure of the benzene molecule. Having pondered the problem of that structure for some time, he dreamed of a snake biting its own tail; when he awoke, he followed up the hypothesis of a ring structure. The usual view of this incident is that Kekulé already was on the verge of the ring hypothesis; he dreamed of a snake biting its tail because of the idea he already (almost) had about the structure of benzene. Yet, why did the idea come to him in this dream form, and not when he was awake? (Is there any plausible Freudian mechanism for his repressing and disguising his hypothesis yet doing this so poorly that he noticed it immediately upon awakening?) There is a different view we can take of this incident. The motif of a snake biting its tail is common in many cultures—no doubt, Jungians have much to say about this. Kekulé dreamed this for some reason or another, just as he had many dreams during the previous nights; he also encountered many things while he was awake. Working on his project, he was extremely alert for any clue to the structure of benzene, any analogy, any detail, that would suggest a solution to his problem. Previous dreams might have suggested other hypotheses that he could reject quickly as not fitting the data at hand. He seized upon this clue of the snake and pursued it further since it fit his task. However, since he must have seen other circles while awake, why didn't these suggest the same new chemical structure? Circles are so commonplace, the ones he saw as part of everyday life would have faded into the background; whereas the dream circle, salient and powerful for other reasons, caught his attention, so that it then was checked for relevance to his project.*

---

* A similar issue is raised by Christopher Ricks, who reports that T. S. Eliot, when he revised his essays, often revised sentences that already contained words pointing in the direction of that sentence's flaw or infelicity (talk at conference, "T. S. Eliot: A Centennial Appraisal," Washington University, St. Louis, Oct. 2, 1988). When he first wrote these sentences did Eliot, as Ricks believes, unconsciously realize something was amiss and so place those reflexively critical words in the sentences?

How many different areas of alertness can one person have? Can someone be entrepreneurially alert, creatively alert, alert to things affecting the well-being of his children, alert to alternative occupations, to possibilities for enhancing international peace, to opportunities for fun and excitement, etc., assessing everything that swims into ken for its relevance to each of these and then examining further the most promising? That is a question for empirical psychological research. I will register my hunch that the number of independent avenues of alertness is very small, not more than two or three. A significant part of the story of creativity, but not the whole, is that creative people have *chosen* to be creative; they have set themselves to be alert that way, making that an important priority, and they have stuck to it in the face of other tempting diversions.

One fruitful kind of alert noticing, emphasized by Arthur Koestler in his book *The Act of Creation,* brings together two previously separate frameworks to produce a new and surprising combination. (Koestler sees this happening in jokes too.) Working within one structure or framework, another is brought to bear and produces a rearrangement of the previous material that suggests new connections and questions. If creativity involves bringing together two existing elaborated matrices in a new and fruitful way, perhaps originality consists in creating a new framework, not completely out of whole cloth but not by simply combining two preexisting ones, however imaginatively. Making new "frame" requires not just daring and alertness but an immersion within, patiently allowing a new

---

Another explanation is possible. Imagine someone revising writing in a room containing a blackboard with two or three words on it which someone else had written in large letters. These words would be salient to the mind, and if they denoted types of flaws in writing or rhetoric, the person revising would be especially sensitized to notice those very kinds of flaws in the sentences he was encountering. So too in revising his own sentences, the words in them or in immediately adjacent sentences which could be read as denoting flaws might have led Eliot's attention to those very flaws if they were present, even though these words were not inserted originally because of any unconscious intimation of flaws. It is not easy to know how to decide between these hypotheses, since each predicts that a higher percentage of sentences containing flaw-words were revised than of sentences without them. If, however, there was an independent criterion for which sentences were flawed and in need of revision, and Eliot himself did not revise all of these, then Ricks's hypothesis predicts that a higher percentage of the flawed sentences will contain flaw-words than of the unflawed sentences, whereas the alternative "sensitizing" hypothesis predicts these percentages are the same.

structure to emerge, without forcing it prematurely into a more obvious form.

Breaking out of an established framework of thinking or perceiving occurs in creating a theory or artistic object, yet it is not restricted to these; it is important to be able to "break frame" in our everyday lives also. Sometimes the breaking of frame will be a direct action, violating a previous framework of expectations that defined which actions were admissible or were allowed to occur, but which excluded the most functional actions or even effective ones. Sometimes the breaking of frame will be in response to some previous less desirable breaking, a quite new action being necessary to repair the situation or transform it so the previous unexpected alteration doesn't continue to hold sway. In acting toward others, your breaking frame can move or force them, too, out of their habitual frame of action. This can be disconcerting but it can also create new opportunities for all parties to escape the traps and cycles of expectable reactions.

The pieces of the frame—others' expectations, cultural traditions, our own habitual patterns of behavior resulting from past reinforcements, our own rules of thumb for acting—affect what range of choice we perceive, which alternatives are salient, which ones come to mind, which get excluded immediately, even whether we think we face a choice rather than simply a direction we must move in. (In a chess sacrifice a player gives up one or a number of valuable pieces for no evident immediate commensurate purpose, in order eventually to step into a winning position. Simply to have contemplated the consequences of *that* route—loss of the queen, say—will have involved breaking the usual frame.)

Creation in life is one portion of a cycle of activities, fed by the others and feeding in return. It is worth lingering on this somewhat. Creating is fed by a person's previous explorings and his responses to what was encountered. Anything can be explored—ideas, natural processes, other people, the culture of the past—and the activity of exploration has a familiar threefold structure. You *venture out* to explore novel phenomena, territory, ideas, or incidents *from a home base,* a place which is familiar, containing fewer novel or uncertain features to reward focused attention, a place of security or comfort that does not call for alertness to danger, and eventually you *return* to this base. Human beings, I want to think, are naturally alert and curious; the question is why some people explore so little. Here we may suspect the operation of particular experiences in early childhood that squelched their natural openness to the novel and interesting.

In their intellectual explorations, philosophers prize daring and freedom from parochialism. Yet even they constantly wield and recur to certain philosophical modalities: the essential, the necessary, the rational, the normative, the required, the objective, the intelligible, the valid, the correct, the provable, the justified, the warranted. Do these modalities provide a conceptual home base for philosophers, something they can depend upon, orient themselves by, and return to as safe haven?

The philosopher Karl Popper has pointed out that the simple command to "observe" cannot be followed simply. There are an indefinite number of things that might be observed; one cannot observe all of them, and so some selection has to be made. Similarly, one cannot just explore. But exploration does not have the structure of a well-designed experiment either, fixed observation among well-defined alternatives. Rather, you explore in a place or direction you think is likely to be fruitful, and you allow things to roll in upon you, prepared to notice within general categories and to pursue interesting facts or possibilities further. You come to new territory with a template of what the normal run of things is like, at least where you come from, but you can notice any deviation from that template and pursue interesting ones further, gathering new directed observations.

What is worth exploring is worth responding to. In a response, some action, emotion or judgment is contoured to the valuable panoply that is encountered, taking account of intricate features and fitting them in a nuanced and modulated way. A response differs from a reaction. A reaction focuses upon and takes account of a constricted, standard, and preset group of features, and it issues as one of a limited number of preset actions. What we call "emotional reactions" fit this description; for example, a flash of anger or annoyance focuses temporarily on only one or a few aspects of a situation and reacts in a stereotyped fixed manner. A reaction is a small piece of you reacting to a small piece of the situation by selection from a small and preset number of stereotypical actions. The button has been pushed.

44

In a full *response,* a large part of you responds to a large part of the situation by selection from a large range of nonstereotyped actions. (Small and large are not precise delimitations, of course, and the three components may not vary together.) The ideal limit of response would be this: The whole of your being responds to the whole of reality by selecting from an unlimited repertoire that in no way limits in advance the contour or fit of your response.* Two people *relate* when they respond to each other. A relationship defined in this way might be quite thin, however; two persons might each give charity attuned to one another's need secretly and anonymously, neither knowing who the source was. More usual and fruitful is a situation of two people with mutual knowledge that they are responding to each other. To be responsive, we should note, is *not* to be in a passive mode; an apt and creative response to a situation can constitute a decided intervention, though one attuned to the context.

Think of ourselves as engaged in a spiral of activities: exploring, responding, relating, creating, and transforming ourselves to do these again; now different, we do them differently—a spiral and not a cycle. Of course, these are not separable activities but aspects that activities can have simultaneously—even when they do come in a sequence, it need not be the very one listed—though often particular activities will have one aspect predominant.

Evaluations will give the activities of this spiral aim and direction—we don't explore or transform randomly but guide ourselves toward certain things—though engaging in the spiral itself may modify the evaluative standards that direct it. The spiral's point is not any single component but the spiral itself.

Others' explorings, respondings, and creatings enlarge us. In Chaucer's time, people did not know of Shakespeare yet were not conscious of missing anything. It is difficult now to imagine a world in which Shakespeare, Buddha, Jesus, or Einstein are absent, in which their absence goes unnoticed. What comparable voids exist now, waiting to be filled? If there is regret in not yet knowing the great reconfigurations to come, there is pleasure in knowing that they will come and that something remains to do.

* In drawing this distinction between reaction and response, I have benefited from
  the writings of Vimala Thakar. See *Life as Yoga* (Delhi, India: Motilal Banarsidass,
  1977); *Songs of Yearning* (Berkeley, 1983).

5

The Nature of God, the Nature of Faith

THE CONCEPT of God, Descartes held, specifies God as the most perfect possible being, and other proponents of the ontological argument for God's existence agreed. This does not get the concept exactly right, yet I don't know how important it is to get this right. When I find myself discussing the concept of God or religious themes, one part of me finds these speculations moving—or at least fascinating as a bit of nonscience fiction—while another part, or perhaps the very same part, wants to dismiss it all as empty. In the twentieth century—or the fifty-seventh—can we really take God seriously? What circumscribes the religious sensibility in our intellectual time is not actual belief—I cannot say that I am a believer—but simply a willingness to contemplate religion or God as a *possibility*.

Must God be the most perfect possible being, as Descartes thought, more perfect than any that can be imagined? Suppose there existed no completely perfect being, but our universe was created by one very high on the perfection scale; then, provided no other being existed that was more perfect or even equally perfect, that creator of our universe would be, despite its falling short of perfection, God.

More accurately, the concept of God is structured as follows: God is (1) the most perfect actual being, (2) who is very high on the scale of perfection, "perfect enough" to be God, and (3) whose perfection is vastly greater than that of the second most perfect actual being, and (4) who is in some way most importantly connected to our universe, perhaps as its creator (though not necessarily *ex nihilo*) or perhaps in some other way. This is the general concept of God. Particular *conceptions* may differ, though, in which dimensions they include under the notion of perfection, as enhancing it, and in the weights these are given; they can differ also in their views of which important way God is connected to the world, and in their views of what else exists and hence of how perfect the most perfect existing being must turn out to be.

Although the concept of God leaves great leeway about what particular attributes God has, one attribute is part of the concept, that of being most importantly connected to our universe. That connection, I have said, need not be that God is our universe's creator. Here are some examples, *stories* meant to test the limits of the concept. If a being perfect enough to be God had delegated the world's creation to a lesser being, one under his authority who acted in general accordance with his plan, yet the first afterward governed the world, directly or through some other intermediary under his authority acting in general accord with his plan, then that first being would be God, despite not actually being the world's creator or even its direct governor. It may be unclear, though, how much slippage there can be; when does a connection to the world become so attenuated as to no longer count as a most important one? One can ring variants on gnostic views to make it unclear which, if any, being is God. Still, a being that greatly surpassed any other in perfection yet had not created our universe or otherwise been most importantly connected to it might be *a* god but it wouldn't be God. On the other hand, simply being the creator of our universe is not enough alone to constitute a being as God; consider the science fiction situation of our universe being created by a teenager living in another dimension or realm, as the equivalent of a high school science and art project. Many other beings would actually be higher. It is all four of the above conditions that make up the concept of God, not just the fourth alone. The four together are sufficient, though. Any being that sat-isfies all four conditions is God.*

The concept of God depicts him as vastly more perfect than any other existing being. Must he always be so or is it enough that he once was? If some other being now surpasses (or comes very close to) the creator God in perfection—because God's perfection has declined or her own has increased—does God then cease to be God? If the term *God* is fixed as a proper name of the being who was the first to satisfy all the conditions, then the creator god continues to be (correctly referred to as) God. However, the story can be elaborated. Suppose that second being who now is more perfect than God is—must he or she also be more perfect than God *was?*—currently stands in a more important relation to the world: governing it now, determining its destiny, and being its supreme artistic portrayer. One *could* continue to say that he or she is not God—the one Michelangelo painted retired that title years ago. Yet one equally well might say that he or she has become God now, the current title holder being whoever currently satisfies the four conditions. No shift of title would occur if the term *God* applied not to whatever being currently satisfies the four conditions or to whatever being first satisfied them, but (only) to whatever being always does, or (more leniently) to whatever being, in the past, present, or future, in fact fits the conditions, that one who is far and away the most perfect, etc., looking at all the beings there ever were or ever will be. (That being need not be the most perfect at each moment, just as the strongest person ever need not be the strongest always.) However, this last leaves open the

* Specifying the concept by the first three conditions above fits the "best instantiated realization" mode of structuring a concept that I discuss in *Philosophical Explanations* (Cambridge, Mass.: Harvard University Press, 1981), pp. 47–58. The complexity of the concept of God, and the intricacies of combining the above view with a theory of proper names and a Kripkean view of names and essence, are discussed in Emily Nozick, "The Implications of 'God' for Two Theories of Reference," unpublished senior honors thesis, Harvard University, 1987; discus-sions with her have helped develop and clarify my ideas here.

One might want to add another condition to the four listed: not merely that God is the very most perfect existing being but that there *couldn't* be one more perfect that coexisted with it (in the same possible world). This further structuring of the concept of God also allows for a perfection that while vastly greater than any other actual perfection yet falls short of being complete and absolute, so it too fits our current line of thought.

possibility that God has yet to appear, the most important connection to the world being one that comes in the future.

I am not trying to invent a new theology or re-present an old one or to dwell in a world of fantasy, but to see how elastic the concept of God is. Like other concepts, this one was shaped by people who presumed certain things about the world and its course—for instance, that particular features and traits were found together and would continue so. Slight deviations in these background presumptions could produce interesting new applications of the concept; in the face of larger deviations, however, the concept might split or dissolve or spontaneously combust.

Why believe there is any such divine being? The history of thought is littered with attempts to prove the existence of God. Since it is not at all easy to imagine how *God* could provide a permanently convincing proof to us of his existence, the failure of people to do so is not surprising.* Any particular signal announcing God's existence—writing in the sky, or a big booming voice saying he exists, or more sophisticated tricks even—could have been produced by the technology of advanced beings from another star or galaxy, and later generations would doubt it had happened anyway. More promising is a permanent signal, one so embedded in the basic structure of the universe that it could not have been produced by any of its inhabitants, however advanced. For instance, suppose the paths of elementary particles spelled "God exists" in English cursive script. Still, thousands of years later, others might think this scientific discovery occurred *before* that written form of the language developed, with both the language and the historical records being altered to induce later religious belief.

What then would an effective signal be like? Understanding the

* This paragraph and the next are drawn from my "God: A Story," *Moment,* Jan.–Feb. 1978. Some people claim demonstrative proof would "take away our free will" with respect to believing in God, and that is why God has not offered it and prevented people from formulating it. (But why is free will about believing that $2 + 2 = 4$ not equally important?) However, that seems to me to be a fallback position; if such proof had been offered or found, would these same people really complain that it removes our free will? Moreover, suppose we do have free will about being rational; then even if the demonstrative proof existed, people still could freely choose not to be rational and hence not to be convinced by conclusive arguments of that sort.

message should not depend upon complicated and convoluted reasoning which is easily mistaken or faulty. Either people wouldn't figure it out, or they would not trust it if they did. To cope with the fact that anything can be interpreted in various ways, the signal would have to show its meaning naturally and powerfully, without depending on the conventions or artificialities of any language. The signal would have to carry a message unmistakably about God, if about anything; its meaning should shine forth. So the signal itself would have to be analogous to God; it would have to exhibit analogues of at least some of God's properties or relationships to people. Having some of the properties it speaks of and itself instancing part of its message, the signal would be a symbol of God. As an object symbolizing God, it would have to command respect—no people traipsing all over it, cutting and analyzing it in their laboratories, or coming to dominate it; best might be for it to be unapproachable. For people who don't yet have the concept of God, it would help if the symbol also *gave* people the idea, so they then could know what that symbol was a symbol of. A perfect signal should be spectacularly present, impossible to miss. It should capture the attention and be available by various sense modalities; no one should have to take another's word for it. It should endure permanently or at least as long as people do, yet not constantly be before them, so that they will notice it freshly. No one should have to be an historian to know the message had come. The signal should be a powerful object, playing a central role in people's lives. To match God's being the source of creation or standing in some crucially important relation to it, all life on earth should depend (mediately) on the signal and center about it. If there were some object which was the energy source of all life on earth, one which dominated the sky with its brilliance, whose existence people could not doubt, which couldn't be poked at or treated condescendingly, an object about which people's existence revolved, which poured out a tremendous quantity of energy, only a small fraction of which reached people, an object which people constantly walked under and whose enormous power they sensed, one they even were unable to look at directly yet which did not oppress them but showed how they could coexist with an immensely dazzling power, an object overwhelmingly powerful, warming them and lighting their way, one their daily bodily rhythms depended upon, if this object supplied energy for all life processes upon earth and for the beginning of life as well, if it were dazzlingly spectacular and beautiful, if it served to give the very idea of God to some cultures that lacked the concept, if it were immense and also similar to billions of others scattered throughout the universe so that it couldn't have been created by more advanced beings from another galaxy or by any being lesser than the creator of the universe, then that *would be* a suitable message announcing God's existence.

Of course, I am being somewhat playful here. The Sun does exist, it is about as good a permanent announcement as one could imagine or devise, yet it has not served to prove God's existence, even though viewing it as a signal does provide a unified explanation of why all those properties listed happen to be conjoined in *one* object. Since we do not find it easy to imagine how God could provide *anything* that would be a permanently convincing proof of his existence, why should we expect to be able to do that ourselves?*

One might believe in the existence of a deepest reality that is divine, on faith. To say that someone believes something on faith marks the kinds of reasons by which he has come to believe (or continues to do so); for instance, it is not because of the evidence or because of what he was taught by parents or traditions. Faith's particular route to belief is the following. There is an encounter with something very real—an actual person, a person in a story, a part of nature, a book or work of art, a part of one's being—and this thing has extraordinary qualities that intimate the divine by being forms of qualities that the divine itself would have: these extraordinary qualities touch you deeply, opening your heart so that you feel in contact with a special manifestation of the divine, in that it has some form of divine qualities to a very great extent.

We might say that the faith is justified, or at least that is is not unjustified, when it can be *paralleled* by a plausible argument to the

---

* Things might be helped if God were infinite in some respects—the structure of the very concept of God does not require this—and we had a capacity to experience or recognize the infinite. However, it might be a lesser being or reality, though still an infinite one, that this capacity encountered; even this might serve somewhat to point toward God, though. A more serious difficulty is that our experiential capacity might be unreliable in distinguishing the infinite from the very large finite, or that the capacity might be detecting some infinite aspect of ourselves instead, perhaps that very capacity itself, one that would not indicate anything else that was deeper. It would be poignant to possess the capacity to detect the infinite while that was the only infinite thing to be found.

best explanation, saying that the thing encountered has certain qualities, and that what best explains this is its existing as a manifestation of the divine, which itself possesses some (intensified) form of those qualities. However, the person who believes on faith does not do so because he has passed through this inferential argument; rather, his belief arises directly out of his being deeply touched and moved in encountering something.

Perhaps the faith involved is a faith *in oneself* and one's own responses, a faith that one would not be *so* deeply touched by something in *that* way unless it *was* a manifestation of the divine. Thereby one also would have a belief that the divine existed—otherwise it could not manifest itself—but the faith would initially not be a faith in *it* but a trust in one's own *deepest* positive responses. To *not* have the belief then would be to distrust one's very deepest responses and thus involve a significant alienation from oneself. It might be, however, that a person's initial deepest response, that one he or she so trusts, is *itself* simply faith and trust *in* something encountered. Faith, at its bottom, in that case, *would* be a faith in something else rather than a trust in oneself and one's deepest responses, although here too one might need also to have a faith in one's faith—that is, a trust in one's own response of faith in the thing encountered.*

* Some might claim their trust is in their religious tradition, not in themselves or their own responses. However, once we notice that people in other cultures equally trust their culture's tradition, and once we infer that had we been born in those other circumstances we too would have had equal trust in those different beliefs, it is difficult to retain the same confidence in our own. Suppose the trust, though, is not simply in one's tradition but in one's own deepest responses in encountering that tradition, from which a trust in that tradition grows. A parallel question arises: Had you been brought up in another tradition, would you have had an equally deep encounter with facets of that tradition, leading to an equally deep trust in those experiences? It is not impossible, however, to retain trust in one's actual responses to a tradition, while realizing other responses would have occurred, equally moving, under other circumstances. Love for a mate is not undercut by realizing that under other circumstances—never having met your actual mate, for example—you would have come to love someone else. That love, however, does not make a claim to truth about the world, and it seems that such a claim will get shaken by the realization that other truth claims would have arisen equally forcefully under other circumstances, unless there is some neutral criterion for deeming those other circumstances untrustworthy. Similarly, those who speak of a "leap of faith" might worry that under different circumstances they would still have leaped, but to a quite different place. However, the trust in oneself and one's own deepest responses does not fall before similar considerations when these responses do not derive from or simply reinforce one's particular preconceptions, but break one's frame instead.

To be sure, a lesser faith in oneself than this is possible, a faith that would not get one all the way to a belief in the divine, namely a faith that no thing would touch you *that* deeply or give you an experience that deep without itself being at least equally deep. However, this focuses only upon the degree of depth and reality of the experience itself, distrusting its content. If there did exist a divine being or realm not directly perceivable by the senses, how else would you come to know it other than by being *open* to it, allowing it to most deeply touch you?

It is not that God (or some other conception of deepest reality) is introduced as an hypothesis needed to explain the special experiences. Rather, we *trust* those experiences. Our fundamental connection to the world is not *explanatory,* but one of relation and trust. The existence of the parallel argument from the best explanation, however, undercuts those reductionist arguments that otherwise themselves would undercut our trust in our own deepest experiences and in what they seem to show; the reasoning serves to show that the faith is not irrational. Compare this to the case of romantic love, caused through encounter, not mandated by reasons, yet (reasons might be introduced to show it is) not irrational. (Another view of faith would concede that it is *narrowly* irrational in that none of the current kinds of reasons we know of support it, yet maintains that it will be supported by a kind of reason still to be discovered—why think we already know all the kinds of reasons there are?—and hence that faith is rational in a broader sense that takes account of all the good reasons there are and will be, timelessly.)

Still, there seems to be a step from trusting one's experience in the sense of not repudiating it, holding it extremely valuable, and letting it shape one's life to making the further claim that there is another existing reality it reveals. To actually deny the further claim about existence, though, would tend to undermine trust in the value and significance of the experience, thus demeaning it. Why not, then, simply suspend judgment? Yet this too would forgo the fullest power of the experience to shape a life; and an affirmation, not merely a suspension of judgment, may also be an important component of that life as shaped.

This affirmation and trust in one's deepest experiences is not the same as dogmatism, holding these experiences to be infallible. Still deeper experiences might undercut these or show something differ-

6

The Holiness of Everyday Life

EACH AND EVERY portion of reality, the Transcendentalists said, when viewed and experienced properly, stands for and contains the whole. Likewise, religious traditions do not always view holiness as removing oneself from everyday life and concerns. In the Jewish tradition, the 613 commandments, or *mitzvot,* raise and sanctify every portion of life just as the people who follow them view themselves as having been sanctified through being given them. The Buddhist tradition, not only in its Zen aspect, brings the meditative attitude of complete attention and focus to all activities. Holiness need not be a separate sphere. There also is the holiness of everyday life.

How deeply might we respond to the everyday things in our lives, for instance to life's ordinary necessities? For the most part, we take in food and air, we eat and breathe, without special attention. How do these activities differ when we attend to them? And are these differences desirable?

Eating is an intimate relationship. We place pieces of external reality inside ourselves; we swallow them more deeply inside, where they are incorporated into our own stuff, our own bodily being of flesh and blood. It is a remarkable fact that we turn parts of external reality into our own substance. We are least separate from the world in eating. The world enters into us; it becomes us. We are constituted by portions of the world.

This raises primal issues. Is the world safe to take in? How do we come to trust it or find this out? Does the world care enough about us to nourish us? The example David Hume used in formulating the problem of induction was whether we can know that bread, nourishing in the past, will continue to nourish us. Bertrand Russell's favored induction example was whether we can know that the sun will rise tomorrow. (He also told of a chicken: the person who each previous morning has fed it this morning has come to kill.) Is it an accident that the problem of induction expresses itself as a worry over loss, of nourishment, of warmth and light, of safety?

Eating food with someone can be a deep mode of sociability— the Romans were offended that the Hebrews would not join them in meals—a way of sharing together nurturance and the incorporation within ourselves of the world, as well as sharing textures, tastes, conversation, and time. Rapport and intimacy thrive when our normal physical boundaries are relaxed to take something in; it is no accident that we often suggest getting together with another over a meal. The loving preparation of food, the visual beauty it presents, sensuousness in eating, the daily sharing of such meals in leisure and loveliness—all these can be a romantic couple's way of being lovingly together, a way for one or both to create a piece of the world they treasure. (For a large number of people in the world, the basic fact about food is how difficult, sometimes impossible, it is to come by. We should remember the biological and personal havoc this produces, even as we study food's social and symbolic significance when it is plentiful.)

Eating has an individual side also, a nonsocial one. What is its character when it is attentive, neither oblivious nor aesthetically distant? First, awareness is focused upon the activity of taking in the food, not simply on the food's qualities. We meet food in the anteroom of the mouth and greet it there. We probe and explore it, surround it, permeate it with juices, press it with our tongues against the roof of the mouth along that hard ridge directly above the teeth, place it under suction and pressure, move it around. We know its texture fully; it holds no secrets or hidden parts. We play with the food, we make friends with it, we welcome it inside.

We open ourselves, also, to the specific character of the food, to the taste and the texture, and so to the inner quality of the substance. I want to speak of the purity and dignity of an apple, the explosive joy and sexuality of a strawberry. (I would have found this ridiculously overblown once.) I have not myself *tasted* that many foods, but the times I did seemed a mode of knowing them in their inner essence.* There is a Buddhist story of a man who, fleeing a tiger, swings on a vine over a precipice and sees another tiger waiting below; then two mice start to gnaw away at the vine. He sees a strawberry near him and with one free hand he plucks and eats it. "How sweet it tasted!" We wonder how the man could have responded thus to the strawberry in that situation. He did because he tasted the berry and knew it. What I don't know—and the story does not go on to tell us—is his knowledge of the tiger.

On the basis of only a very small sample, I think that many foods open their essence to us in this way and teach us. I don't know whether artful concoctions can give us such knowledge, and so I am skeptical about the assumption behind Brillat-Savarin's asking Adam and Eve, "who ruined yourself for an apple, what might you not have done for a truffled turkey?" A creator of an original dish that did impart new lessons *would* be a significant creator. While I do not think the world has been stocked with these substances for our benefit and education, how these foods have come to have such amazing essences is a question worth wondering about. It would be nice to think that by so knowing them and incorporating substances within our flesh we raise them to a higher plane of being and so benefit them in turn.

* I am, in fact, rather ignorant about all this, having carried out only a few experiments. My only excuse for imparting such very limited knowledge and speculations is that I do not find even these in print elsewhere. The literature of Buddhist meditation is relevant, though, perhaps especially that of the Vipassana tradition. Among methods of achieving enlightenment, Eastern tradition includes these two: "When eating or drinking, become the taste of the food or drink, and be filled"; "Suck something and become the sucking." (See Paul Reps, *Zen Flesh, Zen Bones* [New York: Anchor Books], items 47 and 52 in the section on "Centering.")

(Could animal flesh, though hardly the animal itself, be benefited by being incorporated and transformed into the flesh of a being with greater consciousness?)

Eating with awareness also brings powerful emotions: the world as a nurturative place; oneself as worthy of receiving such nurturance, excitement, primal contact with the nurturative mother; the security of being at home in the world, connection to other life forms, thankfulness too—the religious will add—for the fruits of creation.

The mouth is a versatile arena, the location of eating, speaking, kissing, biting, and (in conjunction with the nasal cavity) breathing. Perhaps the first four can be emotionally laden, but isn't breathing uncomplicated and automatic? When one attends to breathing, though, it turns out also to be a full and rich process. Eastern techniques of meditation recommend "following the breath," focusing upon the inhalation, the pause, the exhalation, the pause before the next inhalation, and so on, repeating the cycle. One can also change the rate and tempo of these, prolonging the exhalation in a constant slow process, holding the breath after the inhalation. Remarkably, such simple breathing techniques alter the nature of one's awareness, in part by becoming the simple focus of awareness, bringing it to a nondistracted point and quieting other thoughts. In part, also, the changes in consciousness might be immediate physiological results of alterations in mode of breathing. Yet, there also are the changes wrought by the fact that it is breathing that the attention is focused upon. Breathing, like eating, is a direct connection with the external world, a bringing it inside oneself. It involves immediate changes in the body, including large changes in the size of one's chest cavity and belly. Perceiving one's physical being as a bellows, breathing the air in and out, enlarging and contracting in reciprocal relation to the outside space, being a container of space within a larger space, sometimes unable to distinguish between the held-in breath and the held-out breath until you see what happens next—all this makes one feel less enclosed within distinct boundaries as a separate entity. Breathing the world, even sometimes feeling one is being breathed by it, can be a profound experience of nonseparation from the rest of existence. Within meditative breathing, emotions too can be brought more easily under control and evaluation—they do not simply wash over one to produce unmediated effects.

Moreover, a prolonged attention to breathing, as in meditative practice that "follows the breath," following the rising and falling of the chest and diaphragm, can develop the attention so that it becomes supple and concentrated, not subject to wandering, able to be maintained indefinitely on an object, and this attentiveness to breathing can be interwoven within daily activities too, thereby sharpening the nature of the attention to everything falling within the interstices of the noticed breathing. One can place external things or emotions, if fearful or stressful, within the calm and calming latticework of this attentive breathing, and within this attended-to structure too, subtler bodily rhythms become apparent which in turn can be attended to and followed, forming yet another lattice from which one can be suspended to delve deeper still.

To carry on our eating and breathing in this intense meditative fashion most of the time would insufficiently recognize the relaxed and easy naturalness these activities can have, but it seems important to do so sometimes at least and to carry with us the lessons we have learned thereby, returning on occasion to reconfirm these lessons or to learn new ones.

Attention also can be focused upon other things, inner or outer. The sun can be experienced as a direct source of light and warmth for oneself, and (aided by one's other knowledge) as the major energy source for all life processes here on earth. One's own body and its movement can also be focused upon attentively.

The most ordinary objects yield surprises to attentive awareness. Chairs, tables, cars, houses, torn papers, strewn objects, all stand in their place, waiting, patiently. An object that is displaced or awkwardly placed on purpose is no less a patient waiter. It is as though being an entity, any kind of entity, has its own salient quality, and we can become aware of something's entityhood, its sheer beingness. Everything is right exactly as it is, yet everything also is poised expectantly. Is some grand event being awaited, is there something we are to do besides simply knowing entities? (Are these dignified objects waiting there to be loved?)

Still, to linger on these matters and describe these details may seem "too precious." It would be a shame, though, to pass through one's life oblivious to what life and the world contains and reveals— like someone walking through rooms where wondrous music is playing, deaf to it all. Perhaps, after all, there is a reason why we have bodies.

Holiness is to stand in a special and close relation to the divine. To respond to holy things *as* holy may place us, too, in a more special relation to them. Seeing everyday life as holy is in part seeing the world and its contents as infinitely receptive to our activities of exploring, responding, relating and creating, as an arena that would richly repay these activities no matter how far they are taken, whether by an individual or by all of humanity together throughout its time.

7

✳

Sexuality

THE MOST INTENSE WAY we relate to another person is sexually. Nothing so concentrates the mind, Dr. Johnson noted, as the prospect of being hanged. Nothing, that is, except sexual arousal and excitement: rising tension, uncertainty about what will happen next, occasional reliefs, sudden surprises, dangers and risks, all in a sequence of heightened attention and tension that reaches toward resolution. A similar pattern of excitement also occurs near the end of closely matched athletic contests and in suspense films. I do not say our excitement at these is at base covertly sexual. Yet the sexual is so preeminent an exemplar of the general pattern of excitement that these others also may hold sexual reverberations. However, only in sex is such intense excitement shared with the object and cause of it.

Sex is not simply a matter of frictional force. The excitement comes largely in how we interpret the situation and how we perceive the connection to the other. Even in masturbatory fantasy, people dwell upon their actions with others; they do not get excited by thinking of themselves or of themselves masturbating while thinking of themselves. What is exciting is interpersonal: how the other views you, what attitude the actions evidence. Some uncertainty about this makes it even more exciting. Just as it is difficult to tickle oneself, so too sex is better with an actual partner on the other end. (Is it the other person or the uncertainty that is crucial?)

Sex holds the attention. If any wanderings of the mind from the immediate sexual situation are permissible, it is only to other sexual fantasies. It bespeaks a certain lack of involvement to be ruminating then about one's next choice of automobile. In part, the focus of attention is on how you are touched and what you are feeling, in part on how you are touching the other person and what he or she is feeling.

At times we focus in sex upon the most minute motions, the most delicate brushing of a hair, the slow progress of the fingertips or nails or tongue across the skin, the slightest change or pause at a point. We linger in such moments and await what will come next. Our acuity is sharpest here; no change in pressure or motion or angle is too slight to notice. And it is exciting to know another is attuned to your sensations as keenly as you are. A partner's delicacy of motion and response can show knowledge of your pleasure and care about its details. To have your particular pleasures known and accepted, to linger in them for as long as you will without any rushing to another stage or another excitement, to receive another's permission and invitation to loll there and play together—*is* there such a thing as sex that is too slow?—to be told in this way that you are deserving of pleasure and worthy of it, can bring a profound sigh.

Not only are old pleasures sensitively and delicately awakened and explored, but one becomes willing to follow to somewhere new, in the hands and mouth and tongue and teeth of someone who has cared and caressed knowingly.

It is not surprising that profound emotions are awakened and expressed in sex. The trust involved in showing our own pleasures, the vulnerability in letting another give us these and guide them, including pleasures with infantile or oedipal reverberations, or anal ones, does not come lightly.

Sex is not all delicacy of knowledge and response to nuanced pleasure. The narrative that begins there, and occasionally returns, also moves along to stronger and less calibrated actions, not so much the taking of turns in attentiveness to each other's pleasures as the mutual growth of stronger and broader excitements—the move from the adult (or the infantile) to the animal. The passions and motions become fiercer and less controlled, sharper or more automatically rhythmic, the focus shifts from flesh to bones, sounds shift from moans and sighs to sharper cries, hisses, roars, mouths shift from tongue and lips to teeth and biting, themes of power, domination, and anger emerge to be healed in tenderness and to emerge yet again in ever stronger and more intense cycles.

In the arena of sex, our very strongest emotions are expressed. These emotions are not always tender and loving, though sometimes, perhaps often, they are. Such strong emotions bring equally strong ones, excited and exciting, in response. The partners see their strongest and most primitive emotions expressed and also contained safely. It is not only the other person who is known more deeply in sex. One knows one's own self better in experiencing what it is capable of: passion, love, aggression, vulnerability, domination, playfulness, infantile pleasure, joy. The depth of relaxing afterward is a measure of the fullness and profoundity of the experience together, and a part of it.

The realm of sex is or can be inexhaustible. There is no limit to what can be learned and felt about each other in sex; the only limit is the sensitivity or responsiveness or creativity or daring of the partners. There always are new depths—and new surfaces—to be explored.

The one maxim is to experiment attentively: to notice what excites, to follow the other's pleasure where it is and goes, to lean into it, to play with variations around it, with stronger or more delicate pressures, in related places. Intelligence helps, too, in noticing whether what excites fits into a larger pattern or fantasy, in testing out that hypothesis and then, through congruent actions and words, sometimes ambiguous, in encouraging it. Through fresh experimentation one can bypass routinized or predictable pleasures. How nice that freedom, openness, creativity, daring, and intelligence—traits not always so amply rewarded in the larger world—bear such exceedingly sweet private fruits.

Sex also is a mode of communication, a way of saying or of showing something more tellingly than our words can say. Yet though sexual actions speak more pointedly than words, they also can be enhanced by words, words that name one's pleasure or lead ahead to greater intensity, words that narrate a fantasy or merely hint at exciting ones that cannot comfortably be listened to.

Like musicians in jazz improvisation, sexual partners are engaged in a dialogue, partly scored, partly improvised, where each very attentively responds to the statements in the bodily motions of the other. These statements can be about one's own self and pleasures, or about one's partner's, or about the two of you together, or about what one would like the other to do. Whether or not they do so elsewhere in life, in sex people frequently and unconsciously do unto others as they would have others do unto them. By the placing or intensity or rate or direction of their pressures and motions they are constantly sending signals, often unawares, about what they want to receive. In manifold ways, also, some parts of the body can stand for or represent others, so that what happens, for example, at the mouth or ear (or palm or armpit or fingers or toes or bones) can intricately symbolize corresponding events elsewhere with coordinate excitement.

In verbal conversations, people speak in different voices, with different ideas, on different topics. In sexual conversation, too, everyone has a distinctive voice. And there is no shortage of new things two people can say, or older things that can be said newly or reminisced about. To speak of *conversations* here does not mean that the sole (nonreproductive) purpose of sex is communication. There is also excitement and bodily pleasure, desired for themselves. Yet these too are also important parts of the conversation, for it is through pleasurable excitement and the opening to it that other powerful emotions are brought into expression and play in the sexual arena.

In this arena, everything personal can be expressed, explored, symbolized, and intensified. In intimacy, we let another within the boundaries we normally maintain around ourselves, boundaries marked by clothing and by full self-control and monitoring. Through the layers of public defenses and faces, another is admitted to see a more vulnerable or a more impassioned you. Nothing is more intimate than showing another your physical pleasure, perhaps because we learned we had to hide it even (or especially) from our parents. Once inside the maintained boundaries, new intimacies are possible, such as the special nature of the conversation new partners can have in bed after sex. (Might they engage in sex partly in order to have such unposed conversations?)

Is there a conflict between the desire for sexual excitement including orgasm and the deepest knowing of one's partner and oneself? A rush to immediately greater excitement, a focus upon everything else merely as a means to orgasm, would get in the way of deeply opening to another and knowing them. Everything in its proper time. The most intense excitement too can be a route to depth; people would not be so shaken by sex, so awed sometimes by what occurs, if their depths had stayed unplumbed.

Exciting for itself, orgasm also tells your partner how very pleased you are with him or her. When it takes a deeper form, when you allow yourself to become and appear totally without control, completely engulfed, you show the other, and show yourself too, the full extent of that other's power over you and of your comfort and trust in being helpless before him or her.

Pleasing another feels best when it is an accomplishment, a surmountable challenge. Consequently, an orgasm is less satisfying to the giving partner when it comes too early or too late. Too early and it is no accomplishment, too late and only after very much effort, it states that the giving partner is not exciting and pleasing enough. The secret of success with orgasm, as with comedy, is timing.

Orgasm is not simply an exciting experience but a statement about the partner, about the connection to the partner; it announces that the partner satisfies you. No wonder partners care that it happen. Here, too, we can understand the unitive force of simultaneous orgasm, of feeling the most intense pleasure with and from the other person at the very moment that you are told and shown you intensely please him or her.

There are other statements, less about the whole person, more about parts. The penis can be made to feel a welcome entrant in the vagina; it can be kissed lovingly and unhurriedly; it can be made to feel nurturative; it can be delighted in and known for itself; in more exalted moments its fantasy is to be worshiped almost. Similarly, the sweetness and power of the vagina can be acknowledged in its own right, by tender kissing, long knowing, dwelling in the tiniest crevices and emitting those sounds this calls forth. Knowing a partner's body, meditating on the special energy of its parts without rushing any-where else, also makes a statement the partner receives.

Unlike making love, which can be symmetrical, tender, and turn-taking all the way through, what we might (without any den-igration) call "fucking" contains at least one stage where the male displays his power and force. This need not be aggressive, vicious, or dominating, although perhaps statistically it frequently slides into that. The male can simply be showing the female his power, strength, ferocity even, for her appreciation. Exhibiting his quality as a beast in the jungle, with a lion or tiger's fierceness, growling, roaring, biting, he shows (in a contained fashion) his protective strength. This display of force need not be asymmetrical, however. The female can answer (and initiate) with her own ferocity, snarls, hissing, scratch-ing, growling, biting, and she shows too her capacity to contain and tame his ferocity. It is even more difficult to state in quite the right way matters of more delicate nuance, the special way a woman can at some point *give* herself to her partner.

In sexual intimacy, we admit the partner within our boundaries or make these more permeable, showing our own passions, capaci-ties, fantasies, and excitements, and responding to the other's. We might diagram sexual intimacy as two circles overlapping with dotted lines. There *are* boundaries between the partners here, yet these boundaries are permeable, not solid. Hence, we can understand the oceanic feeling, the sense of merging, that sometimes occurs with intense sexual experience. This is not due merely to the excited feelings directed toward the other; it results from not devoting energy to maintaining the usual boundaries. (At climactic moments, are the boundaries dropped or are they made *selectively* permeable, lowered only for that particular person?)

Much that I have said thus far might apply to single sexual encounters, yet a sexual life has its special continuities over time. There is the extended being together over a full day or several, with repeated and varied intimacies and knowings, scarcely emerging or arising from the presence of the other, with fuller knowledge and feelings fresh in memory as a springboard to new explorations. There are the repeated meetings of familiar partners who scarcely can contain their hunger for each other. There are the fuller enduring relationships of intimacy and love, enhancing the excitement, depth, and sweetness of sexual uniting and enhanced by it.

Not only can one explore in sex the full range of emotions, knowing one's partner and oneself deeply, not only can one come to know the two of you together in union, pursuing the urge to unite or merge with the other and finding the physical joy of transcending the self, not only is (heterosexual) sex capable of producing new life which brings further psychological significance to the act itself—perhaps especially saliently for women, who are able to become the carriers of life within them, with all its symbolic significance—but in sex one also can engage in metaphysical exploration, knowing the body and person of another as a map or microcosm of the very deepest reality, a clue to its nature and purpose.

8

Love's Bond

THE GENERAL phenomenon of love encompasses romantic love, the love of a parent for a child, love of one's country, and more. What is common to all love is this: Your own well-being is tied up with that of someone (or something) you love. When a bad thing happens to a friend, it happens to her and you feel sad for her; when something good happens, you feel happy for her. When something bad happens to one you love, though, something bad also happens *to you*. (It need not be exactly the same bad thing. And I do not mean that one cannot also love a friend.) If a loved one is hurt or disgraced, you are hurt; if something wonderful happens to her, you feel better off. Not every gratification of a loved one's preference will make you feel better off, though; her well-being, not merely a preference of hers, has to be at stake. (Her well-being as who perceives it, she or you?) When love is not present, changes in other people's well-being do not, in general, change your own. You will be moved when others suffer in a famine and will contribute to help; you may be haunted by their plight, but you need not feel you yourself are worse off.

This extension of your own well-being (or ill-being) is what marks all the different kinds of love: the love of children, the love of parents, the love of one's people, of one's country. Love is not necessarily a matter of caring equally or more about someone else than about yourself. These loves are large, but love in some amount is present when your well-being is affected to whatever extent (but in the same direction) by another's. As the other fares, so (to some extent) do you. The people you love are included inside your boundaries, their well-being is your own.*

Being "in love," infatuation, is an intense state that displays familiar features: almost always thinking of the person; wanting constantly to touch and to be together; excitement in the other's presence; losing sleep; expressing one's feelings through poetry, gifts, or still other ways to delight the beloved; gazing deeply into each other's eyes; candlelit dinners; feeling that short separations are long; smiling foolishly when remembering actions and remarks of the other; feeling that the other's minor foibles are delightful; experiencing joy at having found the other and at being found by the other; and (as Tolstoy depicts Levin in *Anna Karenina* as he learns Kitty loves him) finding *everyone* charming and nice, and thinking they all must sense one's happiness. Other concerns and responsibilities become minor background details in the story of the romance, which becomes the predominant foreground event of life. (When major public responsibilities such as commanding Rome's armies or being king of England are put aside, the tales engross.) The vividness of the relationship can carry artistic or mythic proportions—lying together

* A somewhat sharper criterion can be formulated of when another's well-being is *directly* part of your own. This occurs when (1) you say and believe your well-being is affected by significant changes in hers; (2) your well-being is affected in the same *direction* as hers, an improvement in her well-being producing an improvement in your own, a decrease, a decrease; (3) you not only judge yourself worse off, but feel some emotion appropriate to that state; (4) you are affected by the change in *her* well-being directly, merely through knowing about it, and not because it symbolically represents to you something else about yourself, a childhood situation or whatever; (5) (and this condition is especially diagnostic) your *mood* changes: you now have different occurent feelings and changed dispositions to have particular other emotions; and (6) this change in mood is somewhat enduring. Moreover, (7) you have this general tendency or disposition toward a person or object, to be thus affected; you *tend* to be thus affected by changes in that person's well-being.

like figures in a painting, jointly living a new tale from Ovid. Familiar, too, is what happens when the love is not equally reciprocated: melancholy, obsessive rumination on what went wrong, fantasies about its being set right, lingering in places to catch a glimpse of the person, making telephone calls to hear the other's voice, finding that all other activities seem flat, occasionally having suicidal thoughts.

However and whenever infatuation begins, if given the opportunity it transforms itself into continuing romantic love or else it disappears. With this continuing romantic love, it feels to the two people that they have united to form and constitute a new entity in the world, what might be called a *we*.* You can be in romantic love with someone, however, without actually forming a *we* with her or him—that other person might not be in love with you. Love, romantic love, is *wanting* to form a *we* with that particular person, feeling, or perhaps wanting, that particular person to be the right one for you to form a *we* with, and also wanting the other to feel the same way about you. (It would be kinder if the realization that the other person is not the right one with whom to form a *we* always and immediately terminated the desire to form it.) The desire to form a *we* with that other person is not simply something that goes along with romantic love, something that contingently happens when love does. That desire is intrinsic to the nature of love, I think; it is an important part of what love intends.

In a *we*, the two people are not bound physically like Siamese twins; they can be in distant places, feel differently about things, carry on different occupations. In what sense, then, do these people together constitute a new entity, a *we*? That new entity is created by a new web of relationships between them which makes them no longer so separate. Let me describe some features of this web; I will begin with two that have a somewhat cold and political-science sound.

First, the defining feature we mentioned which applies to love in general: Your own well-being is tied up with that of someone you love romantically. Love, then, among other things, can place you at risk. Bad things that happen to your loved one happen to you. But

* For a discussion of love as the formation of a *we*, see Robert Solomon, *Love* (Garden City, N.Y.: Anchor Books, 1981).

so too do good things; moreover, someone who loves you helps you with care and comfort to meet vicissitudes—not out of selfishness although her doing so does, in part, help maintain her own well-being too. Thus, love places a floor under your well-being; it provides insurance in the face of fate's blows. (Would economists explain some features of selecting a mate as the rational pooling of risks?)

People who form a *we* pool not only their well-being but also their autonomy. They limit or curtail their own decision-making power and rights; some decisions can no longer be made alone. Which decisions these are will be parceled differently by different couples: where to live, how to live, who friends are and how to see them, whether to have children and how many, where to travel, whether to go to the movies that night and what to see. Each transfers some previous rights to make certain decisions unilaterally into a joint pool; somehow, decisions will be made together about how to be together. If your well-being so closely affects and is affected by another's, it is not surprising that decisions that importantly affect well-being, even in the first instance primarily your own, will no longer be made alone.*

The term *couple* used in reference to people who have formed a *we* is not accidental. The two people also view themselves as a new and continuing unit, and they present that face to the world. They want to be perceived publicly as a couple, to express and assert their identity as a couple in public. Hence those homosexual couples unable to do this face a serious impediment.

To be part of a *we* involves having a new identity, an additional one. This does *not* mean that you no longer have any individual identity or that your sole identity is as part of the *we*. However, the individual identity you did have will become altered. To have this new identity is to enter a certain psychological stance;

---

* This curtailment of unilateral decision-making rights extends even to a decision to end the romantic love relationship. This decision, if any, you would think you could make by yourself. And so you can, but only in certain ways at a certain pace. Another kind of relation might be ended because you feel like it or because you find it no longer satisfactory, but in a love relationship the other party "has a vote." This does not mean a permanent veto; but the other party has a right to have his or her say, to try to repair, to be convinced. After some time, to be sure, one party may insist on ending the relationship even without the other's consent, but what they each have forgone, in love, is the right to act unilaterally and swiftly.

and each party in the *we* has this stance toward the other. Each becomes psychologically part of the other's identity. How can we say more exactly what this means? To say that something is part of your identity when, if that thing changes or is lost, you feel like a different person, seems only to reintroduce the very notion of identity that needs to be explained. Here is something more helpful: To love someone might be, in part, to devote alertness to their well-being and to your connection with them. (More generally, shall we say that something is part of your identity when you continually make it one of your few areas of special alertness?) There are empirical tests of alertness in the case of your own separate identity—for example, how you hear your name mentioned through the noise of a conversation you were not consciously attending to; how a word that resembles your name "jumps out" from the page. We might find similar tests to check for that alertness involved in loving someone. For example, a person in a *we* often is considerably more worried about the dangers of traveling—air crashes or whatever—when the other is traveling alone than when both travel together or when he himself or she herself is traveling alone; it seems plausible that a person in a *we* is alert, in general, to dangers to the other that would necessitate having to go back to a single individual identity, while these are made especially salient by a significant physical separation. Other criteria for the formation of a joint identity also might be suggested, such as a certain kind of division of labor. A person in a *we* might find himself coming across something interesting to read yet leaving it for the other person, not because he himself would not be interested in it but because the other would be more interested, and one of them reading it is sufficient for it to be registered by the wider identity now shared, the *we*. If the couple breaks up, they then might notice themselves reading all those things directly; the other person no longer can do it *for them*. (The list of criteria for the *we* might continue on to include something we discuss later, not seeking to "trade up" to another partner.) Sometimes the existence of the *we* can be very palpable. Just as a reflective person can walk along the street in friendly internal dialogue with himself, keeping himself company, so can one be with a loved person who is not physically present, thinking what she would say, conversing with her, noticing things as she would, for her, because she is not there to notice, saying things to others that she would say, in her tone of voice, carrying the full *we* along.*

If we picture the individual self as a closed figure whose boundaries are continuous and solid, dividing what is inside from what is outside, then we might diagram the *we* as two figures with the boundary line between them erased where they come together. (Is that the traditional heart shape?) The unitive aspects of sexual experience, two persons flowing together and intensely merging, mirror and aid the formation of the *we*. Meaningful work, creative activity, and development can change the shape of the self. Intimate bonds change the boundaries of the self and alter its *topology*—romantic love in one way and friendship (as we shall see) in another.

The individual self can be related to the *we* it identifies with in two different ways. It can see the *we* as a very important *aspect* of itself, or it can see itself as part of the *we,* as contained within it. It may be that men more often take the former view, women the latter. Although both see the *we* as extremely important for the self, most men might draw the circle of themselves containing the circle of the *we* as an aspect *within* it, while most women might

---

* When two people form a *we,* does this *we* constitute an added entity in the world, something in addition to the people involved and their web of relationships? (Might there be times we want to say that in addition to the two people, the *we* also feels an emotion?) This resembles the question of whether a whole society is an additional entity in the world or merely the sum of the web of the various people's relationships? Is a human body an additional entity in the world or simply those constituent physical parts in a web of relationships? Like a body or a society, a *we* maintains itself and adapts in the face of (a wide range of) new circumstances. Unlike a society or a body, it does not continue existing as the same entity while there is replacement of some constituent parts. However, the two people in a *we* relationship often do interact with the outside world as a unit, one with a distinctive well-being and decision-making locus. Noticing the multifarious features of the *we* and the new activities and value it makes possible is more important than deciding whether it constitutes a new item of ontological furniture in the world. The latter would be an apt marker, though, for that familiar phenomenological experience of contentedly just being together in the space the two make and constitute. (For an extremely detailed and illuminating discussion of the nature of a "we" and of a plural subject, one that appeared after this book was complete, see Margaret Gilbert, *On Social Facts* [London: Routledge, 1989], pp. 146–236.)

draw the circle of themselves within the circle of the *we*. In either case, the *we* need not consume an individual self or leave it without any autonomy.

Each person in a romantic *we* wants to possess the other completely; yet each also needs the other to be an independent and nonsubservient person. Only someone who continues to possess a nonsubservient autonomy can be an apt partner in a joint identity that enlarges and enhances your individual one. And, of course, the other's well-being—something you care about—requires that non-subservient autonomy too. Yet at the same time there is the desire to possess the other *completely*. This does not have to stem from a desire to dominate the other person, I think. What you need and want is to possess the other as completely as you do your own identity. This is an expression of the fact that you *are* forming a new joint identity with him or her. Or, perhaps, this desire just *is* the desire to form an identity with the other. Unlike Hegel's description of the unstable dialectic between the master and the slave, though, in a romantic *we* the autonomy of the other and complete possession too are reconciled in the formation of a joint and wondrous enlarged identity for both.

The heart of the love relationship is how the lovers view it from the inside, how they feel about their partner and about themselves within it, and the particular ways in which they are good *to* each other. Each person in love delights in the other, and also in giving delight; this often expresses itself in being playful together. In receiving adult love, we are held worthy of being the primary object of the most intense love, something we were not given in the childhood oedipal triangle.* Seeing the other happy with us and made happy through our love, we become happier with ourselves.

To be englowed by someone's love, it must be we ourselves

* Another Greek tale, that of Telemachus at home with Penelope while Odysseus wanders, provides a different picture of the family triangle's character. A father is a needed protector, not just someone to compete with for the mother's love. If the mother is as attractive as the child thinks, in the absence of the father other suitors will present themselves before her. And unlike the father, who will not kill the competitive child or maim him (despite what the psychoanalytic literature depicts as the child's anxieties), these suitors *are* his enemies. Telemachus *needs* his father—to maintain the *safe* triangle—and so he sets out to find him.

who are loved, not a whitewashed version of ourselves, not just a portion. In the complete intimacy of love, a partner knows us as we are, fully. It is no reassurance to be loved by someone ignorant of those traits and features we feel might make us unlovable. Sometimes these are character traits or areas of incompetence, clumsiness, or ignorance; sometimes these are personal bodily features. Complex are the ways parents make children uncomfortable about sites of pleasure or elimination, and these feelings can be soothed or transformed in the closest attentive and loving sexual intimacy. In the full intimacy of love, the full person is known and cleansed and accepted. And healed.

To be made happy with yourself by being loved, it must be you who is loved, not some feature such as your money. People want, as they say, to be loved "for themselves." You are loved for something else when what you are loved for is a peripheral part of your own self-image or identity. However, someone for whom money, or the ability to make it, was central to his identity, or for whom good looks or great kindness or intelligence was, might not be averse to love's being prompted by these characteristics. You can fall in love with someone because of certain characteristics and you can continue to delight in these; but eventually you must love the person himself, and not *for* the characteristics, not, at any rate, for any delimited list of them. But what does this mean, exactly?

We love the person when being together with that person is a salient part of our identity as we think of it: "being with Eve," "being with Adam," rather than "being with someone who is (or has) such-and-such. . . ." How does this come about? Characteristics must have played some important role, for otherwise why was not a different person loved just as well? Yet if we continue to be loved "for" the characteristics, then the love seems conditional, something that might change or disappear if the characteristics do. Perhaps we should think of love as like imprinting in ducks, where a duckling will attach itself to the first sizable moving object it sees in a certain time period and follow that as its mother. With people, perhaps characteristics set off the imprint of love, but then the person is loved in a way that is no longer based upon retaining those characteristics. This will be helped if the love is based at first upon a wide range of characteristics; it begins as conditional, contingent upon the loved person's having these desirable characteristics, yet given their range and tenacity, it is not insecure.*

However, love between people, unlike imprinting with ducks, is not unalterable. Though no longer dependent upon the particular characteristics that set it off, it *can* be overcome over time by new and sufficiently negative other characteristics. Or perhaps by a new imprinting onto another person. Yet this alteration will not be sought by someone within a *we*. If someone were loved "for" certain desirable or valuable characteristics, on the other hand, then if someone else came along who had those characteristics to a greater extent, or other even more valuable characteristics, it seems you should love this new person more. And in that case, why merely wait for a "better" person to turn up; why not actively seek to "trade up" to someone with a "higher score" along valuable dimensions? (Plato's theory is especially vulnerable to these questions, for there it is the Form of Beauty that is the ultimate and appropriate object of love; any particular person serves merely as a bearer of characteristics that awaken in the lover a love of the Form, and hence any such person should be replaceable by a better awakener.†)

A readiness to trade up, looking for someone with "better" characteristics, does not fit with an attitude of love. An illuminating view should explain why not, yet why, nevertheless, the attitude of love is not irrational. One possible and boring explanation is eco-

---

* Being loved *for* characteristics seems to go with the notion of love being deserved, the characteristics being the basis of the desert. This notion of love's being deserved is a strange one; no one deserves non-love because they fall short of high standards. We do sometimes say someone is "unworthy" of another's love, but by this we mean that person cannot respond appropriately to being (romantically) loved, cannot respond in a loving way. (The person need not love romantically in return but the genuine love that was offered must at least be turned away in a loving way.) To be worthy of (romantic) love, then, is simply to have the capacity to love in return. Yet if that capacity is not evident beforehand in a person, might it not be created or evoked by that person's being loved? Such is the hope of those who love, convinced that the depth and nobility of their own love will awaken love in the other; it takes a certain experience of the world to discover that this is not always so.

† See Gregory Vlastos, "The Individual as an Object of Love in Plato," in his *Platonic Studies* (Princeton: Princeton University Press, 1973), pp. 3–34.

nomic in form. Once you have come to know a person well, it would take a large investment of time and energy to reach the comparable point with another person, so there is a barrier to switching. (But couldn't the other person promise a greater return, even taking into account the new costs of investment?) There is uncertainty about a new person; only after long time and experience together, through arguments and crises, can one come to know a person's trustworthiness, reliability, resiliency, and compassion in hardships. Investigating another candidate for coupledom, even an apparently promising one, is likely eventually to reach a negative conclusion and it probably will necessitate curtailing or ending one's current coupled state. So it is unwise to seek to trade up from a reasonably satisfactory situation; the energy you'd expend in search might better be invested in improving your current *we*.

These counsels of economic prudence are not silly—far from it—but they are external. According to them, nothing about the nature of love itself focuses upon the particular individual loved or involves an unwillingness to substitute another; rather, the likelihood of losses from the substitution is what militates against it. We can see why, if the economic analysis were so, we would welcome someone's directing an attitude of love toward us that includes commitment to a particular person, and we can see why we might have to trade the offering or semblance of such an attitude in order to receive it. But why would we want actually to give such a commitment to a particular person, shunning all other partners? What special value is reached through such a love relationship committed to particularism but in no other way? To add that we care about our partners and so do not want to cause them hurt by replacing them is true, yet does not answer the question fully.

Economic analysis might even provide somewhat more understanding.* Repeated trading with a fixed partner with special resources might make it rational to develop in yourself specialized assets for trading with that partner (and similarly on the partner's part toward you); and this specialization gives some assurance that you will continue to trade *with that party* (since the invested resources

* This paragraph was suggested by the mode of economic analysis found in Oliver Williamson, *The Economic Institutions of Capitalism* (New York: The Free Press, 1986).

would be worth much less in exchanges with any third party). Moreover, to shape yourself and specialize so as to better fit and trade with that partner, and therefore to do so less well with others, you will want some commitment and guarantee that the party will continue to trade with you, a guarantee that goes beyond the party's own specialization to fit you. Under some conditions it will be economically advantageous for two such trading firms to combine into *one* firm, with all allocations now becoming internal. Here at last we come to something like the notion of a joint identity.

The intention in love is to form a *we* and to identify with it as an extended self, to identify one's fortunes in large part with its fortunes. A willingness to trade up, to destroy the very *we* you largely identify with, would then be a willingness to destroy your self in the form of your own extended self. One could not, therefore, intend to link into another *we* unless one had ceased to identify with a current one—unless, that is, one had already ceased to love. Even in that case, the intention to form the new *we* would be an intention to *then* no longer be open to trading up. It is intrinsic to the notion of love, and to the *we* formed by it, that there is not that willingness to trade up. One is no more willing to find another partner, even one with a "higher score," than to destroy the personal self one identifies with in order to allow another, possibly better, but discontinuous self to replace it. (This is not to say one is unwilling to improve or transform oneself.) Perhaps here lies one function of infatuation, to pave and smooth the way to uniting in a *we;* it provides enthusiasm to take one over the hurdles of concern for one's own autonomy, and it provides an initiation into *we*-thinking too, by constantly occupying the mind with thoughts of the other and of the two of you together. A more cynical view than mine might see infatuation as the temporary glue that manages to hold people together until they are stuck.

Part of the process by which people soften their boundaries and move into a *we* involves repeated expression of the desire to do so, repeatedly telling each other that they love each other. Their statement often will be tentative, subject to withdrawal if the other does not respond with similar avowals. Holding hands, they walk into the water together, step by step. Their caution may become as great as when two suspicious groups or nations—Israel and the Palestinians might be an example—need to recognize the legitimacy of one other.

Neither wants to recognize if the other does not, and it also will not suffice for each to announce that it will recognize if the other one does also. For each then will have announced a conditional recognition, contingent upon the other's unconditional recognition. Since neither one has offered this last, they haven't yet gotten started. Neither will it help if each says it will recognize conditional upon the other's conditional recognition: "I'll recognize you if you'll recognize me if I'll recognize you." For here each has given the other a three-part conditional announcement, one which is contingent upon, and goes into operation only when there exists, a two-part conditional announcement from the other party; so neither one has given the other exactly what will trigger that other's recognition, namely a two-part announcement. So long as they both symmetrically announce conditionals of the same length and complexity, they will not be able to get started. Some asymmetry is needed, then, but it need not be that either one begins by offering unconditional recognition. It would be enough for the first to offer the three-part recognition (which is contingent upon the other's simple two-part conditional recognition), and for the second to offer the two-part conditional recognition. The latter triggers the first to recognize outright and this, in turn, triggers the second to do the same. Between lovers, it never becomes this complicated explicitly. Neither makes the nested announcement "I will love you if you will love me if I will love you," and if either one did, this would not (to put it mildly) facilitate the formation of a *we*. Yet the frequency of their saying to each other, "I love you," and their attention to the other's response, may indicate a nesting that is implicit and very deep, as deep as the repeated triggering necessary to overcome caution and produce the actual and unconditional formation of the *we*.

Even after the *we* is formed, its motion is Aristotelian rather than Newtonian, maintained by frequent impetus. The avowals of love may not stop, and neither may romantic gestures, those especially apt actions, breaking the customary frame, that express and symbolize one's attachment to the *we* or, occurring earlier, the desire to form it.

Granting that a willingness to trade up is incompatible with love and with the formation of a *we* with a particular person, the question becomes one of whether it is rational to love in that particular way. There is the alternative of serious and significant personal ties without a joint identity, after all—friendships and sexual relationships, for instance. An answer could be given by the long and obvious list of the things and actions and emotions especially made possible and facilitated by the *we*. It is not unreasonable to want these, hence not irrational to enter into a *we* including forgoing the option of trading up. Yet it distorts romantic love to view it through the lens of the egoistic question "What's in it for me?" What we want when we are in love is to be with that person. What we want is to be with her or him—not *to be someone who is with her or him*. When we are with the other person, to be sure, we are someone who is with that person, but the object of our desire is not being that kind of someone. We want to make the other person happy, and also, but less so, to be the kind of person who makes her or him happy. It is a question of the emphasis, of how we describe what we want and seek—to use the philosophers' language, a question of the intentional object of our desire.

The way the egoistic question distorts romantic love is by switching the focus of attention from the relation between the lovers to the way each lover in the relation is. I do not mean that the way they are then is unimportant; how good reciprocated romantic love is for us is part of the reason why we desire and value it. But the central fact about love is the relation between the lovers. The central concern of lovers, as lovers, what they dwell upon and nurture, is the other person, and the relation between the two of them, not their own state. Of course, we cannot completely abstract a relation from whatever stands in it. (Contemporary extensional logic treats a relation simply as a set of the ordered pairs of things that—as we would say—stand in the relation.) And in fact, the particularity of a romantic relation does arise from the character of the lovers and then enhances that. Yet what is most salient to each is the other person and what holds between the two of them, not themselves as an endpoint of the relation. There is a difference between wanting to hug someone and using them as an opportunity for yourself to become a hugger.

The desire to have love in one's life, to be part of a *we* someday, is not the same as loving a particular person, wanting to form a *we* with that person in particular. In the choice of a particular partner, reasons can play a significant role, I think. Yet in addition to the merits of the other person and her or his qualities, there also is the question of whether the thought of forming a *we* with that person brings excitement and delight. Does that identity seem a wonderful one for you to have? Will it be *fun*? Here the answer is as complicated and mysterious as your relation to your own separate identity. Neither case is completely governed by reasons, but still we might hope that our choices do meet what reasoned standards there are. (The desire to continue to feel that the other is the right partner in your *we* also helps one surmount the inevitable moments in life together when that feeling itself becomes bruised.) The feeling that there is just "one right person" in the world for you, implausible beforehand—what lucky accident made that one unique person inhabit your century?—becomes true after the *we* is formed. Now your identity is wrapped up in that particular *we* with that particular person, so for the particular *you* you now are, there *is* just one other person who is right.

In the view of a person who loves someone romantically, there couldn't be anyone else who was better as a partner. He might think that person he is in love with could be better somehow—stop leaving toothpaste in the sink or whatever—but any description he could offer of a better mate would be a description of his mate changed, not one of somebody *else*. No one else would do, no matter what her qualities. Perhaps this is due to the particularity of the qualities you come to love, not just a sense of humor but that particular one, not just some way of looking mock-stern but that one. Plato got the matter reversed, then; as love grows you love not general aspects or traits but more and more particular ones, not intelligence in general but that particular mind, not kindness in general but those particular ways of being kind. In trying to imagine a "better" mate, a person in romantic love will require her or him to have a very particular constellation of very particular traits and—leaving aside various "science fiction" possibilities—no other person *could* have precisely those traits; therefore, any imagined person will be the same mate (perhaps) somewhat changed, not somebody else. (If that same mate actually alters, though, the romantic partner may well come to love and require that new constellation of particulars.) Hence, a person in romantic love *could not* seek to "trade up"—he would have to seek out the very same person. A person not in love might seek someone with certain traits, yet after finding someone, even (remarkably) a person who has the traits sought, if he loves that person she will show those traits in a particularity he did not initially seek but now has come to love—her particular versions of these traits. Since a romantic mate eventually comes to be loved, not for any general dimensions or "score" on such dimensions—that, if anything, gets taken for granted—but for his or her own particular and nonduplicable way of embodying such general traits, a person in love could not make any coherent sense of his "trading up" to *another*.

This does not yet show that a person could not have many such different focused desires, just as she might desire to read this particular book and also that one. I believe that the romantic desire is to form a *we* with that particular person *and* with no other. In the strong sense of the notion of identity involved here, one can no more be part of many *we*s which constitute one's identity than one can simultaneously have many individual identities. (What persons with multiple personality have is not many identities but not quite one.) In a *we*, the people *share* an identity and do not simply each have identities that are enlarged. The desire to share not only our life but our very identity with another marks our fullest openness. What more central and intimate thing could we share?

The desire to form a *we* with that person and no other includes a desire for that person to form one with you yourself and with no other; and so after sexual desire links with romantic love as a vehicle for its expression, and itself becomes more intense thereby, the mutual desire for sexual monogamy becomes almost inevitable, to mark the intimacy and uniqueness of forming an identity with that one particular person by directing what is the most intense physical intimacy toward her or him alone.

It is instructive here to consider friendship, which too alters and recontours an individual's boundaries, providing a distinct shape and character to the self. The salient feature of friendship is *sharing*. In sharing things—food, happy occasions, football games, a concern with problems, events to celebrate—friends especially want these to be had together; while it might constitute something good when each person has the thing separately, friends want that it be had or done by both (or all) of them *together*. To be sure, a good thing does get magnified for you when it is shared with others, and some things can be more fun when done together—indeed, fun, in part, is just the sharing and taking of delight in something together. Yet in friendship the sharing is not desired simply to enlarge our individual benefits.

The self, we shall see later, can be construed as an appropriative mechanism, one that moves from reflexive awareness of things to *sole* possession of them. The boundaries between selves get constituted by the specialness of this relation of possession and ownership—in the case of psychological items, this generates the philosophical "problem of other minds." Things shared with friends, however, do not stand in a unique and special relationship to any one self as its sole possession; we join with friends in having them and, to that extent at least, our selves and theirs overlap or the boundaries between them are less sharp. The very same things—experiences, activities, conversations, problems, objects of focus or of amusement—are part of us both. We each then are related closely to many things that another person also has an equally close relationship to. We therefore are not separate selves—not so separate anyway. (Should we diagram friendship as two circles that overlap?)

A friendship does not exist *solely* for further purposes, whether a political movement's larger goals, an occupational endeavor, or simply the participant's separate and individual benefits. Of course, there can be many further benefits that flow within friendship and from it, benefits so familiar as not to need listing. Aristotle held one of these to be most central; a friend, he said, is a "second self" who is a means to your own self-awareness. (In his listing of the virtuous characteristics one should seek in a friend, Aristotle takes your parents' view of who your friends should be.) Nevertheless, a relationship is a friendship to the extent that it shares activities for no further purpose than the sharing of them.

People seek to engage in sharing beyond the domain of personal friendship also. One important reason we read newspapers, I think, is not the importance or intrinsic interest of the news; we rarely take action whose direction depends upon what we read there, and if somehow we were shipwrecked for ten years on an isolated island, when we returned we would want a summary of what had happened meanwhile, but we certainly would not choose to peruse the back newspapers of the previous ten years. Rather, we read newspapers because we want to *share* information with our fellows, we want to have a range of information in common with them, a common stock of mental contents. We already share with them a geography and a language, and also a common fate in the face of large-scale events. That we also desire to share the daily flow of information shows how very intense our desire to share is.

Nonromantic friends do not, in general, share an *identity*. In part, this may be because of the crisscrossing web of friendships. The friend of your friend may be your acquaintance, but he or she is not necessarily someone you are close to or would meet with separately. As in the case of multiple bilateral defense treaties among nations, conflicts of action and attachment can occur that make it difficult to delineate any larger entity to which one safely can cede powers and make the bearer of a larger identity. Such considerations also help explain why it is not feasible for a person simultaneously to be part of multiple romantic couples (or of a trio), even were the person to desire this. Friends want to share the things they do *as* a sharing, and they think, correctly, that friendship is valuable partly *because* of its sharing—perhaps specially valuable because, unlike the case of romantic love, this valued sharing occurs *without* any sharing of identity.

We might pause over one mode of sharing that, while it is not done primarily for its own sake, produces a significant sense of solidarity. That is participating with others in joint action directed toward an external goal—perhaps a political cause or reform movement or occupational project or team sport or artistic performance or scientific endeavor—where the participants feel the pleasures of joint and purposeful participation in something really worthwhile. Perhaps there is a special need for this among young adults as they leave the family, and that in part constitutes youth's "idealism." Linked with others toward a larger joint purpose, *joined* with them at the same node of an effectual causal chain, one's life is no longer simply private. In such a way citizens might think of themselves as creating together, and sharing, a memorable civilization.

We can prize romantic love and the formation of a *we*, without denying that there may be extended times, years even, when an adult might best develop alone. It is not plausible, either, to think that every single individual, at some or another time in his life, would be most enhanced as part of a romantically loving *we*—that Buddha, Socrates, Jesus, Beethoven, or Gandhi would have been. This may be, in part, because the energy necessary to sustain and deepen a *we* would have been removed from (thereby lessening) these individuals' activities. But there is more to say. The particular vivid way these individuals defined themselves would not fit easily within a romantic *we;* their special lives would have had to be very different. Of course, a *we* often falls short of its best, so a prudent person might seek (or settle for) other modes of personal relationship and connection. Yet these extraordinary figures remind us that even at its best a *we* constitutes a particular formation of identity that involves forgoing some extraordinary possibilities. (Or is it just that these figures needed equally extraordinary mates?)

Just as the identity of the self continues over an extended period of time, so too is there the desire for the *we* to continue; part of identifying fully with the *we* is intending that it continue. Marriage marks a full identification with that *we*. With this, the *we* enters a new stage, building a sturdier structure, knitting itself together more fully. Being a couple is taken as given though not for granted. No longer focusing upon whether they *do* constitute an enduring *we,* the partners now are free confidently to build together a life with its own focus and directions. The *we* lives their life together. As egg and sperm come together, two biographies have become one. The couple's first child is their union—their earlier history was prenatal.

A *we* is not a new physical entity in the world, whether or not it is a new ontological one. However, it may want to give its web of love relationships a physical incarnation. That is one thing a home is about—an environment that reflects and symbolizes how the couple feel (and what they do) together, the spirit in which they are together; this also, of course, makes it a happy place for them to be. In a different way, and to a much greater extent, children can constitute a physical realization of the parents' love, an incarnation in the world of the valuable extended self the two of them have created. And children might be loved and delighted in, in part as this physical representation of the love between the parents. However, of course and obviously, the children are not merely an adjunct to the parents' love, as either a representation of it or a means of heightening it; they primarily are people to be cared for, delighted in, and loved for themselves.

Intimate bonds change the contours and boundaries of the self, altering its topology: in love, as we have seen, in the sharings of friendship, in the intimacy of sexuality. Alterations in the individual self's boundaries and contours also are a goal of religious quest: expanding the self to include all of being (Indian Vedanta), eliminating the self (Buddhism), or merging with the divine. There also are modes of general love for all of humanity, often religiously enjoined—recall how Dostoyevsky depicts Father Zossima in *The Brothers Karamazov*—that greatly alter the character and contours of the self, now no longer so appropriately referred to as "individual."

It may not be an accident that people rarely do simultaneously combine building a romantic *we* with a spiritual quest. It seems impossible to proceed full strength with more than one major alteration in the self's topology at a time. Nevertheless, it may well be important at times to be engaged in *some* or another mode of change in the boundaries and topology of the self, different ones at different times. Any such change need not be judged solely by how it substantively feeds back into the individual self, though. The new entity that is created or contoured, with its own boundaries and topology, has its own evaluations to make. An individual self justifiably might be proud to be supple enough to enter into these changes and exfoliate them, yet its perspective before the changes does not provide the only relevant standard. It *is* in the interests of an individual sperm or egg cell to unite to form a new organism, yet we do not continue to judge the new life by that gamete's particular interests. In love's bond, we metamorphose.

to consider an example of a particular emotion: pride. Suppose you say you feel proud that you read three books last week, and I say that you're misremembering; I counted and you read only one book last week. You grant the correction and reply that nevertheless you feel proud that you read three. This is bewildering. Since you no longer believe you read three books last week, whatever you are feeling, it isn't pride, or at least, it isn't being proud *of that*. To be proud of something, you have to think or believe it is the case (well, not exactly, as a general point about emotions, for you might think of a possibility in fantasy and have an emotion about it, without believing it to be the case).

Suppose you did read the books, and when you announce your pride I say it's nothing to be proud of; it's a bad thing to read three books, perhaps because it's bad to do anything in threes, or because books are bad, or it was bad to read the ones you did, or because you should have spent the time doing something else. I negatively evaluate your reading the three books. Suppose you accept this evaluation, agree that it was bad, and say that nevertheless you are proud that you did it. I am bewildered and ask whether there's some good aspect of your act that you are focusing upon, such as the courage to defy convention or whatever. You reply that everything about it is bad, but nonetheless you're proud of having done it. Here, too, whatever you are feeling, it isn't pride. To be proud that something is so is to believe it is so and also to positively evaluate it as somehow valuable or good or admirable. Along with your belief that you read the three books and your favorable evaluation of having done so, there perhaps goes a feeling, a sensation, an inner experience. What makes it an emotion *of pride* rather than of something else is the feeling's connection with this particular belief and evaluation. The simplest connection is when the belief and evaluation give rise to the feeling, when the person has the feeling because of his beliefs and evaluations. More complex is a situation where the feeling arises for some other reason and the person attributes it to that belief and evaluation; if while you're simply thinking positively of having read the three books I electrochemically stimulate you, producing a sensation in your chest, you may identify that as pride. But in whichever direction the connection goes, the emotion is partially constituted not just by the feeling but also by its attendant belief and evaluation:

a different belief or evaluation, a different emotion. (This does not mean we first are conscious of beliefs and evaluations and *then* have an emotion; sometimes we may discover our implicit beliefs and evaluations by pondering the emotions we are aware of feeling.) Emotion, therefore, is much more "cognitive" than one might think, and thus it can be judged in certain respects.

An emotion can be defective or inappropriate in three ways: the belief can be false; the evaluation can be false or wrong; or the feeling can be disproportionate to the evaluation. Suppose, walking along the street, I find a dollar bill and feel ecstatic. You ask whether I think it indicates this is my lucky day or that my fortunes have changed or that I am beloved by the gods, but no, it is none of these things. I simply am ecstatic. But finding a dollar isn't *that* wonderful a thing; the strength and intensity of the feeling should bear some proportionate relationship to the evaluation of how good a thing finding a dollar is—to the measure of the evaluation.

Let us say that an emotion *fits* when it has the above threefold structure of belief, evaluation, and feeling, and moreover when the belief is true, the evaluation is correct, and the feeling is proportionate to the evaluation. When the feeling is disproportionately strong, given the evaluation, this often indicates that the fact believed and evaluated is functioning symbolically; unconsciously the person views it as something else to which his degree of feeling *is* proportionate. (Alternately, the disproportionate feeling may be camouflage for the opposite unconscious emotion based upon an opposite unconscious evaluation.) When we have a positive emotion, one whose component evaluation is positive, we want the components to fit; we want the belief to be true, the evaluation to be correct, and the feeling to be proportionate. (On occasion we might want the belief and evaluation not simply to be true but also to be known to be so.)

In speaking of our evaluations as correct—that is, as something like objectively true and right—I am aware that I have touched upon controversial matters, but these can be sidestepped for now. Perhaps evaluations are not the sorts of things that can be objectively correct. In that case, we can utilize whatever standards and norms are appropriate for assessing them. Evaluations can be informed, unbiased, supported by reasons, justified, or whatever. Provided that not all evaluations are just matters of arbitrary subjective preference, none better grounded than any other, then we can plug in the strongest standards that are appropriate and say that an emotion is fitting only when its component evaluation satisfies those standards. We want the evaluations our emotions are based upon to be the best kind there can be, however that notion of bestness gets specified eventually.*

Intense emotions are the ones with evaluations that are *very* positive (or very negative) and also with proportionately great attendant feelings. Despite the special and central place it has been given by the philosophical tradition, happiness is only one of these intense emotions, roughly on a par with the rest.

An important part of life is having many intense positive emotions that are fitting (including some it would take Rilke to describe). Why? This is not just because the facts evaluated then would hold true; they could hold without being evaluated. Nor is it just because when something is valuable, there is a further value when it is responded to as valuable. For this could occur unemotionally, through correct evaluative judgments that are not accompanied by any attendant feelings. The character Spock in the television program *Star Trek* held correct beliefs, made correct evaluations, and acted on these, yet his life lacked emotion and inner feeling. Inner experiences are not the *only* things that matter, but they *do* matter. We would not plug into an experience machine, but we would not plug into an anesthetizing machine either.

Why are emotions important, above and beyond correct evaluations? (Call this the Spock Problem.) We might want to reply, simply, that having emotions is an essential part of being human. Yet even if having an emotional texture is essential to being human, the question of why we should prize emotions still would arise. Why should we especially prize being human, if *that* is what it is, unless it embodies something that objectively merits being prized? We don't have to prize every trait we have; why then should the fact that the trait is part of our essence make a significant difference? We need to investigate further the special value of having emotions.

---

* We want this, all other things being equal; if these best evaluations can be acquired only at a high cost in time or energy, we might be content to let some emotions rest on somewhat inferior evaluations. The same point also applies to beliefs. We want our beliefs to be based upon the best and most complete evidence or data, but when this comes dear we may be content to let certain beliefs rest upon rougher material, accepting their diminution in accuracy.

Is it that an emotionless life lacks the feelings that go along with correct evaluations and so is less pleasurable? But an emotionless life might contain other equally pleasurable feelings, provided these feelings are not attendant upon beliefs and evaluations, and so are not themselves components of emotions. Consider the pleasurable sensations and feelings of basking in the sun or floating in the water. These may be no less pleasurable than are the feelings that are components of intense positive emotions, and they are available to Spock, as are certain intellectual pleasures. So an emotionless (Spock) life need not be less pleasurable. Emotions might amplify pleasures and help to recall them more easily during pleasureless times, etc., so that it might be more difficult for a life without emotions to be very pleasurable, but I do not think the story is this simple. Rather, a life without emotions would be the poorer. Why?*

Emotions typically involve not only a psychological feeling but also physiological changes in respiration, pupil size, skin color, etc. Hence, they provide an especially close integration of the mind and the body. They integrate the psychological and the physical—belief, evaluation, and feeling. If a unity between mind and body is itself desirable and valuable, as I think it is, emotions provide a unique route.

Emotions also can link us closely to external value. When we positively evaluate a situation or fact, an emotional response links us more closely to the value we perceive than an unemotional evaluative judgment would. By value I do not mean our own subjective experience or liking of something; I mean the quality something has in virtue of which it is valuable. (In particular, the quality something has which makes it valuable in itself, apart from its further consequences and effects—a kind of value philosophers call "intrinsic value.") Value judgments are not all subjective, I am supposing; they can be right or wrong, correct or incorrect, true or false, well-founded or not. It is an objective matter whether something is valuable—that is,

* Emotions inform us of the evaluations we are making, including unconscious ones. Since the feelings involved are present to consciousness, we can use them to monitor, reexamine, and perhaps alter our underlying evaluations. This is a useful function, yet we would not renounce emotions if doing so would afford us an even more effective knowledge of our unconscious evaluations; in any case, that function would equally well be served if we could be aware of our evaluations without any attendant feeling. So this too is not the reason why emotions matter especially.

has the characteristics that make something valuable or exhibits the property that value consists in. I think that something is valuable insofar as it has a high degree of "organic unity," unifying and integrating disparate material. More will be said about this later, but whether or not this particular suggestion about the nature of value turns out to be correct—some of the things it may seem to leave out fall into a wider category than value—for present purposes we need only assume that value is not just a matter of opinion, that it is "out there" and has its own nature. Our current suggestion is that emotions are a response to value (whatever the correct theory of objective intrinsic value might turn out to be).

When we respond emotionally to value, rather than merely judging or evaluating it mentally, we respond more fully because our feelings and our physiology are involved. Emotions are a fitting and appropriate response to value. Emotions are to value as beliefs are to facts. (I will modify this statement somewhat later: Emotions are the fitting response to a wider category which includes value as a part but also includes other things such as meaning, intensity, and depth.) Given the nature of value, given its character—and given ours—we can be most responsive to value, its content and its contours, through emotion. While this strikes me as so, it is less clear why it is so. Perhaps we can use this to learn more about the nature of value. What must value be like if emotions are the appropriate response to it; what is the difference between value and facts if emotions stand to value as beliefs do to facts?

Beliefs are our appropriate response to nonevaluative facts. When our belief about a fact is true, and that belief is further linked to the fact in an appropriate way, then it is a case of knowledge. (Philosophers disagree about the precise nature of this knowledge-connection.) Our appropriate response to facts is to believe them and know that they hold. And just as we can hold false beliefs without impugning the objectivity of the facts out there, so too we can have unfitting emotions, responses to purported values that are incorrect.

I said earlier that emotions are fuller responses to value than are bare evaluative judgments, since emotions involve our bodily responses also. But we may wonder whether more complete responses always are more desirable. Would it be better yet if our heart also pumped out in Morse code a statement of the positive evaluation?

What emotion must provide is not merely an increased quantity of response to value but a response that is peculiarly appropriate.

Emotions provide a kind of picture of value, I think. They are our internal psychophysiological response to the external value, a response that is specially close by being not only due to that value but an analog representation of it.* Emotions provide a psychophysical replica of value (or of a wider, more inclusive category I discuss later). One way this might happen is the following: Something's being valuable involves its having a certain mode of structural organization to a certain degree—for example, a degree of organic unity; the responding emotion would be a psychophysical entity with a similar or parallel mode of organization. The emotion would be or contain something like a map of the value, or of the thing's being valuable. This model need not be an *exact* analog, however; it may be only the best analog we can produce or the best one it is worthwhile producing, given the extent of our other tasks, emotional resources, etc. (Perhaps this leaves it an exact analog, only now by a more complicated mapping.)

More needs to be said, however, about the way, in which emotion provides an analog of value. For suppose some extraterrestrials could dance expressively and represent external value though analog movement yet not have any elaborate feelings or emotions themselves. If this were possible, then we should have to claim that the medium of psychological feelings is an *especially* apt and appropriate locus for people's analog representation of value, or concede that other analog representations would do as well as emotions. However, perhaps the assumption that no emotions are involved here is too quick. If writers sometimes can write expressively without there being any emotions they have that they are expressing, or rather if the writing itself is the place where they have emotions, not in any inner psychological happenings but right there on the page, then perhaps the Martians can have them too in their dance motions. Emotions then might involve not necessarily inner feelings but rather

* Roughly put, an analog model or representation of a process somehow replicates that process rather than merely describing it. The model depicts a continuous process or dimension in the world by corresponding continuous changes in itself. The analog nature of emotions is more complicated than this brief statement can indicate; I have relegated some details to an appendix to this section.

analog representations (produced in a *certain* way) through *any* sufficiently rich personal medium; feelings would be only one way to constitute emotions.*

An intense emotion that is fitting is a close response to particular value, and is valuable in itself. It provides an analog model of the value that depends on the value's existence and perhaps tracks it closely. This combination of emotion in relation to value gives us a further integrated structure, added to the integrated structure of the value itself. If such additional integrated structures count as valuable—as I think they do—that gives us a *second* value. So it is a valuable thing that there exist fitting positive emotions.

But is it valuable for us? Fitting responses to value, which are valuable things, would be taking place within our psychophysiological structure, but are they valuable *for us*? We can (following some recent literature on Aristotle) distinguish between the way you can be that is best, the one whose existence is most valuable, and the way that is best and most valuable *for you*, the way that leaves you best off. Suppose your body could be used as a theater by microorganisms to do an intricate and beautifully interwoven pattern of movement and interaction. That might be the most valuable thing that could happen there; from the point of view of the universe it might be best that it occur. Since that process, however, constitutes a fatal disease for you, it would not be best *for you* that it occur. (Yet might this other fact help reconcile you to its occurrence?) Our question then is: Is it good *for us* to be beings with an emotional life or is it merely valuable from the point of the universe that it take place somewhere while we merely happen to be the theater where these valuable events occur?

This question overemphasizes our passivity, though. Many of our capacities are drawn upon when we respond emotionally to value, capacities of being able to recognize and appreciate value, to make evaluative judgments, and also to feel in tandem. Not just

---

* Gerard Manley Hopkins, we might note, held a particular version of the onomatopoetic theory of the origin of language: A word imitates in its substance and (what he called its) inscape the substance and inscape of what it names, so that some words provide a kinesthetic imitation of their referents. (See J. Hillis Miller, *The Disappearance of God* [Cambridge, Mass.: Harvard University Press, 1975], p. 285.) Words such as Hopkins describes would constitute analog models of what they represented.

anything can be a "theater" for such fine happenings; only beings with a feel for value can do it. But still, when we do it, is it good for us or is it merely a good thing happening? It certainly is good for us if, as Aristotle thought and John Rawls recently has emphasized, it is good for us to exercise our intricate capacities on valuable objects. Emotions then would be an important part of a valuable life. Moreover, these emotions recreate within us the value they respond to; at least, they create an analog model of it, which is also valuable. We therefore possess these intricate structures within ourselves. (Not only do these positive emotions feel pleasurable; they constitute a force we can utilize and in an important way, I think, they provide us with substance.) Moreover, we make them; we have the ability to produce—often we can't help producing—these emotional models of value which have value themselves by having some of the very same qualities they represent and picture. Our emotional capacity, then, constitutes one portion of our value-creating power; and being originators of value is part of our own special value. Emotions give us a certain *depth* and substance, too, a fact that becomes clearer when we also consider emotions that are not positive.

This leads us to an additional even shorter answer to the Spock problem. Emotions make many things—the situation of having emotions, our lives as they include emotions, and also ourselves as beings with emotion—more valuable, more intense, and more vivid than otherwise. Emotions do not simply feel good; intense and fitting emotions make us more.

Appendix: The Analog Nature of Emotion

Why is emotion a peculiarly appropriate response to value? (Because my reflections here are somewhat technical, I relegate them to this appendix; many readers may want to move directly to the next section.) Look, again, at the case of knowledge. In some way we want our response to a fact to track it, to vary subjunctively with it (so that if the fact didn't hold, the response wouldn't occur),* but why must that response be a *belief*? Why not respond with twitches or hummed musical tones, different ones for different facts?

A theory known as the picture theory of meaning provides one answer. According to this theory, sentences of a language state or represent or refer to facts by being pictures of them. (The sentences are able to be such pictures, the theory says, because facts are constituents arranged in certain structures and the sentences also contain corresponding constituent parts arranged similarly.) In this theory, supposing a belief was something like a sentence in the head, it would be the appropriate response to a fact because it would picture it.

The philosopher's picture theory of meaning now has few adherents—Wittgenstein, who first formulated it, rejected it later— but one part still does seem plausible: Language provides us with a systematic (though not a pictorial) way of representing facts. A belief is the appropriate kind of response to a fact then, because unlike an arbitrary item like a twitch or a sound or a flag signal in an (arbitrary) code, a belief represents and states a fact within a structured system of representing other facts; in that way a belief *means* or *refers to* the fact it states and believes in.

As a response to a nonevaluative fact, a belief can be fitting in two ways. Being in part akin to a sentence or proposition, it can represent or refer the content of the fact. Also, by being knowledge, by tracking the fact and being subjunctively related to it, the occurrence of the belief can represent when the fact holds. The belief thus can provide a model of when the fact holds, not simply a digital state-

* See my book *Philosophical Explanations,* Chapter 3.

ment, using bits of information, of the conditions under which it holds. (It does, though, also provide a digital statement of the content of the fact.)

Recall how the terms *analog* and *digital* are used in speaking of computers. An analog computer answers the question of how far something moves in a straight line by having something else within itself move proportionally in a straight line or rotate in an angle proportional to the length of the straight-line motion under scrutiny. It performs a computation by replicating within itself a model, an analog, of that process about which the computation is to be made. An analog computer models a continuous quantity in the world by (what are treated as) continuous changes within the computer itself. A digital computer, on the other hand, utilizes discontinuous bits of coded information which represent the topic of interest (not necessarily in analog fashion). The way the computer processes this information within itself so as to yield a desired answer need not model whatever real-world process is under study.

Thus, we have to distinguish three things: first, a digital statement or process that utilizes discontinuous bits of information and does not model its subject matter; second, a statement or process that represents discontinuous subject matter and models it discontinuously, perhaps in binary fashion; and third, a statement or process that represents continuous subject matter and also models it in some continuous fashion. (Note that whether something falls within this third category may depend on whether we choose to abstract from its minute discontinuous features and treat it as continuous.)

Our belief that a fact holds fits that fact in two ways. It fits its content by stating it digitally. It also fits the conditions under which the fact obtains by tracking that fact; hence, it models the fact when the fact holds. However, since truth (as that notion is involved in knowledge) is a binary notion, the binary notion of tracking is able to model something's being true. (This binary tracking notion is constituted by subjunctives about something's holding or not.) Thus, tracking provides a model of a belief's being true, but not an analog model. (If some nonbinary notion that involves degrees of truth played a role in understanding—as opposed to knowledge— then a binary process such as tracking could not suffice to model something's being understood.)

An emotion is able to be an analog model of value or of some more inclusive relevant category. The emotion's psychophysiological configurations and sequences model or picture the structure of the particular value that emotion responds to. Emotion provides a psychophysical replica of value, perhaps by exhibiting a parallel mode of organization, perhaps also by itself possessing some of the characteristics (such as intensity and depth) involved in value. An emotion would contain or be something like a map of value, of a thing's being valuable. (As we noted earlier, the analog need not be exact, only the best analog we can or should produce, given our emotional resources, our other tasks, etc.) A mere evaluation, unaccompanied by feeling, can state that something is valuable and even track when it is valuable, but it cannot give us a representation or model of the value or of the situation of that thing's being valuable. (Also, since the notion of being valuable is a dimensional notion, in modeling value it helps to have a process that is not simply binary.) The peculiarly intimate connection of emotion to value resides in the way emotion can provide an analog model of value and of its more inclusive salient category.

10

Happiness

SOME THEORISTS HAVE CLAIMED that happiness is the *only* important thing about life; all that should matter to a person—they say—is being happy; the sole standard for assessing a life is the amount or quantity of happiness it contains. It is ironic that making this exclusive claim for happiness distorts the flavor of what happy moments are like. For in these moments, almost everything seems wonderful: the way the sun shines, the way that person looks, the way water glistens on the river, the way the dogs play (yet not the way the murderer kills). This openness of happiness, its generosity of spirit and width of appreciation, gets warped and constricted by the claim—pretending to be its greatest friend—that only happiness matters, nothing else. That claim is begrudging, unlike happiness itself. Happiness can be precious, perhaps even preeminent, yet still be one important thing among others.

There are various ways to nibble away at the apparent obviousness of the view that happiness is the one thing that is important. First, even if happiness were the only thing we cared about, we would not care solely about its total amount. (When I use "we" in this way, I am inviting you to examine whether or not you agree. If you do, then I am elaborating and exploring our common view, but if after reflecting on the matter you find you do not agree, then I am traveling alone for a while.) We would care also about how that happiness was distributed within a lifetime. Imagine graphing someone's total happiness through life; the amount of happiness is represented on the vertical axis, time on the horizontal one. (If the phenomenon of happiness is extremely complicated and multidimensional, it is implausible that its amount could be graphed in this way—but in that case too the purported goal of maximizing our happiness becomes unclear.) If only the total amount of happiness mattered, we would be indifferent between a life of constantly increasing happiness and one of constant decrease, between an upward- and a downward-sloping curve, provided that the total amount of happiness, the total area under the curve, was the same in the two cases. Most of us, however, would prefer the upward-sloping line to the downward; we would prefer a life of increasing happiness to one of decrease. Part of the reason, but only a part, may be that since it makes us happy to look forward to greater happiness, doing so makes our current happiness score even higher. (Yet the person on the downward-sloping curve alternatively can have the current Proustian pleasure of remembering past happiness.) Take the pleasure of anticipation into account, though, by building it into the curve whose height is therefore increased at certain places; still most of us would not care merely about the area under *this* enhanced curve, but about the curve's direction also. (Which life would you prefer your children to have, one of decline or of advance?)

We would be willing, moreover, to give up some amount of happiness to get our lives' narratives moving in the right direction, improving in general. Even if a downwardly sloping curve had slightly more area under it, we would prefer our own lives to slope upward. (If it encompassed vastly greater area, the choice might be different.) Therefore, the contour of the happiness has an independent weight, beyond breaking ties among lives whose total amounts of happiness are equal. In order to gain a more desirable narrative direction, we sometimes would choose *not* to maximize our total happiness. And if the factor of narrative direction might justify forgoing some amount of happiness, so other factors might also.*

Straight lines are not the only narrative curves. It would be silly, though, to try to pick the best happiness curve; diverse biographies can fit the very same curve, and we care also about the particular content of a life story. That thing we really want to slope upward might be our life's narrative story, not its amount of happiness. With these stories held constant, we might then care only about happiness's

---

* It requires some care to accurately delineate the preference, all other things being equal, for the upward slope, to take into account the full complexities as one moves through life of anticipating and recollecting time intervals of changing lengths. However, the preference about the contour of one's children's lives avoids this problem, for you then are evaluating the life as a whole from a point outside it, and their anticipation and recollection will not enter if they do not know the life's contour. If anticipation of a future good pleases us more now than recollection of a past one, thereby affecting where the curves are placed, this fact itself might indicate a preference for the upward-sloping curve. (Similarly, people with amnesia might prefer that a given happiness were in their future rather than their past, even if the memory could be retrieved.) We also need to disentangle the preference for the upward slope from the preference for a happy ending which the upward slope might be taken to indicate. Consider one curve sloping upward until nearly the very end, and another curve sloping downward until nearly the very end, each having the same total area underneath; these two curves cross like an X. At nearly the very end, though, things are more complicated: For a person on each curve there is a half chance of staying at that level, and a half chance of immediately dropping or being raised to the level of the other curve, with life ending soon thereafter. The level of the end cannot be predicted from the course of the curve until then; if under these circumstances the upward slope still is preferred to the downward one, this preference concerns the course of the curves, not just their endings.

That we prefer the upward (and very much dislike the downward) slope might help explain other phenomena. Recently, two psychologists, Amos Tversky and Daniel Kahneman, have emphasized that in making choices people judge the outcomes of actions (contrary to the recommendations of existing normative theories) not by their absolute level but by whether they involve gains or losses as compared to some baseline or reference point, and that they weight losses more heavily than gains. (See Daniel Kahneman and Amos Tversky, "Prospect Theory," *Econometrica*, Vol. 47, 1979, pp. 263–291; "Rational Choice and the Framing of Decisions," in Robin Hogarth and Melvin Reder, eds., *Rational Choice* [Chicago: University of Chicago Press, 1987], pp. 67–94.) If people do prefer an upward-sloping curve, these two features are what one would expect: They will categorize outcomes as above or below a current or hypothetical reference point—are they gains or losses?—and they will give especially great weight to avoiding losses. (If, however, the preference for upward slope varies depending upon where the zero-level was, then that preference cannot be used to explain the two features; in any case, some might try to run the explanation in the other direction, seeing the preference for the upward slope as arising *from* the two features.)

amount, not its slope. However, this too would support the general point that something matters—an upward slope, whether to the narrative line or to the happiness curve—besides the quantity of happiness.

We also can show that more matters than pleasure or happiness by considering a life that has these but otherwise is empty, a life of mindless pleasures or bovine contentment or frivolous amusements only, a happy life but a superficial one. "It is better," John Stuart Mill wrote, "to be a human being dissatisfied than a pig satisfied; better to be Socrates dissatisfied than a fool satisfied." And although it might be best of all to be Socrates satisfied, having both happiness and depth, we would give up some happiness in order to gain the depth.

We are not empty containers or buckets to be stuffed with good things, with pleasures or possessions or positive emotions or even with a rich and varied internal life. Such a bucket has no appropriate structure within; how the experiences fit together or are contoured over time is of no importance except insofar as some particular arrangements make further happy moments more probable. The view that only happiness matters ignores the question of what *we*— the very ones to be happy—are like. How could the most important thing about our life be what it *contains,* though? What makes the felt experiences of pleasure or happiness more important than what we ourselves are like?

Freud thought it a fundamental principle of behavior that we seek pleasure and try to avoid pain or unpleasure—he called this the pleasure principle. Sometimes one can more effectively secure pleasure by not proceeding to it directly; one countenances detours and postponements in immediate satisfaction, one even renounces particular sources of pleasure, due to the nature of the outside world. Freud called this acting in accordance with the reality principle. Freud's reality principle is subordinate to the pleasure principle: "Actually, the substitution of the reality principle for the pleasure principle implies no deposing of the pleasure principle but only a safeguarding of it. A momentary pleasure, uncertain in its results, is given up but only in order to gain along the new path an assured pleasure at a later time."*

* "Formulations on the Two Principles of Mental Functioning," in James Strachey, ed., *The Standard Edition of the Complete Psychological Works of Sigmund Freud,* Vol. 12 (London: The Hogarth Press, 1958), p. 223.

These principles can be formulated more precisely, but technical refinements are not needed here.* Notice that there can be two different specifications of the pleasure to be maximized: the net immediate pleasure (that is, the total immediate pleasure minus the total immediate pain or unpleasure), or the total amount of net pleasure over a lifetime. (This latter goal might fully incorporate Freud's reality principle.) Since pleasure alone seemed too much tied to immediate sensation or excitement, some philosophers modulated the pleasure principle by distinguishing some kinds of pleasure as "higher." But even if this distinction between higher and lower pleasures were adequately formulated—something that hasn't yet been done—this would only add complications to the issue of choice: Can some amount of lower pleasure outweigh a higher pleasure? How much higher are the higher pleasures and do they too differ in their height? What is the overarching goal that incorporates this qualitative distinction? The distinction does not say that something different from pleasure also is important, just that the one thing that is important, pleasure, comes in different grades.

We can gain more precision about what pleasure is. By a pleasure or a pleasurable feeling I mean a feeling that is desired (partly) because of its own felt qualities. The feeling is not desired wholly because of what it leads to or enables you to do or because of some injunction it fulfills. If it is pleasurable, it is desired (in part at least) because of the felt qualities it has. I do not claim there is just one felt quality that always is present whenever pleasure occurs. Being pleasurable, as I use this term, is a function of being wanted partly for its own felt qualities, whatever these qualities may be. On this view, a masochist who desires pain for its own felt quality will find pain pleasurable. This is awkward, but no more so than masochism itself. If, however, the masochist desires pain because he (unconsciously) feels he deserves to be punished, hurt, or humiliated, not desiring pain for its own felt qualities but for what that pain announces, then

---

* Behavioral psychologists offer more precise quantitative versions of the pleasure principle in statements of the law of effect; operations researchers and economists offer formal theories of the (reality) constraints on actions. The reality and pleasure principles together are mirrored in decision theory's dual structure, with its probabilities of alternative possible outcomes of feasible actions, and its utilities of these outcomes; as did Freud, decision theory maintains the priority of the pleasure principle in its own principle of maximizing expected utility.

in that case the pain itself will not count as pleasurable. Someone *enjoys* an activity to the extent he engages in the activity because of its own intrinsic properties, not simply because of what it leads to or produces later. Its intrinsic properties are not limited to felt qualities, though; this leaves open the possibility that something is enjoyed yet not pleasurable. An example might be tennis played very forcefully; lunging for shots, scraping knees and elbows on the ground, you enjoy playing, but it is not exactly—not precisely—pleasurable.

From this definition of pleasure, it does not follow that there actually are any experiences that are wanted because of their own felt qualities; nor does it follow that we want there to be pleasurable experiences, ones we desire because of their felt qualities. What does follow from (my use of) the term is this: *If* experiences are pleasurable to us, then we do want them (to some extent). The term *pleasurable* just indicates that something is wanted because of its felt qualities. How much we want it, though, whether enough to sacrifice other things we hold good, and whether other things also are wanted, and wanted even more than pleasure, is left open. A person who wants to write a poem needn't want (primarily) the felt qualities of writing, or the felt qualities of being known to have written the poem. He may want, primarily, *to write* such a poem—for example, because he thinks *it* is valuable, or the activity of doing so is, with no special focus upon any felt qualities.

We care about things in addition to how our lives *feel* to us from the inside. This is shown by the following thought experiment. Imagine a machine that could give you any experience (or sequence of experiences) you might desire.* When connected to this experience machine, you can have the experience of writing a great poem or bringing about world peace or loving someone and being loved in return. You can experience the felt pleasures of these things, how they feel "from the inside." You can program your experiences for tomorrow, or this week, or this year, or even for the rest of your life. If your imagination is impoverished, you can use the library of suggestions extracted from biographies and enhanced by novelists and psychologists. You can live your fondest dreams "from the

---

* I first presented and discussed this experience-machine example in *Anarchy, State, and Utopia,* pp. 42–45.

inside." Would you choose to do this for the rest of your life? If not, why not? (Other people also have the same option of using these machines which, let us suppose, are provided by friendly and trust-worthy beings from another galaxy, so you need not refuse connecting in order to help others.) The question is not whether to try the machine temporarily, but whether to enter it for the rest of your life. Upon entering, you will not remember having done this; so no pleasures will get ruined by realizing they are machine-produced. Uncertainty too might be programmed by using the machine's optional random device (upon which various preselected alternatives can depend).

The question of whether to plug in to this experience machine is a question of value. (It differs from two related questions: an epistemological one—Can you know you are not already plugged in?—and a metaphysical one—Don't the machine experiences themselves constitute a real world?) The question is not whether plugging in is preferable to extremely dire alternatives—lives of torture, for instance—but whether plugging in would constitute the very best life, or tie for being best, because all that matters about a life is how it feels from the inside.

Notice that this is a *thought* experiment, designed to isolate one question: Do only our internal feelings matter to us? It would miss the point, then, to focus upon whether such a machine is techno-logically feasible. Also, the machine example must be looked at on its own; to answer the question by filtering it through a fixed view that internal experiences are the only things that *can* matter (so of course it would be all right to plug into the machine) would lose the op-portunity to test that view independently. One way to determine if a view is inadequate is to check its consequences in particular cases, sometimes extreme ones, but if someone always decided what the result should be in any case by *applying* the given view itself, this would preclude discovering it did not correctly fit the case. Readers who hold they *would* plug in to the machine should notice whether their first impulse was *not* to do so, followed later by the thought that since only experiences could matter, the machine would be all right after all.

Few of us really think that only a person's experiences matter. We would not wish for our children a life of great satisfactions that all depended upon deceptions they would never detect: although they take pride in artistic accomplishments, the critics and their friends too are just pretending to admire their work yet snicker behind their backs; the apparently faithful mate carries on secret love affairs; their apparently loving children really detest them; and so on. Few of us upon hearing this description would exclaim, "What a wonderful life! It feels so happy and pleasurable from the inside." That person is living in a dream world, taking pleasure in things that aren't so. What he wants, though, is not merely to take pleasure in them; he wants *them to be so.* He values their being that way, and he takes pleasure in them because he thinks they *are* that way. He doesn't take pleasure merely in *thinking* they are.

We care about more than just how things feel to us from the inside; there is more to life than feeling happy. We care about what is actually the case. We want certain situations we value, prize, and think important to actually hold and be so. We want our beliefs, or certain of them, to be true and accurate; we want our emotions, or certain important ones, to be based upon facts that hold and to be fitting. We want to be importantly connected to reality, not to live in a delusion. We desire this not simply in order to more reliably acquire pleasures or other experiences, as Freud's reality principle dictates. Nor do we merely want the added pleasurable feeling of being connected to reality. Such an inner feeling, an illusory one, also can be provided by the experience machine.

What we want and value is an actual connection with reality. Call this the second reality principle (the first was Freud's): To focus on external reality, with your beliefs, evaluations, and emotions, is valuable *in itself,* not just as a means to more pleasure or happiness. And it is this connecting that is valuable, not simply having within ourselves true beliefs. Favoring truth introduces, in a subterranean fashion, the value of the connecting anyway—why else would true beliefs be (intrinsically) more valuable within us than false ones? And if we want to connect to reality by knowing it, and not simply to have true beliefs, then if knowledge involves tracking the facts—a view I have developed elsewhere—this involves a direct and explicit external connection. We do not, of course, simply want contact with reality; we want contact of certain kinds: exploring reality and responding, altering it and creating new actuality ourselves. Notice that I am not saying simply that since we desire connection to actuality the experience machine is defective because it does not give us whatever we desire—though the example is useful to show we *do* desire some things in addition to experiences—for that would make "getting whatever you desire" the primary standard. Rather, I am saying that the connection to actuality is important whether or not we desire it—that is *why* we desire it—and the experience machine is inadequate because it doesn't give us *that*.*

No doubt, too, we want a connection to actuality that we also share with other people. One of the distressing things about the experience machine, as described, is that you are alone in your particular illusion. (Is it more distressing that the others do not share your "world" or that you are cut off from the one they do share?) However, we can imagine that the experience machine provides the very same illusion to everyone (or to everyone you care about), giving each person a coordinate piece of it. When all are floating in the *same* tank, the experience machine may not be *as* objectionable, but it is objectionable nevertheless. Sharing coordinate perspectives might be one criterion of actuality, yet it does not guarantee that; and it is *both* that we want, the actuality *and* the sharing.

---

* One psychologist, George Ainslie, offers an ingenious alternative explanation of our concern for contact with reality, one that sees this as a means, not as intrinsically valuable. According to Ainslie, to avoid satiation (and hence a diminution of pleasure) by *imagining* satisfactions, we need a clear line to limit pleasures to those less easily available, and reality provides that line; pleasures in reality are fewer and farther between (George Ainslie, "Beyond Microeconomics," in Jon Elster, ed., *The Multiple Self* [Cambridge, England: Cambridge University Press, 1986], pp. 133–175, especially pp. 149–157). Note that the phenomenon of satiation itself presumably has an evolutionary explanation. Organisms that don't get satiated in an activity (as in the experiments where apparatus enables rats to stimulate the pleasure centers in their brains) will stick to it to the exclusion of all else, and hence die of starvation or at any rate not go on to have or raise offspring. But in a reality framework too organisms will have to show some self-control, and not simply pursue easy pleasures even when they have not yet been satiated, so a reality principle would not completely fulfill the purpose Ainslie describes, and presumably other quite clear lines also could serve the purpose as well. One line might depend upon a division of the day according to biological rhythms—is sleep the time for easy pleasures and dreams the vehicle? Other lines might depend upon whether you were alone or accompanied, recently fed or not, close to a full moon, or whatever; these too could be used to restrict when the easy gain of pleasure was acceptable. Reality is not a unique means to this, nor is our concern with reality simply a means.

Notice that we have not said one should never plug in to such a machine, even temporarily. It might teach you things, or transform you in a way beneficial for your actual life later. It also might give pleasures that would be quite acceptable in limited doses. This is all quite different from spending the rest of your life on the machine; the internal contents of *that* life would be unconnected to actuality. It seems too that once on the machine a person would not make any choices, and certainly would not choose anything *freely*. One portion of what we want to be actual is our actually (and freely) choosing, not merely the appearance of that.

My reflections about happiness thus far have been about the *limits* of its role in life. What *is* its proper role, though, and what exactly is happiness; why has its role so often been exaggerated? A number of distinct emotions travel under the label of *happiness,* along with one thing that is more properly called a *mood* rather than an emotion. I want to consider three types of happiness emotion here: first, being happy that something or other is the case (or that many things are); second, feeling that your life is good now; and third, being satisfied with your life as a whole. Each of these three related happiness emotions will exhibit the general threefold structure that emotions have (described in the previous meditation): a belief, a positive evaluation, and a feeling based upon these. Where these three related emotions differ is in the object of the belief and evaluation, and perhaps also in the felt character of the associated feeling.*

The first type of happiness, being happy that some particular thing is the case, is reasonably familiar and clear, a straightforward instance of what has been said about emotion earlier. The second type—feeling that your life is good now—is more intricate. Recall those particular moments when you thought and felt, blissfully, that there was nothing else you wanted, your life was good then. Perhaps this occurred while walking alone in nature, or being with someone you loved. What marks these times is their completeness. There is something you have that you want, and no other wants come crowding in; there is nothing else that you think of wanting right then. I

---

* There is a need for an accurate phenomenology of the specific character of these feelings.

do not mean that if someone came up to you right then with a magic lamp, you would be at a loss to come up with a wish. But in the moments I am describing, these other desires—for more money or another job or another chocolate bar—simply are not operating. They are not felt, they are not lurking at the margins to enter. There is no additional thing you want right then, nothing feels lacking, your satisfaction is complete. The feeling that accompanies this is intense joy.

These moments are wonderful, and they are rare. Usually, additional wants are all too ready to introduce themselves. Some have suggested we reach this desirable state of not wanting anything else by the drastic route of eliminating *all* wants. But we don't find it helpful to be told to *first* get rid of our existing wants as a way of reaching the state of not wanting anything else. (And this is not simply because we doubt this route leads to an accompanying joy.) Rather, what we want is to be told of something so good, whose nature is so complete and satisfying, that reaching it will exclude any further wants from crowding in, *and* we want to be told how to reach this. Aristotle projected the quality of the feeling of not wanting anything additional out onto the world; he held that the complete good was such that nothing added to it could make it any better. I want to keep that quality within the feeling.

There are two conditions in which you feel that your life is good now, that there is nothing else you want: with the first a particular want already is satisfied; with the second you are embarked upon a process or path through which the other wants you have will be satisfied, and you have no *other* want than to be engaged in that process. Suppose someone wants nothing other than to go to the movies with friends, which he is doing. To be sure, he wants also to reach the movie theater, that it will not have burned down, that the projector will be operating, etc. However, these things all are included as parts of the process he is engaged in; they will come up in their appropriate turn. It would be different if instead he wanted to be going to a concert alone; then there *would* be something else he wanted. Since few goals are final and terminal—a point emphasized by John Dewey—the first mode of not wanting anything else usually will be found implicitly to involve the second mode, process. The fairy-tale Prince Charming wants nothing else once he has freed and married the princess because this means their living happily ever after.

One might worry that being happy all the time, in this second sense of the emotion of happiness, wanting nothing else, would eliminate all motivation for further activity or accomplishment. However, if what we want nothing other than is to be engaged in a process of living of a certain kind, for example, one involving exploring, responding, relating and creating—to be sure, we may want and expect this process also to include many moments of complete satisfaction of the first (nonprocess) type—then further activities and endeavors will be components of that very process.

When someone thinks, "My life now is good" the extent of time denoted by "now" is not fixed in advance. Hence, one can change its reference according to need. Even in a generally miserable period, you might narrow your gaze to a very particular moment, and want nothing else right then; alternatively, during a miserable moment you can recall that over a wider time period, one you also can call "now," your life is not miserable, and you might want nothing other than to be engaged in that life process, miserable moment and all. On the other hand, during moments of intense happiness we sometimes want to recall other kinds. For instance, within the Jewish tradition, at weddings one recalls and acknowledges the most bitter event, the destruction of the Temple; during school class reunions, one might pause in the celebrations to remember those who have died. We have not forgotten these events or people and even in our most intense happiness we pause to give them continuing due weight.

The third form taken by the emotion of happiness—satisfaction with one's life as a whole—has been explored by the Polish philosopher Wladyslaw Tatarkiewicz.* According to his account, happiness involves a complete, enduring, deep, and full satisfaction with the whole of one's life, a satisfaction whose component evaluation is true and justified. Tatarkiewicz builds so much into this notion—complete and total satisfaction, etc.—because he wants nothing to be superior to a happy life. But this makes it difficult for there to be two happy lives, one happier than the other. Here, we can be more relaxed about the fullness of the satisfaction, and about how high a degree

* Wladyslaw Tatarkiewicz, *Analysis of Happiness* (The Hague: Martinus Nijhoff, 1976), pp. 8–16.

of positiveness the evaluation involves. A happy life will be evaluated as good enough on the whole. A life can be a happy one in another sense, too, by containing many events of feeling happy about one thing or another—that was the first type of happiness emotion. Such a life might frequently feel happy, yet that person need not positively evaluate his life as a whole, even unconsciously. Indeed, he might make the opposite evaluation if he focused upon his life as a whole, perhaps because he thinks the constituent happy feelings not very important. Despite his frequent happy moments, then, he would not be happy in the third sense of being satisfied with his life as a whole.

We would be reluctant to term someone happy at a particular moment or in life in general if we thought the evaluations upon which his emotion was based were wildly wrong. Yet it would be too stringent simply to require that the evaluations be correct. Looking back upon earlier historical times, we may see people making evaluations which (by our lights) are incorrect yet which were understandable and not egregiously unjustified at that time; the incorrectness of the evaluation should not be an automatic bar to its composing happiness. (After all, we hope that recent gains in moral sensitivity to issues such as women's equality, homosexual rights, racial equality, and minority relations will not be the last.) Simply to substitute "justified" (or "not unjustified") for "correct" would misclassify the person whose emotion is based upon correct but at that time, in that context, unjustified evaluations. Perhaps what serves is the weaker disjunction: true or at any rate justified (or not completely unjustified). Someone whose emotion is based upon completely and egregiously unjustified and false evaluations we will be reluctant to term happy, however he feels. He should have known better.*

---

* Notice that an evaluation made now about your life during an earlier time period can differ from the evaluation you made then. The fact that different evaluations can be produced of that period of life—yours then, yours now, and also the evaluation that we, the observers, make—complicates the question of whether that period counts as happy. We are reluctant simply to treat its proper evaluation, for these purposes, as the one the person actually made then. For example, if you then evaluated your life positively and felt accordingly, but now in looking back you evaluate your overall life then in a negative way, were you happy then or not? At that earlier time you *felt* happy about your life then, but now you do not feel happy about your life then. Because of your current negative evaluation (especially if it is one we endorse), we would be reluctant to say, simply, that you were happy then.

This third sense of happiness—satisfaction with one's life as a whole—makes it extremely easy to understand why we would want to be happy or to have a happy life. First, there is simply the pleasure of having that emotion. Feeling happy or satisfied about one's life as a whole is pleasurable in itself; it is something we want for its own felt qualities. (This feeling generally will not be as intense, though, as the joy which accompanies the second notion of happiness, wanting nothing else.) However, other emotions also can involve equally intense pleasurable feelings; why, then, has happiness loomed so central? We also want this emotion of happiness to be *fitting*. If the emotion does fit our life, then the component beliefs about our life as a whole will be true and the component positive evaluation will be correct. Hence, we *will* have a life that *is* valuable, one it is correct to evaluate positively.

The object of this third form of the emotion of happiness is one's life as a whole. That object—life as a whole—also is precisely what we are trying to evaluate when we try to discover what a very good life is, in order to decide how to live. What could be simpler than to focus upon an emotion that does the evaluating for us? Add that the emotion is fitting, and we therefore can be sure the life is a good one.

Consider the corresponding question on the other side. If you then negatively evaluated your life and felt accordingly, yet now in looking back you positively evaluate that time, were you happy then or not? Your negative feelings then mean that you, even in retrospect, were *not* happy then, unless you also had many happy feelings then and your overall negative evaluation then, producing no extensively lasting feelings of unhappiness, was based upon more abstract grounds, perhaps that you weren't an exemplary tragically suffering hero at that time. If you now come to evaluate that period positively, feeling accordingly about it, and it did not contain extensive negative feelings then even though it was then negatively evaluated, might we not conclude that it *was* a happy time then, after all? Such complications make it difficult to offer a sleek and straightforward view of happiness.

Notice also an ambiguity in the notion of one's life as a whole, the object that is evaluated. It might mean the *whole* time slice of your current life, including all its aspects, not just a few; or it might mean the whole of your life until now. (Does it include also the future that is expected?) A person might be happy now, and be a happy person now, because of her current life and how she (correctly) evaluates it, even if her past was unhappy enough to lead her not only to have evaluated it negatively then but to now evaluate all her life until now as (on balance) negative. The question of whether a life is a good one overall does not focus just upon an evaluation of the current time slice, nor does it simply average the contemporaneous evaluations of each time slice (even if these were accurate), for the answer might depend also upon the narrative contours of the life, upon how these different time slices fit together.

(Add only that the evaluation was justified or not egregiously false, and it has a decent chance of being a good one.) However, for all we yet know, the reason a happy life must be a good one is not necessarily because of any feelings it contains but merely because if that evaluation was correct, the life has to be good. To think, because happiness certifies that a life is desirable, that happiness is supremely important in life is like thinking an accountant's positive statement is itself the most important fact in the operation of a firm. (Each statement, though, might produce further effects of its own.)

Another way to make this point: A life cannot just be happy while having nothing else valuable in it. Happiness rides piggyback on other things that are positively evaluated correctly. Without these, the happiness doesn't get started.

Happiness can occur at the metalevel as an evaluation *of* one's life, and at the object level as a feeling *within* the life; it can be in both places at once. No wonder happiness can seem to be the most important constituent of a life. For it *is* extremely important at the metalevel and it does occur (and can have some importance) at the object level too. The central importance of (this third notion of) happiness lies at the metalevel, though, as an evaluation of a life as a whole; hence, the crucial question is what in particular makes a life best. What characteristics must it have to be (correctly) evaluated in an extremely positive way? It is not very illuminating at this point simply to mention emotions of happiness once again.

This conclusion is reinforced if we ask what particular evaluation enters into this third emotion of happiness. Precisely which of the many different possible positive evaluations does happiness make of a life as a whole? Not that the life is a *moral* one, for that needn't make one happy; not that it is a happy one—that circle would not help; not simply that it is valuable that the life exist, that the universe is a better place for it, for someone might make that evaluation without being happy; not simply that the life is good, for you might grudgingly recognize that without thinking it fulfilled your major goals or that it was very good. Perhaps the evaluation of the life must be something like the following: that it is very good, also *for* the person living it, in whatever dimensions he considers most important and whatever dimensions *are* most important. This clearly leaves us with the question of which dimensions of a life *are* the important ones. What does make a life a good one? Once again, it is not illuminating simply to mention the emotion of happiness here. When we want to know what is important, we want to know what to be happy *about*.

There is another sense of the term *happiness:* having a happy mood or disposition. This is not itself an emotion but rather the proneness or tendency to have and feel the three types of happiness emotions just described. A mood is a tendency to make certain types of evaluations, to focus upon facts that can be evaluated that way, and to have the ensuing feelings. In a depressed mood, one is disposed to focus upon negative facts or upon the negative features of otherwise positive situations and hence to have the feelings appropriate to these. A happy person tends to look upon the bright side of things. (However, it would be foolish to want to do this in every situation.) A person's disposition, I think, is a tendency one level up, the tendency to be in certain moods. A person of happy disposition might be in a sad mood on occasion, because of specific factors, but that particular mood will not be an expression of his or her general tendency.

A happy disposition may be a more important determinant of happy feelings than any one of the person's true beliefs and positive evaluations, however large one of these may seem to loom for the moment; it may be more important than the specific character of the actual situation. For example, people frequently pursue goals that they think will make them happy (such as money, fame, power), yet achieving these produces happy feelings only temporarily. They do not linger long in making positive evaluations of these changes, and so the attendant feelings do not last very long either. A *continuing* tendency to look upon positive features of situations and have the attendant feelings—a happy disposition, in other words—is far more likely to result in continuing feelings of happiness.

If there is any "secret of happiness," it resides in regularly choosing some baseline or benchmark or other against which features of the current situation can be evaluated as good or improving. The background it stands out from—hence, the evaluation we actually make—is constituted by our own expectations, levels of aspiration, standards, and demands. And these things are up to us, open to our control. One salient background against which to evaluate is the way things recently were. Perhaps the importance to our happiness of things improving, of some or another upward slope to our lives, is due not, then, to the intrinsic importance of a directional process but to the fact that such a process leads us to judge the present against the recent past, which, happily, it surpasses, rather than against some other baseline from which it might fall short. A person intent upon feeling happy will learn to choose suitable evaluative benchmarks, varying them from situation to situation—he might eventually even choose one that would diminish that very intentness.

Happiness can be served, then, by fiddling with our standards of evaluation—which ones we invoke and which benchmarks these utilize—and with the direction of our attention—which facts end up getting evaluated. The experience machine was objectionable because it completely cut us off from actuality. How much better, though, is aiming at happiness by such purposeful selectivity, which points us only toward some aspects of reality and toward some evaluative standards, omitting others? Wouldn't happiness gained thus be like being on a *partial* experience machine? In the next meditation I consider the issue of which facts to focus upon; while the correct evaluative principles that apply to these facts may not be up to us, the benchmarks and baselines we employ and when we are satisfied in comparison to what are a matter not of external actuality but of our stance toward it. No particular benchmark or baseline is written in the world; when we employ one, even when we select a particular one just in order to be happy, we need not be denying any portion of reality or disconnecting from it. It is in this sense that our happiness is within our own power. Yet just this fact, that happiness depends upon how we look upon things—to be sure, looking upon them in a certain way may be harder in some situations than in others—may make us wonder how important happiness itself can be, if it is that arbitrary. How someone looks upon things, however, might be an important fact about him; people who can never be satisfied, no matter what, may have not simply an unfortunate trait of temperament but a flaw of character. Yet to willfully and constantly shift baselines to suit various situations in order to feel happy in each seems flighty and arbitrary too. Perhaps, although the baselines are not fixed by anything external, we expect a person to show a certain congruence or consistency in these, with only smooth and gradual changes over time. Even so, a person could increase his happiness by setting his uniform sights accordingly.

Moods can affect one's feelings in various obvious ways: by directing attention toward positive (or negative) facts, by resisting dwelling on certain types of facts when they come to attention, by adjusting the benchmarks, by intensifying the degree of the evaluation, by intensifying the degree of the associated feeling by affecting the factor of proportionality, or by lengthening the feeling's duration. What determines the mood, though? Most obvious is the person's general disposition, which is just his tendency to be in certain moods. Another factor—more surprising—is a prediction of what the day's emotions will be. A person wakes up in the morning with some general idea of what emotions are in store for him that day, what events are likely to occur, and how these events will affect him. Of course, this prediction draws upon knowledge of yesterday's conditions and events and of today's likely ones, but it also is to some significant extent self-fulfilling. By setting his mood, the prediction affects what he will notice, how he will evaluate it, and what he will feel, and hence helps to make the prediction come true. A mood is like a weather prediction that could affect the weather. (Moreover, the prediction will not be independent of the first factor, the person's disposition.)

"Anticipation is better than realization," the saying goes. Here is one reason why this sometimes might be so. When we anticipate the occurrence of a likely future event, an event we desire, our current level of felt well-being already gets raised by the amount of that future utility (as the economists term it) we think is coming, discounted by the probability. To make the point clear, let us suppose or fantasize that units of happiness and probabilities can be measured exactly. Then, for example, an event that we initially estimate as bringing us ten units of happiness later and which we think will have a .7 probability of happening raises our level by seven units (.7 times 10) immediately. For that expectation, that expected value, is a current one. When the event itself finally occurs, then, there is room for a rise of only three more units. (This corresponds to the uncertainty that it would occur, the remaining probability of .3 times 10.) Hence the anticipation now might feel better, a rise of seven units' worth, than the realization, a rise of only the remaining three units, when it finally comes; this phenomenon will hold when the probability of that future satisfaction is greater than one half.*

* That this occurs when the probability is greater than one half is a frequent psychological phenomenon, not a law. Some people look ahead with great fear to the possibility of the event's not occurring, and discount the future accordingly. When anticipation of a future good does add an amount to a person's current utility level, how will that person fare when the event doesn't occur?

We have found various reasons for thinking that happiness is not the only important thing in life: the contours of happiness over a lifetime, the importance of some contact with reality as shown by the experience machine example, the fact that other intense positive emotions have a similar status, the way evaluations built into the notion of happiness presuppose that other things too are of value. Still, we might grant that happiness is not the whole story yet wonder whether it isn't *most* of the story, the most important part. How can one try to estimate percentages on a question like this? Judging by happiness's small role in my own reflections—much of my thinking here was called forth by the weight others have given to it—it is only a small part of the *interesting* story.

Nevertheless, I want to recall near the close of this meditation how undeniably wonderful happiness, and a happy disposition, can be. How natural then that sometimes we think happiness is the most important thing in life. Those moments when we want to leap or run with exuberant energy, when our heart is light—how could we not want to have our life full of moments like these? Things feel just right, and with its optimism happiness expects this to continue and with its generosity, happiness wants to overflow.

Of course we wish people to have many such moments and days of happiness. (Is the proper unit of happiness the *day*?) Yet it is not clear that we want those moments constantly or want our lives to consist wholly and only of them. We want to experience other feelings too, ones with valuable aspects that happiness does not possess as strongly. And even the very feelings of happiness may want to direct themselves into other activities, such as helping others or artistic work, which then involve the predominance of different feelings. We want experiences, fitting ones, of profound connection with others, of deep understanding of natural phenomena, of love, of being profoundly moved by music or tragedy, or doing something new and innovative, experiences very different from the bounce and rosiness of the happy moments. What we want, in short, is a life and a self that happiness is a fitting response to—and then to give it that response.

11

Focus

EMOTIONS are to be connected to actuality—according to the second reality principle (discussed in the previous meditation)—as responses to the facts based upon correct beliefs and evaluations. However, there are many facts, many aspects of actuality. To which ones should our emotions connect?

Some things—traumas to those we love, monstrous public evil—must be evaluated negatively. Responding to these with not only negative evaluations but negative emotions will involve sadness, sorrow, horror. This will conflict, of course, with a desire for happiness and intense positive emotions. A proponent of maximizing our own happiness might recommend we ignore these negative portions of reality and focus our attention selectively only upon the positive. Sometimes that might be appropriate; a person in a Nazi extermination camp might focus eventually upon memories of Mozart's music in order to escape the horrors around him. But if this were his preoccupation from the beginning, smiling constantly in fond memory of the music, that reaction would be bizarre. Then he would be disconnected from important features of his world, not giving them emotional attention commensurate with the evil they inflict.

However, the second reality principle would not exclude this kind of disconnection: The person's beliefs about Mozart's music and evaluations of it might be correct and his feelings might be commensurate with the music's beauty. These feelings are appropriate to the music, but focusing upon the music is not appropriate *then*. We need an additional reality principle, concerning not the accuracy of attention's focus—the second principle handled this—but its *direction*. Just as our feelings should be proportionate to our evaluations when our attention is focused, so too in the focusing we should pay attention to the things around us in proportion to their importance, not simply to the things but to the aspects that make them important. This principle—call it the third reality principle—has been only gestured at here, not formulated precisely. (Could the person in the extermination camp argue that Mozart's music *is* more important to him, and should be so, than what is happening right then?) How should the balance be struck between looking at things from your perspective, so that what is "around you" occupies the foreground of importance, and taking the widest and most general view "from the standpoint of the universe"? Perspectival balance is not the only issue that needs to be resolved to adequately formulate the third reality principle. What precise notion of importance does this principle use, toward which our attention should be proportionately focused?

Questions about selective attention pertain to knowledge of nonevaluative facts too, not just to emotions. It sometimes is said that all knowledge is intrinsically valuable. Yet some truths are completely trivial. There is *no* value or importance in knowing the number of grains of sand on Jones Beach—as an isolated fact, that is. (It would be different if you were testing or constructing a theory of beach formation; that bit of information then might aid in discovering a deep scientific law or general principle.) What balance should be struck between pursuing deep or general truths and evaluative principles on the one hand, and pursuing particular details of practical import for us on the other? When I speak later of the third reality principle, I shall mean an adequately formulated principle concerning the focus and direction of attention, in the spirit of the present paragraphs.

The fundamental evaluative activity is selectivity of focus, focusing here rather than there. We can imagine a theory, though, that maintains that everything is equally important, nothing more important than anything else, so that anything can be attended to, to whatever extent. This might seem to be a noble, nonelitist view, finding equal value everywhere. (Will it object, though, if we pay it no attention?) But what makes it an *evaluation* of things as valuable—mustn't an evaluation be something that directs our attention and concern? To be consistent, it would have to maintain also that partial or cloudy attention, or inattention itself, is no worse or less important than fullness and sharpness of focus, and that we should think that about our own case too. It would constitute an evaluation, then, not by directing our attention in any way but by giving it permission to be every way, any way at all. (Here, if not earlier, the supposition diverges from Buddhist views.) Whether or not it is good economics, laissez-faire does not constitute an acceptable attitude toward life in general.

The example of the experience machine shows we do not want to be completely disconnected from actuality; we do not want zero percent contact. But how have I gotten from our wanting *some* contact to our wanting the maximum amount, 100 percent? Perhaps some amount greater than zero percent but considerably less than 100 percent would be enough to satisfy our desire for contact with actuality; beyond that amount the happiness principle could have full sway. Above that threshold percentage, happiness would not be forgone to further increase contact with actuality, but rosy illusions would be welcome if they increased happiness. To say there is intrinsic value to contact with actuality can mean three things of increasing strength: first, that there is intrinsic value to there being *some* (nonzero) contact; second, that there is a finite value to every bit of contact there is, even above the threshold, though this value sometimes can be outweighed by other things; or third, that there is a value to contact with actuality that cannot be overridden, hence that amount or degree of contact is to be maximized. Since I believe the concentration camp prisoner may not ignore his surroundings completely, concentrating mainly upon Mozart—no doubt he also will focus upon other less immediate actualities too that bring him above some threshold—I do not stop with the weakest of the reality principles, mandating merely some nonzero contact. But since I also believe the prisoner need not focus completely upon the horror of his surroundings, that he may escape them in imagination or alternative focus, I cannot endorse the strongest form of the principle, which mandates the maximum amount of contact with actuality. I rest, then, somewhere in between, holding that each bit of contact with actuality does have its intrinsic weight, the more significant the actuality the greater the weight, but that other considerations (including considerations of happiness and of asserting autonomy by refusal to be victimized completely) sometimes can outweigh the value of the most complete focus upon the actuality one finds oneself amid. Attention can be focused upon different parts of actuality, however, so we might contemplate a reality principle *slanted* toward focus upon the positive insofar as this is possible without significant detachment from the actuality one is amid.

Advertising is an interesting case to consider. Besides its functions of giving information and catching attention and its less happy one of sidestepping rational evaluation, advertising can manipulate images to differentiate a product—cigarettes or beer, for example—in a way that is not based on any relevant differences in the objects' actual characteristics. One cigarette or drink is not "really" more rough and Western, another not really more elegant. We can see this differentiation as performing a useful function, though, not only for the sellers of products but for their buyers too. We all might like, upon occasion, to feel an unusual way or to reinforce ways we would like to be. We sometimes do this with fictional or film characters, moving through life somewhat in their aura. With their style of movement or standing, dress or speech, we feel more like them, tough or elegant, sophisticated or sexy, daring, adventurous or rough-hewn. We also might welcome products with chemicals added that temporarily could make us feel these ways, enabling us to relax (or tense) into certain roles and moods. Advertising expands our range of opportunities in these ways, even when it is not based on any actual differentiating characteristic of the product. By creating symbolic props we can utilize in our fantasy life, advertising functions as the added chemical would. Armed thus with the right cigarette or car or drink, we can play at being a certain way or more easily imagine we are that way. (Even when products do differ, part of their qualities' function might be to fit into and prompt further fantasies.) Sometimes when we behave thus, others will produce fitting responses and thereby make our role more comfortable, even eventually, more authentic. This mode of creating and utilizing illusion need not come into conflict with the reality principles if the person remains aware it is an induced role. This does not mean, however, that he must constantly be aware of it as false. If the symbolic prop gives him the confidence to exercise the wit or courage he has, then he does become more witty or courageous. However, advertising should not aim to convince someone that a product will make her invulnerable to bullets or detection, for example. Few people growing up in our society are that simple, though, and most advertisers wisely stick to creating pleasant illusions that can be sustained or at least that cannot be disconfirmed obviously and bluntly.

The ability and opportunity to focus our attention, to choose what we will pay attention to, is an important component of our autonomy.* Voluntary control over our attention also is an important feature of our psychological well-being. An impairment in ability to focus attention marks some neurotic disorders.† In general, we need to be able to alter our attention's focus as appropriate, back and forth from the general picture to details, from confirmation to things that don't fit, from the surface to what is deep, from the immediate to the long-term. Call this the *zoom lens* ability. In addition to focus near or far, I mean to include also control over the direction attention points in. Without such control of the mode and object of our attention, it would be difficult to behave effectively or to have a rounded emotional life.

Emotions therefore do not, or need not, simply wash over us. We can have a certain control over them by modifying the beliefs we

---

* What we presently focus upon is affected by what we are like, yet over the long run a person is molded by where his or her attention continually dwells. Hence the great importance of what your occupation requires you to be sensitive to, and what it ignores *de jure* or *de facto,* for its pattern of sensitivities and insensitivities—unless a continuing effort is made to counterbalance this—will eventually become your own.

† See the descriptions of the various neurotic personalities in David Shapiro, *Neurotic Styles* (New York: Basic Books, 1965).

hold, through rational criticism or further thought; by changing our evaluations through probing further facts or rethinking the nature of value itself; and by controlling the focus of our attention, deciding which of our beliefs and evaluations to bring into emotional play. We also can embed an emotion's component belief and evaluation in a wider network of interconnected plans, evaluations, beliefs and goals that modify or relocate the emotion. I do not say these things are fully within our control, or that this would even be desirable. Nevertheless, philosophy can have a quite practical impact on our emotional lives by providing us with operative principles of rational belief and evaluation, and perhaps even principles for selectively directing, as well as for intensifying or diminishing, our attention.

There also is control of whether to undergo intense emotion on particular occasions. We can treasure such emotions yet not want to be awash in them constantly. Calm, equipoise, and detachment also have their place and function. Moreover, these might be utilized to make oneself less subject to operant conditioning. Pleasures and pains can sometimes be experienced and observed with a certain detached attentiveness; by keeping them discrete, one might control their tendency to spill over into wanting more or wanting again. Through selective focusing of attention and shaping the response, we mold our emotional lives.

Someone is said to be "philosophical" about something when he avoids negative emotions by displacing or diminishing negative evaluations, either by taking the very widest perspective or by selective focus of attention upon facts. Sometimes, though, philosophy—or the third reality principle, at any rate—tells us to focus *upon* the negative. The conflict between this reality principle and our desire to avoid intensely unpleasant feelings may be less severe than it appears. That principle sometimes mandates negative emotions; however, the feelings that form part of negative emotions, while they cannot be pleasant, need not themselves be unpleasant precisely. Let us look first at positive emotions. The feeling component of an intense positive emotion is itself something pleasurable; it is desired in part because of its own felt qualities. It would be awkward if attending positive evaluations were feelings one felt negatively about, unpleasurable ones we wanted to *avoid* because of their own felt qualities. Only a feeling viewed positively could form an integrated whole with a positive evaluation and so appropriately express it.

When something is correctly evaluated *negatively,* as unharmonious or ugly or destructive or evil, what feeling appropriately attends *this* evaluation? Not, surely, a pleasant one; that feeling should not be one you desire partly for its own felt qualities. (It is inappropriate to relish making negative evaluations or to attend these with pleasurable feelings, or in *this* context to have a good feeling about one's ability for evaluative discernment and its skillful exercise.)

The feeling accompanying a positive evaluation is to be proportional, its felt quality matching the evaluation. It feels as good as the evaluation says that thing is.* That feeling represents the value (or some more inclusive category) in its structure and also in its positive character. The feeling's positive character provides an analog model within us of the positive character of the thing evaluated. Earlier, we speculated that the feeling, in its structure, provided an analog model of the *structure* of that particular value. Here, we add that the feeling, in its positive character, provides an analog representation of the positive *character* of the value. By this route, the value is responded to *as* valuable, as positive value. If negative evaluations, on the other hand, were attended by pleasurable feelings, the (*positive*) character of those feelings would not provide (as complete) an analog representation of the (negative) character of what they evaluated. Implicitly, by the character of his feelings, the person would be saying these negative values were a good thing; at least as objects for him to negatively evaluate, he would be glad they existed.

If it cannot be positive must it be negative and unpleasant feelings, then, that accompany negative evaluations—this was our question earlier—or can the conflict be mitigated between the third reality principle and our aversion to intensely unpleasant feelings? Must the negative evaluations, even when embodied in emotions and not simply bare evaluations, be accompanied by feelings that are

---

* To put it more laboriously, the positive magnitude of the felt quality is proportional to the measure of value the evaluation ascribes. The factor of proportionality, though, the constant the evaluative measure is multiplied by to yield the felt quality, may vary from person to person, or from mood to mood. Is it legitimate to use a different multiplicative factor with the negative emotions than with the positive?

unpleasant in proportion to how negatively the evaluation judges? That would certainly remove incentive for making correct negative evaluations! However, there are dimensions of experience other than unpleasantness that we can call upon and utilize in responding to negative value and in providing its analog representation. We can have experiences that are powerful, moving, gripping, or memorable. By their magnitude along these and other dimensions, emotions can be responsive to negative value, to the magnitude of the suffering or loss or tragedy or injustice or horror. In a theater too we can respond to tragedy powerfully and deeply with emotions, although in their own dimensions an analog to what occurs onstage, that we do not find it (precisely) unpleasant to have.

Yet the response to tragedy in the theater differs from our responses to the tragedies of life. Sadness in life, unlike sadness in the theater, *feels* unpleasant, and this truly is a difference in how the experiences feel, in their phenomenology, and is not simply constituted by the different contexts. (Inside a theater we know approximately when the experience will end; no action of ours can alter anything; we know we are secure. At a horror movie, when the experience turns actually unpleasant, people cover their eyes or leave.) When certain facts or events in life make us unhappy, this is not simply the absence of happiness (in any one of its senses) but an existing emotion with its own accompanying feeling: sad, flat, depressed. Wouldn't it be best not to feel *these* feelings when we respond with emotion to facts we evaluate negatively? Perhaps these feelings are simply part of the package of our general emotional capacity. Still, wouldn't it be better if we could separate the package's parts, feeling happiness in response to facts evaluated positively and, as in the theater, feeling some strong emotion in response to facts evaluated negatively—just not unhappiness? Could the third reality principle be satisfied by this sort of experience a theater audience has, powerful and moving and sad even, yet not unpleasant? (Upsetting, though?) Or would this be yet another kind of detachment from actuality that called for the statement of a further reality principle? Is unhappiness necessary as an appropriate response to certain negative facts?

Pleasure is too impoverished a term, anyway, for the desirable felt qualities of experience, unless we keep remembering the technical use of *pleasure* to denote not any single quality but whichever felt qualities are in part desired for themselves. The question then becomes one of listing the qualities of experience that should be desired for themselves. Emotions and experiences can be rich, varied, profound, intense, nuanced, complex, ennobling, exhilarating, powerful, authentic, intimate, memorable, full, uplifting, and so forth. There are many desirable dimensions of emotional experience; to want to have intense positive emotions (that are fitting) just is shorthand for wanting an emotional life that contains the whole panoply.

We want to love some people, and hence to be someone whose own well-being is linked with theirs. When they are worse off, it is not enough simply to make a dispassionate negative evaluation of ourselves as worse off too, for in what way *are* we worse off then? Can we say simply that the way we are worse off is simply that *they* are worse off? That does not seem adequate. So the emotion of unhappiness we feel is what makes us worse off when they are; it constitutes the way we are worse off and links our well-being directly with theirs.

This explains why unhappiness sometimes is a necessary response to certain situations involving those we love, but it does not explain why we need be unhappy too over our *own* situations. For example, when a parent dies or a project fails, isn't the way we are worse off just and simply that we now no longer have that parent alive or that project proceeding? We don't need any further emotion to make us worse off—we already are, just by virtue of the fact. (But can this very fact link our well-being to the parent's loss of his or her own life?) So why do we want to be constituted as beings who are made *unhappy* over our own situations—wouldn't different strong emotions connect us sufficiently yet be more desirable?

In your own case, toward your own suffering, you might strive to win through to the attitude of a theater audience, whose emotions are felt deeply but not felt as painful. (We already have seen that this would not do toward people one loves. With them, we do not merely feel deeply in some way or other, we hurt when they do; not to do this is not to be connected to them in the bond of love.) Yet these deep feelings, while not leaving one completely detached from the events, leave one a spectator. Perhaps your feeling unhappy (or happy) at certain events is what makes these events part of *your* life or what makes you feel they are. The question then would become:

Why do we want to live our lives, rather than be spectators of (part of) them? Why do we want to be the kind of beings who live our whole lives? Perhaps actual unhappiness or happiness is what makes our lives serious—not just play or a game. But why do we want our lives to be serious, then?

Part of the answer may reside in the way we can gain also from intense sadness, even tragedy. Such experiences etch us sharply; they deepen us. Why then have I placed any emphasis at all upon *positive* emotions, rather than simply upon having intense emotions of whatever kind? The perception of virtues in what is negative usually occurs after the fact. True, we would not, even if we could, change all of that negative past which has shaped and deepened us, made us what we are (though this is not to say we would not change *any* of it); yet few of us therefore seek out even more of the negative to gain further deepening still. Intense negative emotions, then, get valued not *for* their negativeness but only because of what they make of *us;* we don't choose them.

12

Being More Real

WE ARE NOT merely empty buckets to be stuffed with happiness or pleasure; the self's nature and character matter too, even matter more. It is easy to fall into an "end-state" conception of the self, demarcating some particular condition for it to reach and maintain. As important as the self's constituents and structure, however, are the ways it transforms itself. And this is not simply because it is important to reach that end result. Just as a nation is in part constituted by its constitutional processes of change, including the means of amending that constitution, so the self is in part constituted by *its* processes of change. The self does not simply undergo these processes, it shapes and chooses them, it initiates and runs them. Part of the self's value dwells in its ability to transform *itself* and so be (to a considerable extent) self-creating; part too dwells in the special texture of its own processes. It is beneficial, I think, for the self to identify itself in part as the nonstatic agent of its own change, a locus of processes of transformation. These processes can be replaced later by still other ones. At the highest level, perhaps there will be some constant processes of change, yet these too might someday be applied to themselves and thereby undergo self-change.

Because our lives continue over time, we can experiment and try out choices or modify them. We also can pursue some traits intensely without having to forgo others permanently; these can await another time. We thus can aim to have a self that develops, one that over time includes and integrates the most important traits. This may explain the sense in which certain tasks and traits are most appropriate at certain ages or stages. With many to be fitted in over time, some may be done more fully or easily when they come before (or after) others; some sequences may flow more easily than others.*

At some times a person feels more real to himself or herself. Stop, now, to ask, and answer, this question: When do you feel most real? (Stop, now, to actually think about it. What is *your* answer?)

Someone may think the question is confused. At all the times when a person exists, he does exist then and so must be real then. Nevertheless, though we may not be able yet to state what notion of reality is involved, we do seem to be able to distinguish degrees of reality.

First, consider literary characters. Some literary characters are

---

* Later in life, after childhood and adolescence, people say that time moves more quickly. Do we assess an interval of time by the fraction of our life until now that it takes up? Time then would fly faster and faster as we grow older, since any fixed interval—a year, say, or five years—will constitute an increasingly smaller fraction of that life. Distortions of an adult's sense of subjective time might in principle produce extraordinary effects. Suppose a half minute can be experienced subjectively as the length of a normal minute, and this phenomenon is successively doubled over the following time intervals, so that the next quarter minute feels like a normal minute, the next eighth minute too feels like a normal minute, as does the next sixteenth minute, etc. At the end of the one minute of objective time, there will have been an infinite sequence of decreasing intervals of time, $1/2$, $1/4$, $1/8$, $1/16$, $1/32$ . . . , each of which will have been experienced subjectively as if it were one minute long. That infinite sum, then, of subjective minutes would seem like a subjective eternity. And if one then returned in the next minute to the usual sense of time, it would seem as though an experience of infinite subjective duration lay behind one. Might something like this—we might call it Zeno's eternity—be a model for an enlightenment experience, or for the experience of dying? If our consciousness survived biological death for (only) one minute, but that minute subjectively felt like eternity, would that constitute a satisfactory form of immortality?

more real than others. Think of Hamlet, Sherlock Holmes, Lear, Antigone, Don Quixote, Raskolnikov. Even though none of them exist, they seem more real even than some people we know who do exist. It is not that these literary characters are real because they are "true to life," people we could meet believably. The reality of these characters consists in their vividness, their sharpness of detail, the integrated way in which they function toward or are tortured over a goal. Even when their own focus is not completely clear, they are intent on focusing or are presented (as Flaubert presents Madame Bovary) in clear focus. These characters are "realer than life," more sharply etched, with few extraneous details that do not fit. In the characteristics they exhibit they are more concentrated centers of psychological organization. Such literary characters become by-words, paradigms, models, epitomes. They are intensely concentrated portions of reality.

The same features that make some literary characters more real than others, clicking them into paradigmatic focus, apply outside the literary realm also. Works of art, paintings or music or poems, often seem intensely real; their sharply etched features make them stand out against the usual background of blurry and vague objects. In a mode of organization more tight and coherent, or at least having a more evident mode of organization and a more interesting one, they constitute more integrated wholes. The beauty of works of art or of natural scenes, the dynamic balance of the array, makes it more vivid, more real than the usual jumble we encounter. Perhaps this is because beautiful things seem right as they are; they show a perfection of their own. Or perhaps it is because, on their own merits, they hold and repay our attention more enduringly. In any case, they are perceived as in sharper balance and focus; they are more vividly perceived. Features other than beauty, such as intensity, power, and depth, also lead to vividness of perception. Artists are trying, I think, to create objects that, in one way or another, are more real.

Mathematicians also delineate objects and structures wherein sharp properties interlock in a densely layered network of combinatorial possibilities, relations, and implications. To ask, "Do mathematical entities *exist?*"—the question put by philosophers of mathematics—does not capture the saliency of their vivid reality. The Greeks could not fail to be captivated by such objects and the intricate patterns they exhibited so definitely and sharply, even in the case of "irrational" numbers, which were incommensurate. Tradition reports that Plato held that Forms—according to his theories, the most real entities—were (like) numbers. The mathematical realm, a vivid one, grips our attention because it is so real.

Just as some literary characters are more real, so are some people. Socrates, Buddha, Moses, Gandhi, Jesus—these figures capture our imagination and attention by their greater reality. They are more vivid, concentrated, focused, delineated, integrated, inwardly beautiful. Compared to us, they are more real.*

We, too, however, are more real at some times than at others, more real in some modes than in others. People often say they feel most real when they are working with intense concentration and focus, with skills and capacities effectively brought into play; they feel most real when they feel most creative. Some say during sexual excitement, some say when they are alert and learning new things. We are more real when all our energies are focused, our attention riveted, when we are alert, functioning completely, utilizing our (valuable) powers. Focusing intensely brings us into sharper focus.

Consider a second question: When do you feel most yourself? (This is different from the question of when you feel more of *a* self also from the question of when you feel most *alive*.) The answer will not be exactly the same as when you feel most real. People feel most themselves when they are "in contact" with parts of themselves usually not saliently present in their consciousness, dwelling in unaccustomed emotions, integrating these into closer connection with the more familiar portions of themselves. In thoughtful walks in the woods, contemplating the ocean, meditation, or intimate conversation with a friend, deeper parts of oneself are brought into awareness

---

* Some lives give new *meaning* to recurrent human phenomena—for example, Jesus to suffering—by the way they incorporate and transfigure it. From then on, it means something different when we suffer, because of what the suffering was and meant then; ours becomes associated with that. Similarly, fiction gives added depth and meaning to what we encounter. We can meet someone and think he is a Dostoyevskian character; we now are able to see him against the whole landscape of Dostoyevsky's characters, with their not fully stable emotional intensity, just as we can see suffering against a landscape of Jesus's life. These meanings are perpendicular to our ongoing life, and enrich it.

and integrated with the rest, producing a greater serenity of self, a sense of a more substantial self.

This increase in (awareness of) integration of previously isolated parts enables one to act with more power and a wider band of intense focus, and thus to feel more real.

The realm of reality, what has reality to more than a certain degree, is not the same as what exists. Literary characters can be real though they do not exist; existing things may have only that minimal degree of reality requisite for existing. It seems plausible to locate reality's lower bound at existence; nothing *less* vivid and focused than what exists will count as real. Reality comes in degrees, though, and the reality that especially interests us here lies above this minimal lower boundary.

According to this notion, reality has many aspects; there are various dimensions that can contribute to a higher degree of reality. To have a higher position or score along one of these dimensions (holding constant the position on the other relevant dimensions) is to have a higher degree of reality. These other dimensions may be connected with clarity of focus and vividness of organization, but they are not simply an instance of it. We have already mentioned beauty in discussing works of art; the more beautiful something is, the more reality it has. Another dimension of reality, I think, is (greater) value. The greater something's intrinsic value, the more reality it has. Greater depth also brings greater reality, as do greater perfection and greater expressiveness. We shall have to investigate these and other dimensions, and their combined structure, later.

I want to say that you are your reality. Our identity consists of those features, aspects, and activities that don't just exist but also are (more) real. The greater the reality a feature has, the more weight it has in our identity. Our reality consists partly in the values we pursue and live by, the vividness, intensity, and integration with which we embody them. Our values alone, even our value, is not the whole of our reality, however; the notion of reality in general includes dimensions other than value. In saying that we are constituted by our reality, I mean that the substance of the self is the reality it manages to achieve. One view of immortality might be that what survives our death is our reality, whatever reality we manage to realize.

We can now formulate a fourth reality principle; it commends being more real. The figures who most exemplify this, such as

Socrates, Buddha, Moses, Jesus, and Gandhi, had the greatest and most enduring impact, an impact that stemmed (in large part) from their greater reality. Not every application of the fourth reality principle is this high-flown, though: engaging in the activities of exploring, responding, and creating is a way of being more real; so is having intense positive emotions and intimate bonds. We should notice here the theoretical possibility of a conflict between the second and the fourth reality principle; is it possible to become a more real self by, in part, disconnecting from external reality, and do some delusional persons who think they are Napoleon, for instance, attempt to achieve the greatest reality open to them by simulating a very real person, even at the cost of breaking contact with actuality?*

To say that some people are more real than others, or become so, may seem objectionably elitist. Yet mustn't this way of speaking follow from one person's judging that she herself can become more real than before; if she becomes that way, won't she then be more real than someone else who now is as she used to be? However, this does not follow strictly. It is possible to have an intellectual structure that makes comparisons for one person—she can be more real one way rather than another—without making any comparisons of degrees of reality *between* people. (An analogous structure is put forward by those theories of economists that make intrapersonal comparisons of utility without making interpersonal comparisons.) This situation might obtain because in making comparisons that just involve one person being two different ways, all other factors, including whatever mysteries there are to the human person, are assumed to be held constant and so to be equal and so to cancel out. This cannot be assumed, however, *between* people who may vary in reality in unknown or nonevident or incomparable ways. (Even this rationale seems to assume some differences in people's respective reality, though, whether or not we can tell which way the difference goes.) Hence, it is conceivable that differences in reality might be *intrap*ersonal, serving as a guide or goal or standard within each person's life, yet not obtain between people. Most of my reflections would remain unchanged under this narrower view; yet I shall follow the

---

* The fourth reality principle, unlike Abraham Maslow's principle of self-actualization, does not assume there is any one particular self or any particular talents or destiny lurking inside waiting to be realized and thus determining what would count as self-actualization.

wider interpersonal reading. It feels less than honorable to fail to acknowledge the greater reality of figures such as Socrates, Buddha, Jesus, Gandhi, and Einstein. And, in knowingly honoring that greater reality, we can have the pleasure of realizing that, at least, we are not *blind*!

I have formulated the fourth reality principle as one that commends being more real; however, it does not mandate maximizing one's reality or even increasing it. Perhaps someone is real enough already. The level of aspiration, what counts as real enough, is a separate question we each must decide.*

Circumstances, however, may affect our prospects and available routes for reaching a certain level of reality. It would be nice to think that whatever is most important cannot be affected by external social circumstances, yet it would minimize the seriousness of societal inequalities to deny that they affect people's prospects in the most important ways. This does not mean that class position or income or family upbringing must place unalterable limits—suffering can etch people, dignity can be shown in coping with hardships, and enormous wealth may constitute an enormous barrier to becoming real— yet these will affect one's chances and make some lives, early on, a steep uphill battle at best. We might be tempted, then, to turn to another measure, not a person's degree of reality but rather the degree to which he has achieved the maximum reality possible in his particular circumstances. With this *percentage* measure of how well someone has coped, everyone starts equal. Yet to term this the most important measure would be to deny how very deep the costs of social class can be. (For this reason, too, it would not be adequate to say that in relation to others we should simply be responsive to the degree of reality they have; sometimes we must try to increase that, or change the particular conditions or societal structures that limit it.)

Since the reality of a self can change over time, there is a question of how to assess its *overall* reality. Suppose we could graph a self's degree of reality in each period of time—as earlier we imagined graphs of happiness over a lifetime. Which is the most real self; which

* In any case, we need to be aware of our limitations, our particular ones and those of general human nature. We are not perfect and do not need to be; perfectionism is simply an additional flaw. Won't the absolute level of all our accomplishments look trivial anyway to beings from another galaxy with vastly greater capacities?

pattern through time should we strive to follow? The one with the highest peak somewhere on its lifetime graph of reality, even if it maintains that highest degree only briefly? Or the one with the largest total of reality over an adult lifetime, as measured by the area under the curve? (Or, noticing different lengths of life, is it the one with the greatest *average* reality?) Or should we seek a reality curve of upward slope, even at some cost in the total score?

The reality of the self over time, I think, is that largest chunk of reality it is able to maintain most consistently. We can give this a sharper formulation. On our imagined graph of the self's reality over time, draw a horizontal line (parallel to the x-axis, the time axis) and consider the area under that horizontal line in all and only those places where that line also is underneath (or identical with) the reality curve. We can set various horizontal lines at different heights. Consider now the horizontal line A at the height that, for a given curve, yields the greatest area bounded by it under the curve. (In Figure 1, this area is the crosshatched area.) Call this greatest area the *primary bulk* of the curve. This primary bulk will constitute our criterion of choice. For two reality curves of two different lifetimes (or of selves

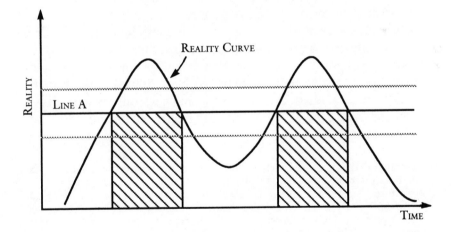

Figure 1. The reality of a self over time. The crosshatched area is the primary bulk of the curve—the largest chunk of reality the self is able to maintain consistently.

135

over time), let us stipulate that the one with the greatest primary bulk counts as the one with the greatest overall reality. (When and only when two curves tie in their primary bulk, we can look to their secondary bulk; this is determined by that second horizontal line—which must be above the first horizontal line—which yields a maximum area under *both* it and the reality curve, after excluding all overlap in area with the primary bulk. The limit of iterating this process—tertiary bulk, etc.—is the total area under the curve.) A self's reality is the largest chunk of reality it maintains most consistently.

This primary-bulk criterion is an appealing one (in comparison to the other candidates). However, questions about our future reality overall do not arise saliently as we make choices, perhaps because the very making of a particular choice among alternatives involving differing future contours of reality significantly affects one's degree of reality *now*. Moreover, any notion of someone's degree of reality at a particular time must take account also of significant stretches of his past and future, or else risk incoherence.*

In passing, we now might understand why people often feel excitement in the presence of celebrities. Magazines, television, and films bring many faces to our attention. Do these people seem more real and vivid to us; does the focused light of public attention enhance their reality? What people find exciting is not only to be close to a celebrity but to be noticed by one, to come into his or her ken. It is as if, because they are the subjects of so much public attention, when they take congnizance of us, all that attention for a moment gets turned upon us, reflected toward us. We bask, however briefly, in the public attention they have received, and feel our own reality is enhanced. The general public, craving heightened reality, does not say, even when fed the most empty glitter, that "the emperor has no

---

* The appealing criterion of primary bulk, perhaps not so necessary in the context of the self's reality, can usefully be applied also to other topics exhibiting a similar structure. For instance, Aristotle asked whether we should develop all of our desirable capacities in some well-rounded fashion or instead concentrate on developing our highest capacity to the utmost. Supposing we could measure each developed capacity against some external scale of worth, one answer might be to develop in whichever direction maximized our total capacities' primary bulk. Whether this is rounded development or maximal concentration on one capacity will depend upon facts about each particular person and her capacities.

clothes." But why doesn't it cry out that the clothes contain no emperor? Or is it the very reality without substance that the public craves, excited by the power of its own attention to create reality *ex nihilo?*

Is "reality" the most fundamental evaluative category, or is there another even more fundamental one to use in understanding and evaluating it? The most basic category, as I see it, is that of reality.* This category has various subdimensions. Along these dimensions (all other things being equal) a higher position makes something more real. Consider, now, the question of whether it is more valuable to be more real. As one of the component dimensions of reality, being more valuable is *one* way of being more real. It does not follow, however, that whenever something is more real it is more valuable. It may possess its high degree of reality because of its high place along another dimension of reality, one different than value. Value is a particular dimension which, although of great inclusiveness, does not encompass everything good. To seek only value is like seeking only beauty in a work of art while caring nothing for power of statement, depth of insight, surprise, energy, or wit.

Reality is a general notion that encompasses value, beauty, vividness, focus, integration. To say of any one of these—for example, beauty—that it yields greater reality is not merely to say repetitiously that more beauty brings more beauty. There is a general notion of reality that includes beauty as one strand; seeing beauty as a way of being more real places it within the pattern of this general notion, alongside the other strands, to their mutual illumination. But why think these various dimensions all are aspects of one thing and not simply separate; isn't it arbitrary to group them together as dimensions under one broader notion and call that reality? These dimensions do not constitute an unconnected list, though. As we shall see, they intertwine in an intricate structure of cross-connections

---

* Reality is so inclusive a category, it encompasses so many others as subdimensions, that it is not clear what more general category could be used in understanding *it*. We might ask: Why should we care about reality? But caring about something, seeking it, and trying to realize it are themselves states of increased vividness, intensity, and focus—that is, states of increased reality. If reality isn't important, why bother to ask what you should care about? (This snappy question is no adequate answer; I shall return to this topic later.)

that bind them together in a family, as dimensional aspects of one broader notion.

Can we really distinguish reality from actuality, though; is not something real precisely when it exists, when it is actual? Nevertheless, despite our temptation to make this objection, reality does lend itself to being spoken of in terms of *degrees;* while one thing does not exist more than another (which also exists) and is not more actual than another, one thing can be more real than another. We speak of someone as "a real friend," not simply in contrast to a false friend, for there are intermediate cases also of friends who are less than real friends. We speak also of a someone's being a real ballplayer, a real poet, a real man, and in each case the term *real* is used as a grading notion that compares and admits of degrees.

Plato's theory of Forms specified differing degrees of reality; the Forms were more real than those particular existing things which instantiated or participated in them. Plato's theory involved separate *realms* of reality—the Forms existed, as people like to say, in "Platonic heaven"; the view we are led to here involves just one realm where things may differ in how real they are. Religious views, too, some-times speak of God as "more real" than we are, and mystics say their experiences are more real than ordinary experiences—*of* something more real and also more real themselves. One reason the mystic gives his experience such credence, and maintains it to be so valuable, is because it is (or seems) so very real. My point now is not to endorse any of these particular claims, but rather to notice that (the notion of) reality does lend itself to being structured this way, in degrees or levels; it can comfortably be used to grade or rank things, to evaluate them comparatively.

Even if this notion of reality is not yet a completely precise one, we want to be patient with it and not dismiss it too soon. The history of thought contains many notions it took centuries to clarify and sharpen, or even to remove the contradictions from, notions of such undoubted importance and fruitfulness as the mathematical ones of *limit* and *proof.* It may seem awkward that this notion of reality seems to straddle the fact/value gap, or the descriptive/normative gap, yet that straddling is an advantage. For how could we ever hope to surmount these gaps if not through some basic notion that has a foot solidly on each side, a notion that shows there is not a gap all the way down, a notion that lives and functions *beneath* the level of the gap? And the notion of reality certainly is basic; it *looks* as basic as can be on the factual side—whence the temptation to identify reality with actuality and existence—yet it also has an evaluative and grading role; what is more real is somehow better. Hence this notion of reality offers some hope of progress on the otherwise intractable fact/value problem. It would be foolish, then, to dismiss this notion too quickly or to sharpen it prematurely so that it falls on only one side of the gap.

I am led to worry, though, about treating greater reality as an end to be desired and pursued, for what guarantees that reality will be something positive? Is the positive simply an additional dimension of reality, one aspect among others, so that usually increased reality involves a turn toward the positive, but not always? Wasn't Iago real? Wasn't Hitler? How then do I exclude dark paths?

In each of our own cases, at least, we do not want simply to increase the quantity of our own reality, we want that reality to grow in a certain direction, becoming higher or becoming deeper. (Height and depth are not polar opposites; the opposite of deep is superficial, of high, low.) We want our own reality to become higher or deeper, or at any rate we want greater reality to come without any loss in height or depth.

An *ideal* is an image of something higher, and having an ideal, pursuing it, lifts us higher too. We want to have ideals—some ideals, at least—and not simply desires and goals; we want to envision something higher and to seek it. Does anything stand to depth as an ideal does to height, being an image of it that moves us in that direction? Understanding does. Really to understand something is to know it in its depth; the understanding makes us deeper too. Emotions also can deepen us when they connect with something deep and spring from our depths. To want our reality to grow in the directions of height and depth is to want our lives to be marked by ideals, understanding, and deep emotion, to be governed by these and to pursue them.

Is this talk of height and depth simply a spatial metaphor misleadingly extrapolated, its special evaluative resonance simply a transfer from some other situation?* It is implausible, I think, that the Himalayas are so exhilarating, seeing them (even in pictures) so—as we say—uplifting, simply as an extrapolation from some childhood situations, or that we term some musical notes higher than others for that reason. Height and depth are independent dimensions with evaluative potency. (A full explication of these two notions would explain why we speak of deep or profound understanding, loftiness of spirit, high ideals, and so on.) The very greatest things people have prized involve both height and depth to a considerable extent: meditative ecstasy, religious experience, sublime music, overwhelming love. Is what we most want this: for our deepest parts to connect with the highest things there are?

It is plausible that a directedness toward height and depth will exclude increasing reality in evil directions; someone can be deeply evil, that is, thoroughly so, but being evil will not increase his depth. However, it is not yet clear why height and depth themselves should be important enough to mandate direction to our greater reality. What underlies those directions; what resides at their limits? We shall return to these questions later.

---

* Barry Schwartz speculates (in *Vertical Classification* [Chicago: University of Chicago Press, 1981]) that in all cultures "upper" and "higher" are applied to the better and more powerful—*upper* classes, kings sitting higher than subjects, company presidents having offices on higher floors than *sub*ordinates, etc.— because children everywhere begin literally looking upward to adults for information and succor, and reinforcement of the infant or child often is connected with its being lifted up.

13

Selflessness

PROCESSES of development can make the self more real and more whole, intimate bonds alter the self's boundaries and topology, and—as we shall see later—enlightenment can be viewed as radically transforming the self in its nature and relation to reality. Yet according to the Buddhist view, that self does not exist at all! For this "no-self doctrine" Buddhists adduce the support of argument and of disciplined meditative observation. Their arguments do have some force against a view of the self as an unchanging piece, a soul-pellet, but not against a view of the self as an ongoing, changing, and evolving unification of psychological traits, plans, bodily features, etc., whose identity is maintained at the level of the ongoing whole, not by some part that never changes. (In the first chapter of my book *Philosophical Explanations,* I present a theory of this sort, the closest-continuer theory.) Even if there had been such a pellet-soul at the beginning, as things were added and changed it would become just one piece of the self among others; it would not remain predominant simply because it alone did not alter. Even if the grain of sand about which a pearl formed somehow were the only part whose molecules remained absolutely constant, it would not stay the most important factor in the pearl's continuing identity.

Still, it may be a liberating insight to notice that the self need not be organized like a Tinkertoy construction, with all pieces stuck directly onto one central piece—even if the earliest parts did begin in that relation—and that no one piece need remain unchanging. The most illuminating view of the current composition of a city need not see each part in relation to the initial center, possibly now quite unimportant, from which it grew. More salient are the present interrelations, and the current geographical center and hub might not be the ancestral part. Correspondingly, a person's psychology need not be organized by tying each trait directly to one central characteristic; a person can be serious without every part being serious or merely one step away. This more ample view of possibilities for organizing a self at the level of the whole is not the same as denying the self's existence, however.

The observational support for the no-self view is rooted within Buddhist meditative practice. However, this practice also is guided by the doctrine itself—part of the practice consists in meditating *on* various pieces of doctrine—so the reports of what gets observed are themselves to some degree a product of the theory already held, hence somewhat contaminated. This does not disbar these observations from supporting the theory to some extent, since even when one is looking with the searchlight of a theory, there is no guarantee of automatic success in finding data that fit that theory; hence, such a finding can constitute some support after all.

More to the point, one cannot simply assume that things are as they are observed to be, even through a carefully disciplined mode of observation. That assumption itself is a bit of theory, not of observation. For instance, followers of Buddhist meditative practice report flickering and gaps in observing the external world—everything exists discontinuously. What is the explanation of this observation? Perhaps that things are discontinuous, whether because of the nature of things or of time, and so not as real as we thought, not as real as they would be if continuous. But another and more likely explanation is that things actually are continuous, although our perceptual and introspective apparatus involves just noticeable differences and imposes discontinuities.

Compare the example of a movie film, which registers frame by frame. What is photographed, the subject of the film, exists (let us assume) continuously. It is represented on the film discontinuously, in discrete frames, but our *ordinary* mode of perception sees the film when projected as depicting continuous movement and existence. Our perceptual acuity simply is not sharp enough to detect the gaps between the frames. Suppose, though, that someone trains himself to notice the gaps between frames. It would be a mistake for him to conclude on this basis that the objects filmed existed only intermittently or that reality really was gray, like the "between-frame" projections he has managed to observe on the screen. Moviemakers, aware of that psychological phenomenon whereby we experience discontinuities as continuous, are able to represent the continuous external things in a discontinuous and gappy manner on film, confident that when we watch the film we will experience it all as continuous. If there were some more expensive process of filming whereby the objects were somehow represented continuously, it would not be efficient for filmmakers to use it if that made no difference to the viewer's experiences and beliefs.*

Similarly, we may suppose that the processes of evolution were that efficient also. They gave us a limited level of perceptual acuity along with a discontinuous psychological mechanism to represent external objects; both of these together in interlocking combination give us continuous experiences of the external objects which do in fact exist continuously. The middle discontinuous phase of the process goes unnoticed. Now, it would be a neat trick to train oneself to be aware of these discontinuities in psychological representation—perhaps the Buddhist meditative practice does sharpen acuity in this way—but it would not be warranted to infer from this that external things really are discontinuous or less real than they appear. At best, the Buddhist mode of the meditative observation would have uncovered a fact about how our perceptual representations operate, not a fact about how physical existence contains gaps.

The insubstantiality of the external world is of a piece with the

* Others have used a movie analogy differently, to explain the Buddhist doctrine and make it plausible by asking whether reality could not be like what it is on the screen, containing gaps although appearing to us continuous.

Buddhist doctrine of the insubstantiality of the self, and while the reported observations of the latter are more inchoate than the ones we have discussed, they seem to fall under similar strictures. Despite claims, meditative practice has not shown or discovered that the self is nonexistent. Yet still such disciplined practice might lead to a reorganization of the self, or to greater control in wielding the self's structure.

In theory, having a self might come into tension eventually with the reality principles, increasing one's reality up to a point, but beyond that point hampering achieving even greater reality or connecting with it. However, if the self is just one among the possible modes of organization, then we can investigate whether some other mode of structural organization might facilitate a connection with reality that is deeper. (Hold, for a moment, the question: *Who* is to be more deeply connected to reality, and mustn't that be a self?) One doctrine rooted in the Indian tradition holds that being a (delimited) self is not the most real way to be, and not a necessary way either. I want to investigate that doctrine, reconstructing it in my terms.

Let us look more closely at the self's organization and particular functions. (Since this requires a certain amount of abstract theorizing about the nature and underlying structure of the self, some readers may prefer to skip over the next ten or so paragraphs.) It is reflexive self-consciousness that constitutes and organizes the self. Self-consciousness is reflexive when it knows itself *as itself,* not just when it thinks about what happens to be itself. An amnesiac might know that someone had painted the wall without knowing that person was himself. When Oedipus looked for the person whose deeds had brought disaster upon the city of Thebes, he didn't realize that he was that very person; he was not looking for himself *as* himself. Reflexive self-consciousness is the kind of consciousness someone has when he thinks of "I," "me," or "myself," not just of someone fitting a certain general description (whom he might be mistaken about).

Let us begin, then, with many bits of consciousness: experiences, thoughts, etc.—isolated bits. Some of these bits of consciousness are about other bits—for example, one bit might be a memory of an earlier conscious event. One of these bits of awareness, however, is very special. This bit is an awareness *of* many of the other bits of experience and thought, *plus* an awareness of itself, a reflexive self-awareness. Let us hypothesize that the self *is* or *begins* as that special awareness: aware of other contents of consciousness and also reflexively aware of itself *as* being aware of these other contents of consciousness and also of itself. It knows itself as aware of other things and as aware of itself too. This particular piece of consciousness, this "self," groups various experiences and bits of consciousness; these are the ones it is aware of—including itself. There also may be other bits of consciousness it is not aware of; these do not fall within the group. Thus far, all the self is entitled to say is "I know of, I am aware of, bits of consciousness, experiences, thoughts, feelings, etc., including this very self-reflexive bit." Somehow the step gets made from being aware of these bits of consciousness to *having* or *possessing* them. The self comes to think of these as *belonging* to it. The self is born, then, in an act of appropriation and acquisition. How does it do this? And when it claims what amounts to ownership over these other bits of consciousness, is that claim legitimate?

As a grouping principle, the bit of reflexive self-consciousness is set apart. Other bits of consciousness may know of still others and thereby group them, but the reflexive bit is special in that it groups others *and* itself (which it knows of as itself). When many other bits fall within its purview of awareness, it groups them in more intricate ways than simply placement on an unordered list of things it is aware of. It interrelates and integrates them; it is aware of how some follow others or form subgroups together, etc. In providing this further structuring to, and for, the otherwise unordered bits of experience, it creates (or becomes aware of) a new interrelated unity. (This goes beyond the unity it gives them merely by knowing of each of them— what Kant called the formal unity of apperception.) There may be something about the phenomenology or character of asymmetrical knowing—when the reflexive bit of consciousness knows of all the others but many of these do not, however, know of it—which makes it feel of a different and superior order, something that is reinforced by its not merely knowing *of* the others but organizing them *into* a complexly interrelated unity. The story of the self and its organizing

145

can be carried beyond just contents of consciousness to the body and its parts, but that is not necessary for our purposes here.*

Is all this enough to constitute *possession*, though, to make the self an entity that *has* all those other experiences? What new factor is introduced when the self, the bit of reflexive consciousness, takes the step from being aware of other bits of experience and their interrelations to possessing or owning them? Perhaps there is an assertion of superiority to other experiences or power over them, but what does this actually amount to, above and beyond those activities of awareness and integration which the self already engages in at the prepossession stage?

The self not only stands in an asymmetrical relation to the experiences it "has," which are its contents, but it stands uniquely in that relationship. Nothing else does also, not to those particular contents. The self does not just possess its experiences, it is the sole owner. Sole ownership does not follow simply from how reflexive self-consciousness groups experiences by being aware of them. Those groupings could overlap. You might have a thought and I might have it too; you might be aware of a pain and I might be aware of that pain too; you might have a pain and I might have it too. To this last, one wants to object, "Not the *very same* pain, perhaps a very similar one, but not the same identical pain in the sense that if we are counting pains there is only one of them there, not two, and both of us have *it*." But this distinction between what philosophers call being numerically identical—there is only *one* thing there—and being qualitatively identical is introduced in order to facilitate property claims over experiences. It is born of the desire to be able to establish separate selves. The experiences are partitioned in order to be separate, so as to fall into separate and nonoverlapping groups.

How do I know what another person is feeling? Sometimes I feel it myself, empathetically. And sometimes I share my feelings. "You

---

* The above paragraphs describe a process within which the self gets constructed. A more extreme view would see the self as an illusion generated in this process, perhaps along the lines of the completion of an incomplete gestalt. Just as circles with slight gaps are seen as complete circles, with the visual system supplying closure, so might the self be a closure of gaps in experiences that actually are not "had" by anything. Apparently an object of direct and constant awareness, the self would not, under these circumstances, exist at all. There would simply occur one additional bit of experience, an illusioning of closure.

can't share one and the same feeling; you cannot be directly aware of his. Yours belongs to you and his belongs to him!" So it is the notion of "belonging to" and "possessing" that creates a separation between minds that must be total, thus also creating the philosophical "problem of other minds."*

Since the self is built upon reflexivity and appropriation, it is not surprising that these spill over into the self's external activities, often in ways that are unfortunate. The reflexive energy of the self takes pleasure in being exercised; a self thinks about itself, about what others think of it, about its impact on others, about what others might say about it, about how to present itself to others. During much of the time, perhaps most of the time, the self engages in self-chatter—we might say it is *addicted* to it. It appropriates external objects and sometimes people; in some instances it seems to be intent upon acquisition without surcease. The centrality of exclusiveness in possession does not tend to lead the self to share its external goods or inner feelings either. All these spillover effects are not strictly necessary but, given the origins of the particular formation that is the self, they are unsurprising. They simply extend the very processes that gave rise to the self in the first place. The even simpler processes that compose and underlie reflexive self-awareness, the self's initial bit, only reinforce this point. For one such process involves the *power* of reflexive self-awareness to refer to itself in virtue of its having a feature it creates and bestows upon itself—it *imprints*—in that very act of referring.† We have gone some way toward explaining, in terms of the processes through which the self originates, why it is self-interested, often even selfish. It would be theoretically satisfying if we also could explain the self's attachment to pleasure: Why would a self thus constituted tend to adhere to the pleasure principle? And why would the self have not merely desires but (to use the language of Eastern theories) *attachments*? I do not see these issues clearly enough yet.

---

* Might women's notion of themselves, the constitution of their *selves,* be less wedded to notions of exclusive partitioning and ownership of experience, and is some part of the greater concern for acquisition, appropriation, and power over external things that is observed among males to be explained by the particular—and not obviously admirable—notion of exclusively appropriating experience that underlies their mode of self-constituting?

† See my *Philosophical Explanations,* pp. 90–94.

The self has a particular character, that of an entity—rather than of a space, say; moreover, it is an entity with a particular partitioned and appropriative structure. If the self is not us but rather only a particular structure through which we experience the world, a pair of Kantian glasses that structures the world of our experience and makes us experience the external world in a way that is self-centered and self-focused, then we can question whether that structure should be kept as it is.

Some Eastern theories condemn the self on three counts: First, the self interferes with our experiencing the deepest reality, and also with experiencing things in general as they are; second, it makes us unhappy or it interferes with our having the highest happiness; third, the self is not our full reality, yet we mistakenly believe it is.

The terse recommendation of these Eastern doctrines, then, is to end the self. This is peculiarly difficult to achieve (short of ending the life also) and this difficulty gets attributed to the wiles of the self: We are attached to the self—an attachment the self encourages—and we won't let it go. There are at least two other explanations of the self's tenacity, though, more respectful of the self. Although the self may not be optimal overall, it may be a somewhat good structure—what economists call a local but not a global optimum. Here is an often-used analogy. Imagine a person who is trying to reach the highest point in an area standing now at the top of a small hill with another taller hill nearby. He is at a local optimum: any small change will take him downhill; but he is not at a global optimum: a greater height is feasible. Even someone who is merely close to the top of the first smaller hill reasonably might proceed upward to its top, thereby improving his situation, rather than first going far downhill to attempt a trip to the distant very highest point. Local optima have a certain stability. Second, even if the self were suboptimal overall, it might be the very best and most efficient structure for certain de-limited functions, functions we do not want to give up. Therefore, to end the self would have significant drawbacks.

The self does have its appropriate and necessary functions. It acts as a central monitor, a funnel through which information can pass and be examined, compared, and evaluated, and out of which decisions can be consciously made. The self functions as an intelligence agency, as knower and noticer and inquirer; it examines perceptions, motives, and beliefs, noticing discrepancies, reorganizing their structure, noticing reactions, etc. This intelligence function need not happen constantly, though. The self is not an omnipresent secret police. The formation that is the self is available to be used as needed; it always engages in very light monitoring to notice if anything has popped up that requires attention, occasionally intensifying its action for specific tasks and purposes. (We might speak of this as the "night-watchman" theory of the self.) The self also integrates its explicit verbal understanding with other modes of understanding, and transmits the result internally to those semiautonomous portions that can make use of it. Complete central planning is no more appropriate or efficient for an individual than for an economy.

While it might be useful for theoretical purposes to list all the legitimate and delimited functions of the self, the ones to be called upon and utilized only when they genuinely help, it is not necessary to be able to do this. The self does not have to know everything about its own proper functions for these to be employed; we can place some trust in our own unconscious or implicit understanding of when such special functions are most needed. Perhaps the self comes to be distrustful of the vast reservoir of its unconscious processes or contents in general because of the nature of some of them, those repressed thoughts or emotions it has banished to the unconscious— that place, after all, was the only one it knew it could send them to whose specific contents it then wouldn't know. Not only might such repressed material continue to operate in ways delineated by Freud, the conscious mind might naturally become distrustful of *everything* in the unconscious—after all, it has placed *some* fearful material there. And although it at most needs to distrust only those things it has placed there to be rid of, because it cannot control perfectly which part of the unconscious gets used, it may in effect end up distrusting *everything* unconscious and hence insist that everything must pass its own conscious scrutiny and monitoring.

The zoom-lens principle we formulated in the meditation on "Focus" for the phenomenon of attention can apply to the self as well. The self structure too can be under our control, utilized in its different modes as needed and appropriate, one part of a reportoire to call upon and wield. Perhaps meditative techniques might help to schedule the self, to direct it toward its best activities and functions and also allow it to rest—surely it has earned some vacation—when other endeavors or ways of being would best be carried out with it in abeyance. (Is this "nonself" posture a role that the self is able to take on, or is the self a role the nonself can utilize? Or could either equally well be said?) These techniques also might dampen or eliminate whatever ugly characteristics result from the self's reflexivity and exclusiveness.

Our own reality is effectively organized within the self and by it, even if after some point it bars the way further. When the extreme heights of reality are to be scaled, perhaps having more of a self will be a hindrance. The self then would be a local, not a global optimum, to be forgone carefully only for other more difficult ways of becoming more real still.

14

Stances

THERE ARE DISTINCT stances toward value which shape a choice of what things are important and the role these then play within life.* The three basic stances are the egoistic, the relational, and the absolute. (Later we consider a fourth that might integrate these.) The first stance sees the primary location of value (or whatever is deemed evaluatively good) as within the self; things are important because of how they enhance or develop or expand or benefit the self. A view that the only important thing is your own happiness locates the thing of value within you—as something you have (happiness) or a way you are (happy)—so unsurprisingly it counts as egoistic. However, the egoistic stance is able to focus upon something external too; when it does so, though, it locates what is valuable not within that thing but rather in the self's having it. For this egoistic stance, the value of your creating something lies not in the nature of what

---

* I have benefited from Thomas Nagel's treatment of two similar stances playing a somewhat different role in his *The View from Nowhere* (New York: Oxford University Press, 1986).

is created or in the act of creation itself but in *your* being a creator; the value of loving someone lies in being the kind of person who loves or in having the kind of identity you acquire when you and another love each other. The goal of the egoistic stance is a person's own reality; he pursues that reality as it is within his self (gaining things such as pleasure or happiness) or as it clothes his self (gaining things such as power, wealth, fame), or he pursues the reality of the self directly (in self-delineation, self-expression, activities of self-projection).

The second lifestance sees the primary location of value in relations or connections, primarily within relations of the self with other things (or other selves). Value gets located *between* the self and something else. According to this relational stance, the value of helping someone lies not in your being a helper (or solely in the other's improved situation) but in the relationship of helping; the value of scientific understanding consists in the way it connects a person to (portions of) nature. The relational stance sees a person's goal as her most real connection to reality—to external reality, to other people's, and to her own. For both of these first two stances, though, the egoistic and the relational, value is somehow connected to the self, either within it or between it and something else.

We can ask, however: What makes the self or its relations valuable; what are the aspects or features in virtue of which these things have value? These general features, once they are identified, might also exhibit themselves elsewhere than in the self and its relations, and then *any* situation that exemplifies them will count as valuable. The third stance, an absolute one, locates value as an independent domain, not initially within us or our relations; this is the stance of the Platonic tradition. We then relate to valuable things (and characteristics) or gain them *because* they are independently valuable. The primary locus of value does not thereby shift to us, though. Like a baby monkey clinging to its mother's fur, we latch on to what is valuable and ride along.

According to the absolute stance, our goal is specified by reality wherever and whenever it occurs, including but not limited to what the other stances speak of. It is the reality that is important; our relation to it is important only insofar as this relation has a reality of its own. Taking the absolute stance, we would count reality equally wherever it is found, not only the reality of lives and selves other than our own and the reality of their relations to external reality but also that of animal life, paintings, ecological systems, clusters of galaxies, social systems, historical civilizations, divine being(s). The goal of the absolute stance is specified by the total amount of reality there is, anywhere.

The three stances are different perspectives on the same things, and although they do not make the same things central, each will have its view on what is central to the others. The egoistic stance, for example, will see the interconnections and relationships central to the relational stance as one of the ways a self enhances itself, while the absolute stance will see those relations as an instance of a general and more extensive kind of value.

We should not construe the stances simply as theories about where value is located; while they all might grant that strictly speaking it can be anywhere, they provide different weightings of how much we are to take account of it depending upon where it is. Each stance specifies how things are to *count* for us. The egoistic stance is prone to undercut itself, though, as a theory of what we are to *value*. If reality is worth relating to, if it is worth having, then it is valuable also even when a person doesn't have it or relate to it. Otherwise, why bother relating to *it,* and trying to gain *it*? Since the egoist is striving to enhance his own reality, the greater reality of other people also is something worthwhile in the same way; since his relating to such reality involves appreciating it, enhancing it, responding to it, etc., he must do this also with the reality of other people. To diminish or scorn the reality of other people undercuts the presumption upon which the egoist's *own* life's direction is built. It announces that reality is something not worth enhancing and respecting—not to mention the way this behavior also diminishes his own reality and the extent to which he relates to other reality. When he acts on the egoistic stance he says, therefore, that his own life is worthless and meaningless in its own intrinsic character and also in what it orients itself by and toward, for he announces that the reality constituting these is not worth respecting and responding to generally.

The reply to an egoistic stance, then, is not that it is necessarily inconsistent as a theory of *wants* but that it undercuts itself as a theory of *value,* a philosophy of what is important in life (this in addition to the ways it stunts the egoist). Because the philosophical tradition has given much attention to egoism—to the task of understanding and isolating its particular defects—let us dwell upon this here. The question of what is important can be answered only by reference to value (such as reality) that is general; what is important is linking or connecting with that value, thereby realizing by a positive relation to it some of what also can be realized elsewhere, in other lives. The importance- or value-giver cannot be worthwhile just in one person's life, "for why is your blood redder than theirs?" It must be something that bestows value wherever it goes; any given person's life is valuable by virtue of falling under this value-giver, participating in it, becoming more infused with it. If the egoist denies its value elsewhere he denies its capacity to bestow value, hence he undercuts his own, which can only be based upon that. To demarcate its self as valuable, not merely to shape desires, the egoistic stance has to transcend its own egoistic orientation.*

---

* These considerations do not presuppose that *reality* provides the appropriate standard. Whatever standard someone adopts, he must acknowledge that this gives importance to the lives of others, or else undercut his view of his own life's importance. I am saying not merely that to deny the importance in the others' case would involve him in an inconsistency—someone may not care very much about avoiding inconsistencies—but that he cannot view his own life as having what is important unless he views others in the same light, so that the same standard can give them the same importance. To distinguish himself from the others is to undercut whatever he has, in its character of being worthwhile and worthy to seek. Nor can he simply care about the standard's getting realized in external things, works of art perhaps, but not other people; what he needs to acknowledge, *for himself,* is that it is important in people too—for otherwise it might be the kind of thing that gave value only to *objects;* what is not important in people generally is not important in him either.

The position here has two parts: (1) someone's recognizing in others and responding to whatever most general standard gives his own life importance/ meaning/value; (2) reality's being that standard. This form of reasoning, I have said, is not dependent upon reality's being the particular standard chosen, yet *some* distorted but imaginable standards—for example, that it is intensity of *suffering* that gives someone's life importance—might, when generalized by (1), lead to quite *un*ethical behavior toward others. The direction of the reasoning might be reversed, though, to find and support a specific standard; starting with the structure of (1) and (2), we can ask which particular standard under (2) would, when combined with (1), give rise to ethical behavior.

The absolutist stance specifies the locus of value as the total of reality in the world; this includes one's own reality and that of one's connections—the egoist's and the relationist's concerns—as portions, albeit tiny ones. In its maximizing mode, it mandates acting so as to maximize the total (amount and degree of) reality in the universe. By the breadth and neutrality of its concern, reality everywhere and anywhere, the absolutist stance extends its purview far beyond the traditional focus of ethics. Planetary systems, stars, galaxies, immense and far-flung intelligences—who knows what the universe might contain whose intense reality might be greater than ours and, in situations of conflict, outweigh our own (one person's or even that of all of humanity together) according to the absolutist stance. I do not say that one cannot take this stance and think humanity should sacrifice itself and the rest of its history for the sake of some vastly greater nonhuman reality, but while it might be noble for us all to choose to do so, it hardly seems required! (Might the absolute stance specify the appropriate focus of our attention and appreciation, even if not of our goals?)

Leaving such macrocosmic contexts aside, can the three stances be reconciled? We can increase the reality of the world by creating very real entities, by preserving or enhancing the ones there are, by helping or enabling other people to increase their own reality, and by increasing our own too. The absolute stance sometimes may be in tandem with the other stances, therefore. These relations of increasing or maintaining the world's reality, or creating some reality, will count heavily within the relational stance, obviously. More interesting, the degrees of reality a person is responsible for in the world, that external reality she creates or increases, gets *imputed* back to her as an increase in her own reality too.* By doing those things, having them as notable events and achievements within her biography, she adds to her

---

* It is a subtle task to delineate what of the reality a person produces also gets imputed back to her, and precisely how this depends upon various factors: what she intends to do, the effort she has to expend, the role of accident and coincidence, how self-expressive and self-projective these activities of increasing external reality are, the various ways in which others are led to respond to her actions, what portion of the total ensuing effects get attributed as consequences of her actions, etc.

life and to her own reality. Increasing the total reality in the world therefore might also be her route to most increasing her own.

Although acting on the absolutist stance might increase a person's own reality and hence serve the egoist stance without this being the actions' object, still, not all conflict among these two stances can thereby be avoided. In general, although the produced reality gets imputed back *to* the self, it does not all get imputed back as a feature *of* the self. Also, when the self does gain in reality, that gain might be less than the egoistic stance would yield. Imagine two alternative and increasingly divergent courses of action, one involving little effort yet great ensuing reality in the world, the other expressing or developing the self more but less externally productive. The mere act of recognizing these facts yet choosing the first might involve some gain in that individual's reality but less than the loss in forgoing the second course of action. The absolutist stance gives the relational stance much shorter shrift. It does not countenance giving special weight in action to your own mate, children, or friends, or to maintaining the special reality these connections have. (It might try to give these some derived special weight by saying that due to someone's greater localized knowledge and sphere of impact, he best serves the total overall reality by especially serving those close to him.) Moreover, it too easily countenances relationally undesirable immoral actions if these serve the greater overall total reality.

While each of the three stances is faulty by itself, each has its appeal, I think, and also its legitimate claim. "If I am not for myself," Hillel asked, "who will be? And if I am only for myself, what am I?" Each portion of reality has its own value, meaning, intensity, vividness, holiness, depth, etc.; each portion is worthy of being enhanced, maintained, created, or known (by being explored and responded to). Such is the appeal of the absolute stance. Yet our own reality does seem to have a certain priority for each of us, and properly so. We do not think we are required to give every other bit of reality, wherever it may be, the same weight as the reality of our selves (or of those we love, and of our relations with them), focusing upon our own lives only insofar as they are a small portion of the whole.* Is there some way the three stances can be combined to captured each one's strengths? An unsatisfactory way would be to maintain the absolute primacy of one of the stances, admitting the others only after that one has been satisfied fully. This makes the subsidiary ones too subordinate; not given enough weight ever to override the verdict of the primary stance, in practice they rarely would get paid any attention at all. A second way of combining these stances would be to alternate among them, keeping each one in your repertoire and using different ones at different times. However, while this enables you to throw yourself fully within each stance at different times, the combination seems *ad hoc*.

A more adequate way to combine the stances would give each one some weight in specifying the overall goal. How should this be done? The three partial goals are one's own reality, the reality of one's relation to other things, and the total reality there is (from which total, to avoid double counting, we may exclude the first two). Shall we simply add them up and guide ourselves by the resulting sum? Since the total reality is vastly greater than that of your own reality or relating—it includes the reality of other people and their relations and everything else there is as well—in the above simple sum that total reality would effectively swamp the rest. Assessing alternative actions or life courses by how they affect the simple sum of what the three stances care about in effect gives the first two stances no weight at all; it turns out to be, in practice, just the absolute stance.

Each of the three partial goals, however, can be given *some* weight without these weights being equal. (Many readers may wish to skim quickly over the remainder of this paragraph, which treats the form of the weighting.) First, normalize the measurements of the

---

* This special weighting of ourselves is an illusion perhaps motivated by selfishness or produced by a general cognitive bias, says the absolutist stance. We and our own lives are by necessity of special salience to ourselves, occupying the foreground of our attention, and there is a general psychological phenomenon that what is most salient will be thought, even inappropriately, to be most important. However, we think that *every* person properly can give special priority to his own life and self and to his own relations with reality; we do not think merely that *we* can and that everyone else must give *our* lives that special priority too! This general position would not easily be produced by merely a cognitive bias centering around ourselves.

three partial goals, and only afterward combine them with weightings. With normalized measurements, the different scales of measurement are set so that they have the same maximum and minimum values. The largest amount of reality someone can produce for his self, his connections and relations, or throughout the universe, will each get assigned the same positive number, 100, say, and the smallest amount of each such kind of reality will get assigned the same number, 0, say. (The scales are different because since the total reality in the universe is vastly greater than his own reality; measuring these each on scales having the same maximum value of 100 in effect greatly scrunches down the universe's reality or inflates his own.) Once the measurements have been normalized so that no one type of reality can automatically swamp the others, we face the question of what weights to give to these three different factors to yield the goal as their weighted sum. Different weights will enable us to tilt somewhat toward different stances.

Since all combinations of weights are possible, it may seem that the correct position must be in there someplace or other. (The simple and pure stances—egoistic, relational, and absolute—can be viewed as limiting cases that give their own factor some positive weight while giving the other two factors zero weight.) And indeed, once positively relevant things or dimensions are identified, a linear weighting often can be a good approximation to whatever it is that we want. However, in the present case, no matter what weights were assigned, the simple weighted sum of the three factors would not capture our feeling that each of the factors should be present. A life that neglects any one of the factors, even when that lack is numerically counterbalanced by a quantity of the two other factors, will be inadequate.

Each factor—someone's own reality, the reality of his relations, and the total reality there is—gets amplified by the presence and magnitude of others. Given a measurement of the three factors on a normalized scale, we need to *multiply* the factors together, not add them, or perhaps we need to weight the factors and then multiply them. Thereby the presence and magnitude of each amplifies the others' magnitudes. We can call this fourth stance a combined stance. It can be stated more precisely in the following formula (which some readers may prefer to skip). When a given person relates to reality on a given occasion, let us suppose there are three measures: a measure of how much his self's reality is brought to bear in that instance of relating, a measure also of the portion of total reality he relates to, and finally a measure of how real his relation to this reality is. (All of these measures are normalized, with the same possible maximum and minimum values.) Then the reality of his relating thus in that instance to that portion of reality will be the arithmetical product of these three measures, the three (weighted) measures multiplied by each other, the reality of his self brought to bear multiplied by the reality of the relation multiplied by the reality related to. And the reality of *all* of his relating to reality will be a sum of three products, the combined total of what is involved in each of the individual instances he participates in: the product in the first instance, plus the product in the second, plus . . . (However, if in a given instance the three factors do not all play a role, there still will be the measure mentioned earlier of whichever separate ones are operating; this weighted sum [using appropriate weights] should be added to the sum of the previous products, to complete the formula.)

This combined stance unites the three previous stances in a mutually reinforcing way. (I wish I could term this combined stance an *integral* stance, but although it brings the three stances together, it does not sufficiently place them within one unified conception to merit this title. In the meditation on Darkness and Light we shall investigate a mode of integrating the stances more tightly than by a multiplicative formula.) The whole this stance is concerned with, not just in each instance of relating but summed over a lifetime, might be called your-relating-to-reality. Given the factors' large mutual rein- forcement within the above sum of their products, to concentrate solely upon any one factor (as each of the previous three stances recommended) would lead to a great loss in overall magnitude, a loss not counterbalanced by the (unmultiplied) addition of a significant quantity of just one factor. The combined formula does not require us to relate to *all* of external reality, although it may encourage us to do this as much as possible, but it does require us to relate to some portion of significant external reality, intensely and with a significant portion of ourselves, in order to add some large multiplier.*

Someone who adopts the combined stance will extend it past

---

* A later section discusses the notion of proportionality; this might be included within the combined stance if, in acting, a person attempted two acts of calibration, adjusting how much reality of his self is involved in a relation, and the reality of the relating too, proportioning both to the magnitude of the reality related to.

the form described above. Just as the egoistic stance, if it is to be a position about value, must recognize and prize reality and value everywhere, not just within the boundaries of one self, so too someone taking the combined stance will eventually be led to focus not simply upon *his*-relating-to-reality, but upon *our*-relating-to-reality. What determines the boundaries of this "us" is an intricate question; ultimately, it may become all those beings who have the capacity to relate to, appreciate, and respond to the characteristics of reality *qua* reality. However, while we can help other people to relate to reality *qua* reality, we cannot *force* them to, the ensuing relation would not be real: it would not draw upon an extensive reality of theirs, and it would not relate them to reality *qua* reality.

A first generalization of the combined stance, as it shifts the goal to the impersonal one of our-relating-to-reality, still keeps a personal perspective on this new goal; a person acts to enhance *his* relating to our-relating-to-reality. He therefore would try to maximize his own connection to that general goal. A second generalization is not concerned especially with *his* relating to that general goal. Cumbersomely put, it focuses upon *our* relating to our-relating-to-reality. A person would think it just as good, when he takes this latter perspective, if somebody else advanced the general goal. The first generalization might be seen as a compromise which captures some force from the egoistic stance and some from the absolute one.

The broadest version of the combined stance generalizes the previous formula to now encompass all people and their relations to portions of reality. For each single person, it takes—as before—the sum of the products representing that person's instances of relating to reality, and then it adds these sums up for all the people together. It is a double summation of those factors that amplify each other by being multiplied together. This general combined stance is concerned with each and every person's relating to reality; the whole it nurtures is our-relating-to-reality.

The reality someone produces or aids in others gets imputed back to his own reality. Might an egoist be led to follow that generalized formula which incorporates a concern for others' relating to reality too, solely *because* he calculates that when the produced reality gets imputed back to his own self, this will best serve his own reality? We may doubt, however, whether reality produced for *that* reason can get imputed back sufficiently. (As in other cases, though, a disreputable original motive may fade in time, with the actual pattern of behavior then generating and displaying its own most appropriate motive.) Taking the egoistic stance is not the most effective route to anyone's greatest reality; that stance is not a global optimum—even when judged by the stance itself!

Talk of different stances casts new light on the problem of free will. This problem stems from worry that previous causal factors— our upbringing or neurophysiology or the past states of the world— drive and control our actions. However, we might wonder whether it is the egoistic stance itself that gives rise to the traditional free-will problem. If I pose the question of how I can be free, isn't this very notion of freedom—independence of external things—a concept rooted in the egoist stance? The relational stance would not prize that independence or find value there, and so it would not ask how to gain it or worry over how it might be possible. Instead, the relational stance asks how one can be related to other things and to external reality. Moreover, being determined to act by specific causal factors might even constitute a specially strong way of begin related to those factors! Hence, determination of action might be something the relational stance prizes. This stance might seek the widest possible causation of action—that is, determination by as many factors as possible in as strong a way as possible. *Its* ultimate goal would be determination by the whole state of reality, nothing left out, each of our actions linked to everything else in the most powerful and multifarious ways. What would be regrettable, on this stance, would be a determinism that was only partial, one that was not complete enough.

15

Value and Meaning

THE NOTION of reality has various aspects or dimensions. To be more intense and vivid is to be more real (holding other things equal), to be more valuable is to be more real, and so on. To have a higher score along any one of the various dimensions that make up the notion of reality (holding everything else constant) is to be more real. The dimensions specify the notion of reality by describing its aspects, and these same dimensions also provide the criteria for evaluating each object. I want to examine the dimensions in their evaluative aspect or role, turning later to their metaphysical status and interrelations as aspects of reality. In this meditation I will consider two dimensions—first, the dimension of value.

The notion of value is not simply some vague laudatory term. Some things have value only as a means to something else that is valuable. And some things have a value of their own, an intrinsic value. (Some things have both kinds of value, value as a means to something else and also a value of their own.) This notion of intrinsic value is the basic one; other kinds of value exist by their relation to intrinsic value. But what does intrinsic value consist in; what gives rise to it?

Let us consider things frequently said to be valuable in themselves. We begin with works of art. Recall what happens in art appreciation classes. You are shown how the different parts and components of a painting are interrelated, how the eye is led from place to place by forms and colors, how it is brought to the thematic center of the painting, how these colors, forms, and textures fit the theme, etc. You are shown how the painting is a unity, how the diverse elements constituting it form an integrated and united whole. A painting has aesthetic value, theorists have held, when it manages to integrate a great diversity of material into a tight unity, often in vivid and striking ways. Such a "unity in diversity" was termed an *organic unity* because organisms in the biological world were thought to exhibit the same unity wherein diverse organs and tissues interrelate to maintain the life of the organism. (An extreme form of this doctrine holds that no part of the work of art can be removed or altered without destroying its character or reducing its value.)

Earlier writers had seen a scale of value exhibited throughout the natural world, beginning with rocks at the bottom, plants next, then lower animals, higher ones, human beings, and (they continued the scale with) angels and finally God. The rankings in this traditional "great chain of being" also can be understood via the degree of organic unity each thing exhibits. The farther you move up the scale, the more diversity there is to get unified in even tighter ways. Rocks exhibit intermolecular forces; plants exhibit these along with organic processes; animals show most of these (although not photosynthesis) and add locomotion; higher animals have their activities integrated over time by intelligence and consciousness, and in the case of human beings, this integration occurs in even tighter ways through self-consciousness. (Much of this corresponds with an evolutionary scale too. However, the point is not that the more evolved is more valuable *because* it's more evolved; rather, the notion of degree of organic unity fits the value ranking we make, one that is roughly evolutionary, and this fact of so fitting is evidence that the notion of organic unity does capture our sense of what is valuable.)

In science also, theories are evaluated by invoking some notion of unity in diversity. Scientists speak of the degree to which a vast amount of data and diverse phenomena are unified by being explained in terms of a small number of simple scientific laws. It was a triumph of Newton's laws that they explained both the motion of bodies on earth and the apparently unrelated motions of heavenly bodies; a similar goal now leads physicists to search for a unified field theory to provide one explanation of the major forces of nature.

It would be a major task to define precisely this notion of degree of organic unity and to specify a way to measure it. For our purposes here, we can proceed with a rough and intuitive understanding. The greater the diversity that gets unified, the greater the organic unity; and also the tighter the unity to which the diversity is brought, the greater the organic unity. A monochromatically painted canvas would show a high degree of unity, but since no diversity of color, form, or theme would thereby have been unified, it would not possess a high degree of organic unity. Thus a resultant organic unity depends upon two things, the degree of diversity and the degree of unity to which that diversity is brought. The task of achieving organic unity is difficult because these two factors tend to vary inversely and so pull in opposite directions. The greater the diversity, the harder it is to bring it to a given degree of unity. Organic unities can be built up out of elements which do not themselves have organic unity; there can be unified "molecules" without there being organically unified "subatomic particles."

Something has intrinsic value, I suggest, to the degree that it is organically unified. Its organic unity *is* its value. At any rate, it is a structure of organic unity that constitutes value's structure. Perhaps, in some special areas, additional specific characteristics (such as pleasurable hedonic tone) also play a role in value, but the common structure of value across different areas, and the major dimension that underlies almost all value, is the degree of organic unity.

Given this, we can understand why we hold other particular things to be valuable in themselves—for example, whole ecological systems with their complexly interrelated equilibria. Also, we can understand why we find it difficult to place in one single ordering of value paintings and planetary systems and people and theories. Even though the same structural notion of organic unity is involved, we are not able to compare the degree of organic unity (or the component degree of diversity) of such different things. Our vagueness in comparing these degrees of organic unity fits (and explains) our hesitancy in making these comparisons of value.

One major problem discussed by philosophers, "the mind-body problem," asks what the connection is between mental events and neurophysical events in the brain and body. Are these merely correlated, or two aspects of the same thing, or are they really the same thing referred to by different words? Thus far no satisfactory solution has been found. The problem is made especially difficult by the apparent extreme difference between mind and body, one which led Descartes to hold that mind and matter were separate substances. The apparent difference between mind and body would not create such a problem, however, were it not for the tightness of the unity that exists between them. Consciousness and the mind not only enable an organism to unify its activities over time; at any given moment, consciousness is tightly unified with the physical/biological processes then occurring. What we have, then, is an apparently enormous diversity which is unified to a very high degree—that is, we have an extremely high degree of organic unity, hence something extremely valuable. If (degree of) value is (degree of) organic unity, the mind-body problem shows that people are very valuable. Solving this problem will require understanding how this very high degree of value is possible.

In wanting ourselves to be of value and our lives and activities to have value, we want these to exhibit a high degree of organic unity. (Plato viewed the proper state of the soul as a hierarchical arrangement of three parts—the rational, the courageous, and the appetitive—with each part subordinate to the one before it and harmoniously performing its own proper function. If such a view is appealing this is because it strikes us as a valuable way to be, not because that soul must turn out to be happy. What Plato describes is *one* organically unified mode of being, though; there are others that have a different character.) We want to encompass a diversity of traits and phenomena, uniting these through many cross-connections in a tightly integrated way, feeding these productively into our activities. Some entities will be the agents of their own organic unity, or some of it, shaping and developing it from within, while others will have it wholly arranged externally; this may make a difference to the kind or extent of value the entity has.

Note that a regimented society of individuals will not have the highest degree of organic unity or value. It will be less valuable than a free society wherein the major relations of people are voluntarily undertaken and modified in response to the particular changing conditions around them, giving rise to complexly interrelated and ever-shifting equilibria such as economic theory describes. Therein is the largest diversity of activity intricately unified. (However, some complications do need to be introduced to handle those entities whose goal or purpose is the destruction of some other innocent or nondestructive organic unities.) Building modes of solidarity, fellow feeling, and sharing into the fabric of the society adds greater unity still to that provided by the market.

Value is one particular kind of thing; there are other dimensions of evaluation also. We can understand, though, why the usual custom is to use the term *value* differently, as denoting the overarching category for everything good; the different ways something can be good then are counted as various kinds of value, not as something else other than value. Is this issue merely verbal? To value something is to stand in a particular close, positive psychological and attitudinal relation to it, a relation itself marked by high organic unity. *Valuing* something is doing that particular relational activity. You might then say that every thing or trait to which we do that specific activity therefore has "value," but that is to project the unity of the psychological evaluative activity onto whatever differing objects that activity was directed toward. The view of value as degree of organic unity, on the other hand, keeps value as just one kind of phenomenon, the activity of valuing being an instance.

Value is not the only relevant evaluative dimension. We also want our lives and our existence to have meaning. Value involves something's being integrated within its own boundaries, while meaning involves its having some connection beyond these boundaries. The problem of meaning itself is raised by the presence of limits. Thus, typically, people worry about the meaning of their lives when they see their existences as limited, perhaps because death will end them and so mark their final limit. To seek to give life meaning is to seek to transcend the limits of one's individual life. (Are there two ways to transcend our current limits and hence two modes of meaning: connecting with external things that remain external, and connecting with things so as somehow to incorporate these things, either within ourselves or into an enlarged identity?) Sometimes this occurs by leaving children behind, sometimes by advancing some larger aim that is beyond oneself, such as the cause of justice or truth or beauty.

Yet for each such larger aim (or aim combined with a person) we can notice the limits of this in turn. Even when we consider the universe as a whole, we can see it is limited. Thus, some people wonder how anything about human existence can have meaning if eventually, millions of years from now, it all will end in some massive heat death of the galaxy or universe. About any given thing, however wide, it seems we can stand back and ask what its meaning is. To find a meaning for it, then, we seem driven to find a link with yet another thing beyond its boundaries. And so a regress is launched. To stop this regress, we seem to need something that is intrinsically meaningful, something meaningful in itself, not by virtue of its connection with something else; or else we need something which is unlimited, from which we cannot step back, even in imagination, to wonder what *its* meaning is. Thus it was that religion seemed to provide a stopping place for questions about meaning, an ultimate foundation of meaning, by speaking of an infinite being which was not properly seen as limited, a being from which there could be no place to step back in order to see its limits, so that the question about *its* meaning could not even begin.

Meaning cannot be gained by just any linkage beyond boundaries, for instance, with something that is completely worthless. But that thing linked with to gain meaning need not itself be *meaningful*. (That way the regress begins.) We already have seen that there is another way for something to be worthwhile: it can have *value*. Value is a matter of the internal unified coherence of a thing. That thing need not be linked with anything else, anything larger, in order to have value. We need not look beyond something to find its (intrinsic) value, whereas we do have to look beyond a thing to discover its meaning. When we look beyond, though, what we may find is a connection with value, with something having its own organic unity. The regress of meaning is stopped by reaching something with a kind of worth other than meaning—namely, reaching something of value. (Other dimensions considered in subsequent sections also may constitute worth and thus provide a ground for meaning.)

Meaning and value, as we have explained them here, are coordinate notions that stand in interesting and intricate relationship. Meaning can be gained by linking with something of value. However, the nature of the linkage is important. I cannot give meaning to my life by saying I am linked to advancing justice in the world, where this means that I read the newspapers every day or week and thereby notice how justice and injustice fare. That is too trivial and too insubstantial a link. (Still, knowing external things and understanding how they are valuable may constitute a nontrivial link.) The greater the link, the closer, the more forceful, the more intense and extensive it is, the greater the meaning gotten. The tighter the connection with value, the greater the meaning. This tightness of connection means that you are interrelated with the value in a unified way; there is more of an organic unity between you and the value. Your connection with the value, then, is itself valuable; and meaning is gotten through such a valuable connection with value.

Meaning and value also can interweave over time. Consider those processes in the arts or the sciences where a unity is achieved at a certain stage, only to be overturned by new elements that do not fit in, whereupon a new unity gets formed to incorporate these new elements (plus most of the old ones), and so on. The new elements might be new data in the scientific domain, or new materials or themes in the artistic one. Many will see the point and goal of the process in the achieving of the unities, and hence see the breaking apart of the previous unities merely as a means toward better and more adequate new ones (I am referring to changes where these further unities do get reached, not to cases we would classify as decay), while others might see the transcending of the previous unities and limits as the point of the process wherein people exercise and demonstrate their nature as beings who strive and transcend. We can, of course, see each stage as of coordinate importance, neither simply a means to reaching the other. Both alternate to constitute what is most important, that continuing process itself.*

Are these two notions of value and meaning a sufficient basis for evaluating a self, its life, works, and relations with other people and things? Or do some important evaluations involve further notions? Value and meaning are notions so broad that it might seem anything can be fitted under them. Even then, it would be unilluminating to place other evaluative notions under just these two categories if doing that distorted or hid their most salient features.

---

* This section draws upon the discussion of value and meaning in my earlier book *Philosophical Explanations,* where further details are given. There is a tenuous and somewhat far-flung application of the concepts of value and meaning to sexual relating that is theoretically intriguing, but which I would not place great weight upon. In sexual union, an intense unity is created, a linking across boundaries, an interpenetrating through them. The notions of value and meaning, the reader may have noticed, are not without their own sexual overtones. Bringing oneself into an internal unity and connecting beyond oneself not only describe the notions of value and meaning respectively, they also seem to fit modes of sexual connection. More speculatively, value and meaning have, so to speak, a gender. Bringing oneself into an internal unity seems to fit a female way of relating sexually, connecting beyond oneself a male. Is value to female as meaning is to male? Since these evaluative dimensions are of great and coordinate importance, this would be a satisfying result. I do not claim that these two central evaluative dimensions are merely our sexual notions sublimated and writ large. However, the parallelism certainly would add to the power of the evaluative notions, as perhaps it would add—were any adding needed—to the dignity of the sexual orientations.

Even at this high level of abstraction, though, it may not be obvious which of the notions, value or meaning, to apply to which sex. In sexual orientation, men go to link outward and women incorporate inward. Yet in the nature of their self-conceptions, women often are described as oriented around notions of relationship and connection, while men view themselves as more autonomously contained within their own boundaries. Wouldn't this locate women more along the meaning dimension, men more along that of value? It would be interesting if men and women tended to define the notions of value and meaning after their own case; then they might differ in their *conception* of these notions, with women modeling value after vaginal incorporation, meaning after relationship with others, and men modeling meaning after phallic connection, value after separate individuation. This need not mean, though, that they must get or find value and meaning, as they define it, by different routes.

16

Importance and Weight

WE WANT to be important in some way, to count in the world and make a difference to it. Importance is an additional, separate dimension of reality. It might seem unnecessary to count importance separately. Since to have effect involves being connected to other things, don't all the features of importance fall under the notion of meaning? Moreover, don't the ways that something counts and the kinds of effects that make it important themselves have to be valuable and meaningful? How, then, can importance be a distinct and additional dimension of reality? The notion of importance is not reducible to that of value and meaning, however. Some activities may have value without being important, while other important, impactful activities will have neither value nor meaning.

An example of value without importance is chess. In chess, it is possible to create valuable, even beautiful structures, unifying themes from earlier games, modifying well-known strategies, exhibiting daring or cunning or patience. The game also reverberates for some with themes of combat between opposing forces. By connecting up with larger themes of combat, games might be said to have meaning also, in addition to the value of their particular developments, combinations, and surprises. But the game is not, I think, important. It does not have any impact beyond itself, even though it is an activity that can dominate someone's life; its play on larger themes of combat does not alter the way we see or engage in other combat. I want to say not that chess has no further effect at all but that, given the immense amount of intellectual power and energy that is put into it, it has disproportionately little. The people who know of and appreciate wonderful chess games do not have their lives deepened or their perceptions altered; there is only the appreciative experience of the game itself and the memory of it. (This is not to deny—remember—that chess has *value*.) Mathematics, a similar structural enterprise, is utilized within scientific theories, and even when it is not put to practical use it can unify a vast amount of other mathematical details and facts, giving a deeper understanding of these structures. (The British mathematician G. H. Hardy, however, gloried in working in mathematics *because* his specialty, he thought, had no further applications or connections.)

It is most desirable to have value and importance together, but even if this is not possible, we want to make some difference sometimes and to have some effect, so we will settle for impact and being important to something, even if this thing is not valuable or meaningful and our impact isn't either. Better some importance than no importance at all. One defect of the experience machine is that it gives us no effect or impact on the world, it gives us no importance. Another machine which, unlike the experience machine, gave a passive contact with reality would have this defect as well. These would not satisfy a further reality principle, coordinate with the others—call it the fifth reality principle—that calls for connecting with actuality in a way that has some impact on it.

Not that one should rank importance above value and meaning, maximizing it whatever the cost. (It would be little comfort if history's monsters were not bent upon evil in its character as evil but rather pursued large impact upon others in the only way they could.) The best sort of importance also has value and meaning. Yet making a difference does have claim of its own; it is a separate evaluative notion. We especially notice that when people invoke and pursue importance in the absence of value and meaning, but the claim is present even alongside these.

However—a further complication—we cannot completely disconnect the notion of importance from the concepts of value and meaning. An important event or action need not itself have positive value or meaning or affect anything positively, but it must have some effect on value or meaning; in this case, then, its importance will lie in its large *negative* impact on value and meaning. To say that something has impact does not merely count the *number* of its effects. Every action perhaps has an indefinitely large number of effects; when I speak I am moving and changing the position of millions of air molecules, and these effects continue to cascade down in time. Yet that does not by itself guarantee importance to the utterance. In identifying something as having impact, then, it is not the number but the kind of effects that matter. To specify that kind of effect will invoke the notions of value or meaning, or yet further evaluative dimensions. An important event, I think, is one with effects that matter, ones that make a large difference to (the amount or character of) value or meaning, or to some other evaluative dimension (This difference may operate in a negative direction, remember. The notion of importance refers to other evaluative dimensions but is not reducible to them.) It is not possible to eliminate the reference to value, meaning, or some evaluative dimension.*

* This means that when historians term some events important, and study them, their claim is not evaluatively neutral. An historian might think she means by an important historical event or action an event with many effects that people know of, many effects that enter people's consciousness even when they do not know what earlier event these effects are due to. A major war or institutional change will have many effects people will be aware of. This criterion focuses upon human knowing; it could be widened to include other intelligent consciousness in the universe or some animal consciousness on earth. Important events in the universe would be those whose effects are widely known. (The notion of "effect" here is not transitive. The historian can think Napoleon's life was historically important without treating the mating of Napoleon's great-great-grandparents as historically important too. How will she exclude this? Does that mating fail to be historically important simply because all of its known effects funnel through one later event? Yet some historically important events are such merely by causing a later event of importance.)

The criterion of the number of known effects functions, I think, as an approximation to another one that invokes evaluative notions. First, imagine that all molecules have some rudimentary form of consciousness. Would that make all of

Feeling important can take strange shapes. Some people feel important not because of the effects they engender but because of the causes that have engendered them, as when descendants of note-worthy people take pride in that fact. Do they believe the earlier accomplishments were genetically based and so feel entitled to pride in recessive traits they possess but do not exhibit? Or do they feel that a biological link with accomplishment gives them meaning, even though the link goes in the less preferred direction? Notice my assumption that it is better to be a cause of something wonderful than an effect of it. Wonderful causes can have trivial effects, whereas it is less easy for a trivial event to cause a wonderful one; then the wonderfulness of the effect gets imputed back, in part, to its cause. The wonderfulness of a cause, however, does not get imputed forward to its effects. The fact is, the notion of impact is a fundamental evaluative dimension; it is not derivative merely from the connections exhibited under the notion of meaning.

The kind of impact we most wish for makes a large positive difference to something's value or meaning (or to some other appropriate evaluative dimension). We want this difference to stem from something nontrivial in us. To accidentally bump into someone with large and cascading effects—a positive version of "for want of a nail . . ."—is not enough. We want the large effect to be due to a characteristic we value, better yet, to an integrated combination of them. When caused by our action, we want that action to be inten-

---

our utterances important simply because the millions of molecules were aware of their new positions caused by our speaking? Wouldn't we instead hold those awarenesses weren't so important and so neither was the event which caused them? Other events also have effects that are widely known but (we would say) trivial; a popular record can be heard by millions but have no other discernible impact upon their lives. The knowledge criterion is inadequate in other ways, too. If the solar system suddenly were obliterated, wiping out all human knowing consciousness, that event, the end of human history, would be historically important even though no occupant of the solar system had any knowledge of it or of its later effects. (However, the knowledge criterion could be improved to say that an historically important event makes a difference to knowledge-events; an explosion that prevents the many knowledge events which otherwise would have occurred thereby would count as important.) The initial plausibility of the knowledge criterion stems from the fact that usually when something matters people will know of it; hence, the knowledge criterion roughly approximates the more accurate view about importance, making a difference along an evaluative dimension.

tional and self-expressive, stemming from and exhibiting valuable characteristics. Perhaps this is because all ensuing differences in value and meaning will get selectively imputed to earlier traits and activities having value and meaning themselves. At any rate, we gain more in importance when such traits play the causal role. By and large, impact is effected by action, not by refraining from it. Your refraining from harming someone counts as an important effect only when something makes your harming that person the expected or appropriate course of action. You are not constantly having important effects on passing pedestrians merely by not running them over.

I want to look more closely at importance, including material wealth and power as forms of it. Like the tradition in philosophy, I have tended to be dismissive of these forms of importance despite the fact that many people pursue them assiduously. Philosophers are people who value being thinkers and writers. Few books say the writing of books is completely worthless, just as few intellectual arguments denigrate the value of intellectual argument. If you think that, you just don't make those things. The people who thought that only wealth and power mattered, that intellectual understanding and clarity did not, didn't leave essays behind (convincingly) stating their case. My impulse still is to dismiss worldly wealth and power, yet I want to look more closely.

Importance has two aspects. The first involves having external impact or effect, being a causal source of external effects, a place from which effects flow so that other people or things are affected by your actions. The second aspect of importance involves having to be taken account of, counting. (Even if being taken account of is one kind of impact or effect, it is worth mentioning separately.) If the first aspect of importance involves being a causal source from which effects flow, the second involves being a place toward which responses flow, responses to your actions, traits, or presence. In some way they pay attention to you and take you into account. Simply being paid attention to is something we want.

Being the focus of other people's attention often is a prerogative of the powerful; * the desire for power, fame, and wealth is, in large part, a desire for importance. Of course, power, fame and wealth are

* See Charles Derber, *The Pursuit of Attention* (New York: Oxford University Press, 1983), pp. 21–35, 65–86.

desired in part as a means to what follows in their wake—material goods, pleasurable experiences, interesting social encounters. Beyond these discrete things, though, power, fame, and wealth also significantly involve importance in its two modes, the having of effect and being taken account of. Moreover, they also symbolize *being* important. A connection to importance is clearest in the case of power; a powerful person is able to affect outcomes in nature, herself, or other people. It is possible to classify the various forms of power—something I relegate to a footnote—and perhaps it even can help or be somewhat comforting, when a particular mode of power is exerted upon us, to see its place in a pattern of alternatives.*

* To measure the extent of power (social scientists tell us) we have to identify the other people, which of their actions are involved, what resources of power are used, and what the costs are to the user of power. Power can take different forms. The behavior of others can be affected through bypassing their choices, as when people are physically carried off or locked in a cell. Or the affecting can occur through their choices. You can raise the probability or disutility of negative outcomes contingent upon a person's behavior, and thereby *force* him to do something else; or you can raise the probability or utility of positive outcomes for him contingent upon behavior and thereby *induce* him to do it. Or you can affect the person's judgment of the probabilities and utilities, while leaving them actually unchanged, by providing him with information. Thereby, you have *influence* over his actions. (When people speak of the power and influence of the media, they are using this sense and perhaps the next.) You *manipulate* another when you give him information you believe to be either false or a biased sample of correct information in order to lead him in a certain direction. (Is it manipulation when, without believing it to be false or biased, you don't believe it true and unbiased, caring only to lead the other person along?) When you influence those actions through which someone exerts power over third parties, you yourself have power over those third parties. To have *authority* is to have the right to demand that someone do something, giving them a duty to obey; this authority has *legitimacy* to the extent that those commanded feel obligated therefore to obey.

A *leader* is able to weld people's diverse aspirations and activities into a coordinated pattern directed toward particular goals. There are many worthwhile things people can do together. A nation can concentrate upon reducing poverty or advancing serious culture or developing new technology or maximizing individual liberty . . . ; a group of teenage friends might conceivably go to a movie together or to an amusement park, or to a fight, or wander the streets, clean up the neighborhood, patrol the streets, or produce a play. The list of possible desirable goals is very long, but all cannot be done simultaneously. Somehow, amid the clamor of the merits of the competing desirable goals, the people or group will have to decide which one to pursue wholeheartedly together. A leader functions to resolve this competition of goals; he provides a vision of a desirable goal, articulates a feasible plan for reaching it, and inspires enough people to move along that path, following him. Only under very special conditions, then, can a society avoid the need for leadership of some sort.

The social scientists who study power—the ability to affect outcomes—often concentrate on situations where other people diametrically oppose those outcomes. Max Weber went so far as to *define* power as "the probability that one actor within a social relationship will be in a position to *carry out his own will despite resistance*."* To be sure, the situation of unalterable resistance may be one situation faced, but it too often is quickly assumed that this case is present. The ability to affect outcomes also can be exercised in other ways: through persuading the other person, proposing cooperative compromises, coming up with a new alternative that better satisfies every party's desires, and so on, through participating in (and affecting the direction of) the myriad array of alterations parties undergo in a continuing association. Social scientists speak of the power to affect actions and behavior; there also is the power to affect emotions, ideas, and modes of perception—the realm of artists and thinkers—and to affect people in their core selves—the realm of spiritual teachers.

Wealth, too, is desired for the importance it brings, as well as the things it buys. In Western society, as in most, wealth makes one important; a wealthy person is (generally) treated as important and can have a large effect. Moreover, for many people wealth is a symbol of being important; we might say it is the currency of importance. Luxury, too, apart from its actual soft comforts, is a symbolic representation of importance. It is as though people think: Anyone the world treats this well must be important. (The relative scarcity of a luxury item—as Veblen realized—enables it to stand for something special and to symbolize importance.)

I want to say that no one, neither others nor that person himself, should assess someone's importance by his wealth. Is it that the mere possession of money cannot be self-expressive, unlike actions that utilize personal qualities? Yet money could be spent to create a home that is self-expressive; this expenditure also can have an impact upon architects, builders, and furniture makers. And cannot the activities of amassing money be done in a way that is self-expressive and also has an impact upon others? Yet to the extent a person focuses his

* Max Weber, *The Theory of Social and Economic Organization* (New York: The Free Press, 1964), p. 152 (my italics).

attention upon the money, a means, rather than upon the substance of his productive activities or the exercise of his own talents, his mind will be occupied with content of no intrinsic value. Money and wealth, by themselves, are not a vehicle for nuanced expression; they lack the convolutions and texture to mirror anything complicated.

Why do we think it is ignoble when money is an activity's primary motive? (This does not mean we think the motive of feeding one's family or oneself is ignoble.) To be motivated in an activity primarily by money is to rank what money brings above the value and meaning of the activity itself. This then denigrates those activities whose value and importance we deem above that of money. If a philosopher tells us that he thinks for the money, a doctor that she cures illness for it, a violin maker that he does it for the cash, then we feel their activity is somehow soiled. And if they understand the meaning and value of their work so ill as to hold that beneath the making of money, how could they then be able to do work of quality? Even the male writers Freud speaks of who are motivated by the desire for fame and the love of beautiful women—Freud did not specify which ranked first—desire fame *for* doing that kind of writing; the quality is internal to their desire. Money, on the other hand, featureless, need not represent or express anything valuable. Therefore it is not simply that money as a predominant motivation distracts the agent's attention from the contours and quality of his activity, though it may well do that. The higher ranking money is given shows him with a distorted view of his activity, a distortion that must affect the way it will be carried on. Might the distortion be only in his view of money, though, not his view of the activity? Life cannot be partitioned thus. It is one integral person who values those other things and does this activity; the activity then is the kind of activity done by that kind of person with that scale of values. Someone who loves money more than he loves a person does not love that person.

Power can be utilized and exerted expressively in ways that have large effects upon others. If importance is indeed a dimension of reality, must we then say that merely possessing power does give someone greater reality, even if that power gets exercised in dominating others or foreclosing some alternatives to them simply because the power-holder wants to force his will upon them and *make* them act in a certain way? If having an effect through the possession and exertion of power itself may bring someone greater reality, it can diminish his reality to an even greater extent in other ways. This is a piece of the corruption that power tends to bring—no one gets away with very much. (Just *look* at the faces of those people who wield power or devote their lives to amassing money or influence or prestige.)

It is because importance was defined neutrally—as having impact, no matter what kind—that we have been forced through these thickets of reasons to show the obvious: that certain modes of such importance do not make someone more real. Wouldn't it be simpler to specify initially that only certain kinds of impact, and only certain types of reasons for being taken account of, constitute an "importance" that is important? In a later meditation on Darkness and Light, we shall reconsider the present neutral specification of reality's content.

Coordinate with value, meaning, and importance, there is a fourth evaluative aspect or dimension of reality, that of *weight*. The weight of something is its internal substantiality and strength. It may help to think of the opposite. What is meant when a person is called a "lightweight"? It might be impact and importance that are being talked about here, but usually, I think, what are meant are those qualities that importance is (or should be) based upon. People are commenting on how substantial the person is, how considered his thoughts, how dependable his judgment, how that person holds up under buffeting or deeper examination. A weighty person is not blown by winds of fashion or scrutiny. The Romans called it *gravitas*.

We might specify weight as a resistance to external change of certain sorts. (Fuller elaboration specifies three components: something has weight in a specified characteristic with respect to specified changes in the face of specified forces.) Weight would be an equilibrium notion. Something in stable equilibrium resists outside forces or reestablishes itself in its previous state or a similar one. So too a person, an opinion, a principle, or an emotion has weight if it maintains and reestablishes itself in the face of outside pressures or forces. This characterizes the internal notion of weight externally, by how it resists external forces. We have not said what the inside substance is like which enables something to maintain itself this way.

Sometimes weight will depend upon how tightly something is

integrated in a network of relations. A weighty opinion is one that has been duly considered and takes account of many facts, larger issues, and possible objections that might be raised. An emotion has weight, it is not a passing fancy, when it connects with the person's other strivings, plans, goals, and desires, and becomes integrated with them; perhaps the emotion has undergone some modification to fit this tightly and well. Such a network of multifareous connections holds something fast in the face of outside pressure. Moreover, that thing with weight already has taken account of and so become integrated with many of the things that otherwise might overturn it.

It would be nice to find a general internal characterization of weight, one that would serve for a person, a belief, and an emotion. To speak of (amount of) substance or density is simply to mark the phenomenon, not to characterize it. Perhaps different types of things are substantial in different ways, sharing in common only some external characteristics and the ability to maintain and reestablish themselves in the face of external pressures. Weight, however, is an internal phenomenon, despite our providing a criterion for it that is external. It is the internal property, whichever that is in a particular case, that is the basis of maintaining equilibrium.

Importance involves external connections or relationships, as does meaning. Weight involves internal organization, as does value. Weight stands to value as importance stands to meaning. Importance is external or relational strength or power, while weight is internal, inherent strength. Value is the inherent integration of something, while meaning is its relation and integration with external things. Thus, from the neat-looking formula weight/value = importance/ meaning, we can form a table:

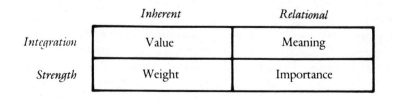

	Inherent	*Relational*
Integration	Value	Meaning
Strength	Weight	Importance

This simple picture of these four evaluative dimensions of reality—value, meaning, importance, and weight—places them in illuminating and satisfying relationship. We might hope, then, to discuss and evaluating everything whatsoever in terms of just these four dimensional criteria. Unfortunately for theoretical purposes, however—but perhaps fortunately for life—these four do not exhaust the relevant kinds of evaluations we want to make.

Depth is a quality we also prize. Whether in a work of art, an emotion, a scientific theory, a mathematical theorem, a person, or a mode of understanding, the deeper, the better. People on a spiritual path seek to connect with the very deepest reality. Shallowness and superficiality are not in general, desirable qualities, although there may be occasions when nothing deeper is needed.

It is tempting to try to reduce depth to width, thereby leaving everything flat. A deep scientific theory connects with many other theories and problems, a deep emotion reverberates across many others and produces many changes. Can we understand depth, then, simply as a nexus of wide-ranging connections, all on the same plane? Everything lies on the same surface, but when some things have more wide-ranging and extensive surface connections than others, we project this aspect as depth. (Compare how Flatland's inhabitants infer curvature from features of the surface geometry.)

But why bother with this one reduction when so many other dimensions quickly flow in upon us? If depth is an appropriate dimension, what about amplitude, the size and scope of something? A larger work, a larger domain, a larger self—with all of these, sheer size, the enlarged capacity to encompass that accompanies it, is a positive feature. In evaluating a self we can care about its spaciousness and volume, the scope of its inner space. If we are willing to speak about value, meaning, importance, weight, depth, and amplitude, should we add height to our list also, because there are higher emotions, higher works of art, and higher pleasure? If height, then why not intensity too?

If we are going to list all the evaluative dimensions by which we might want to judge anything—a self, its life, emotions, or activities, and its relations with others—then shouldn't we also list originality, vividness, vitality, and completeness? And if all these, then why not creativity, individuality, and expressiveness? Why not—once all the stops are being let out—beauty, truth, and goodness too?

Enlarging the number of evaluative dimensions affects our view of intense positive emotions, for emotions are positive precisely when they embody positive evaluations. One positive evaluation invokes the dimension of value, but we can also positively evaluate something as having meaning, weight, importance, depth, intensity, vividness, etc. Not only are emotions based on evaluating things along these varied dimensions, but our having these intense positive emotions itself contributes to the value, meaning, intensity, depth, etc., of our lives. This provides the truest answer to the Spock problem. These emotions not only respond to evaluative dimensions, they help constitute *us* along these dimensions.

It is not surprising that we have encountered a plethora of evaluative dimensions, an explosion. The growing list of evaluative dimensions simply lists the dimensions of reality. These are the dimensions that make something more real. To rank higher along any of these dimensions (holding the others constant) is to be more real. And emotions, we now can say in expansion of an earlier theme, are our analog response to reality. We saw previously that reality has many aspects, many dimensions. Why then should we expect only some of these to constitute relevant dimensions of evaluation? Won't each and every dimension of reality be relevant to evaluation and to our striving?

17

The Matrix of Reality

IN THE PREVIOUS meditation we expanded the list of dimensions of reality from the initial four—value, meaning, importance, and weight—to include many others as well. Let us consider the widest possible list of relevant evaluative dimensions. It contains (take a deep breath): value, meaning, importance, weight, depth, amplitude, intensity, height, vividness, richness, wholeness, beauty, truth, goodness, fulfillment, energy, autonomy, individuality, vitality, creativity, focus, purpose, development, serenity, holiness, perfection, expressiveness, authenticity, freedom, infinitude, enduringness, eternity, wisdom, understanding, life, nobility, play, grandeur, greatness, radiance, integrity, personality, loftiness, idealness, transcendence, growth, novelty, expansiveness, originality, purity, simplicity, preciousness, significance, vastness, profundity, integration, harmony, flourishing, power, and destiny. (Let us not ask whether anything has been left out. It is relevant to ask, though, which of these dimensions are realizable by the experience machine and which ones serve to exclude it.)

This list of dimensions is exhausting. A long list cannot provide us with much understanding if it remains unordered, a jumble. We need to structure the list to gain some intellectual control. The list is not sacrosanct, though. In the course of structuring it, we may be led to omit some dimensions that do not fit the form that is emerging or to include some additional ones this form might require.

How shall we order and categorize these many dimensions of reality? I would like to arrange the dimensions in a table, a matrix with rows and columns. (Is there a reason other than familiarity for choosing a matrix? What configuration would you expect the dimensions of reality to have: a doughnut in fourteen-dimensional space or an infinite-dimensional sphere giving off rays?) With only four dimensions, we had the following two-by-two matrix:

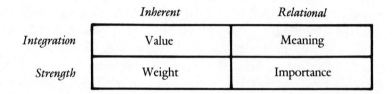

	Inherent	*Relational*
Integration	Value	Meaning
Strength	Weight	Importance

Constructing a larger matrix to encompass all the dimensions serves many theoretical purposes. The labels on its rows and columns will be the categories of reality. (In the two-by-two matrix, the columns were labeled *inherent* and *relational,* the row labels were *integration* and *strength.*) We then can investigate, in turn, the question of why there are precisely those headings of the rows and columns. What is reality like if its more fundamental categorization involves those labels and headings? If the matrix we construct contains some empty boxes, we can ask what other dimensions, not yet on our list, would properly fill them. (Thus we get a check on the completeness of our list of dimensions.) We also might realize a particular category is important when we see it as the appropriate label for a row or column already filled in. Moreover, the matrix can reveal relationships among the dimensions that we had not seen before, namely, the similarities in virtue of which several are in the same column (or row). Also, for each individual dimension, we can see it under the two aspects that correspond to the headings of its column and row. Organizing a chaotic list into a matrix is illuminating; it gives us better understanding of the component dimensions as we see them in new relationships and investigate why the matrix possesses that structure. The organizing of dimensions into a matrix should proceed without too much forcing, without too many arbitrary decisions about precise placement. It would be too much to hope, however, that we will manage without *any* forcing or arbitrariness at all.

We can begin to construct the new matrix by utilizing the previous two-by-two matrix that was appropriate and illuminating when we considered only the four dimensions: value, meaning, importance, and weight. We can use this matrix as the nucleus of an enlarged matrix, building out. Do any other dimensions on the list naturally fit within columns headed *inherent* or *relational*? If so, what new rows do they suggest? Do any other dimensions fit naturally within rows headed *integration* or *strength;* if so, what new columns do they suggest? Positive answers yield a larger matrix; similar questions can then be iterated to continue building the matrix. At times, adding a dimension that seems naturally to fit alongside others might lead us to modify the labeling of a row or column in order to more saliently capture the enlarged grouping.

There are other functions as well, served by constructing a matrix of the dimensions of reality, functions other than strictly theoretical ones. If only we could construct a sleek and satisfying matrix—a glance ahead shows we haven't yet—then we might call these other functions aesthetic ones. The matrix embodies the desire that the various dimensions of reality be unified and illuminatingly interrelated, that the realm of reality exhibit its own organic unity. We might think of this matrix as a *table of values*. I am not confident that the chart that follows is on the right track. The remainder of this section, I admit, contains strange and sometimes bewildering pieces of theorizing, very much against the grain of contemporary philosophy. Omitting it would save me much grief from the current philosophical community—writing it already has cost me uneasiness.

Yet however eccentric, the chart also is a symbolic representation of the unity within reality, or our desire for that, whether or not it is an accurate theory of that unity. See the chart, then, as something like a metaphor, or an object to represent and evoke the inner structuring of reality, or, at least, as something to hold a place for a more adequate symbol of reality until the time that it appears. The table of reality presented here may not be accurate, but it needs to be real.

Now to array the dimensions of reality within a matrix.* Two of the other dimensions, completeness and perfection, seem naturally to fall under the label of *integration*. Completeness seems to be the *telos* or goal of integration, its fulfillment, while perfection seems to be something more. Beyond even a thing's fulfillment, there is its ideal limit. (The ideal limit itself may be a kind of fulfillment, yet fulfillment also can be found short of that ideal limit.) Completeness is a fulfillment of something in its aspect of integration, while perfection is integration that is carried to its furthest possible point and perhaps even beyond, to its ideal limit.

Our initial two-by-two matrix now is enlarged to this one:

	Inherent	*Relational*	*Fulfillment or* Telos	*Ideal Limit*
Integration	Value	Meaning	Completeness	Perfection
Strength	Weight	Importance		

What might fill the two empty boxes? The ideal limit of strength is a trait traditionally ascribed to God, omnipotence, being all-powerful. It is not surprising that the ideal-limit column will gather many characteristics theologians have discussed, for a divine being or

---

* Some readers will not find this section reverberative; they may have heard more than enough about "reality" already or they may find what follows exceedingly abstract. If so, I suggest they move directly to the following section, saving the two of us unnecessary pain. It might help those remaining readers to see what is happening, though, if they were to draw the two-by-two matrix and build it gradually outward as the discussion proceeds. Or readers might find it helpful to look ahead to the finished matrices, p. 189 and p. 190.

the conception of one represents and realizes the ideal limit of many attributes and modes of being.

What is the goal or fulfillment of strength? Two things on the list might fit: power—but isn't this last simply a wider term to describe strength?—and greatness. Our discussion of importance distinguished its two aspects: external impact, and being taken account of. We could try to continue this division across the strength row. Greatness, the fulfillment of strength, would therefore have two aspects. Power fulfills strength in its aspect of impact; what fulfills how something is taken account of? Are autonomy and being loved the fulfillment of being taken account of? Omnipotence is the ideal limit of the impact aspect of strength; what is the ideal limit of its being taken account of? I suppose it is being worshiped.

When being worshiped and being loved are included as subentries in the row, then *strength* no longer appears the best label for that row. *Substantiality* or *substantialness* would serve better. How substantial is something? The inherent nature of its substantiality is its weight, the relational nature of its substantiality is its importance, the fulfillment is its greatness, etc. Perhaps we should speak more simply not of something's substantiality but of its *substance*. If you are not sure of what substance is, perhaps this will help: The inherent nature of something's substance is its weight, the relational nature is its importance, the fulfillment of substance is greatness, etc.

In general, we can clarify the heading of a row through understanding the column headings and the matrix entries for that row; for example, substance is what has those entries for those columns. Similarly, we might clarify our understanding of a column heading by building on our clearer understanding of a row's label and that column's matrix entries; for example, fulfillment is what integration achieves when complete. Even going around the matrix in a circle can increase our understanding, just as we can learn a subject by reading something that we only dimly understand, using this scant understanding to grasp somewhat a second and third essay, then returning to the first and understanding it better, afterward returning to the second and third and understanding these better yet. Constructing and structuring this matrix, though, can feel, I confess, like building a house of cards. Even when it stands, it seems to totter precariously.

Three of the dimensions on our list often are grouped together

and said in a spurt: beauty, truth, and goodness. It would be pleasing to place these together in the same line. The presence of truth in this grouping is puzzling, though, given the usual views of philosophers. They apply the term *true* to propositions or sentences or statements—that is, to something like a linguistic item; such a thing is true when it corresponds to the facts, when it describes how things are. The humblest of declarative statements can be true—for instance, the statement that the preceding page contained at least one occurrence of the letter *a*. Since, for every well-formed statement, either it or its negation is true, we have more true statements than we know what to do with or want to focus upon. (Consider these: "The previous sentence did not contain 942 words." "It is not the case that an elephant is chewing my pen right now.") Do things as humble and commonplace as true sentences belong on a list with beauty and goodness? Perhaps only the fundamental or important true sentences are intended, the ones greatly worth knowing. However, when the term *truth* rolls trippingly off the tongue along with *beauty* and *goodness,* I do not think that it is best construed as something metalinguistic, as a property of a sentence or proposition or anything like that, at all. Whether or not Keats was right in holding truth and beauty identical, *truth* applies to the same kinds of things as beauty and goodness; it is not restricted only to sentences and propositions.*
Indeed, I do not think that truth is even best thought of as primarily relational, whether that relation be corresponding or cohering or disclosing.

A thing's truth is its inner being. Its truth is its inner essence, which can shine forth (although it does not always do so). Its truth is the deepest truths about it—you may understand this metalinguistically if that helps—truths about its inner nature. A thing's truth is its inner light. (That is why truth shines forth.) But cannot some-

---

* Among contemporary philosophers, Martin Heidegger has construed truth more widely. In his view, truth is a kind of stating or nonstating, a disclosure or nondisclosure. You might see it as a virtue of Heidegger's theory that, although his notion of truth applies more widely, it is understandable why we tend especially then to apply the term to sentences. Disclosure and nondisclosure was a personal theme for Heidegger too—he never managed to tell us how very deep was his involvement with Nazism. See Thomas Sheehan's discerning essay "Heidegger and the Nazis," *New York Review of Books,* Vol. 35, No. 10 (June 16, 1988), pp. 38–47.

thing's inner nature, its deepest essence, be darkness? If Erik Erikson can write of "Gandhi's truth," can we also speak of Stalin's or Hitler's? It would be better to avoid this, yet not simply by *stipulating* that a thing's truth is its admirable or desirable nature (if any).

For some row to go underneath integration and substantiality on the chart—a category or mode whose label we don't yet know— truth will go in the first column of the matrix under *inherent*. If goodness and beauty are to be arrayed alongside, then goodness belongs in the relational column. For that category whose inherent nature is its truth and whose relational nature is its goodness, its fulfillment is beauty. It seems, even, beautiful that this should be so. Adding beauty to truth and goodness seems not only a continuation of that list but its fulfillment.

We have posited a category or mode of being whose inherent aspect is (a thing's) truth, whose relational aspect is goodness, whose fulfillment is beauty. What would be the ideal limit of so exalted a category; what *could* be its ideal limit? The ideal limit, I think, is holiness. That sequence can continue without letdown: truth, goodness, beauty, holiness.

What category is it that begins with truth as its inherent aspect and ends at its ideal limit with holiness? It does not get things exactly right to label it *excellence* or *essence*. I am tempted to say it is the category of *light*. The inherent light of something is its truth, the relational light is its goodness, the fulfillment of light is its beauty, while holiness is the ideal limit of its light. This saying is evocative yet, I admit, unclear. Rather than reject it, we wait for fuller understanding.

Some of the dimensions concern a thing's size and *scope*, its depth, height, amplitude, infinitude. Depth seems inherent, infinitude an ideal limit, height a fulfillment, so let us tentatively (though hesitantly) place amplitude as relational. Other dimensions refer to a thing's *energy*, its intensity and vitality; intensity I think of as inner, vitality spills outward. Perhaps creativity fits here as the fulfillment of energy. (For the ideal limit of energy, infinite energy, I know of no special term.) Our initial discussion of reality (in the meditation on Being More Real) began by considering sharpness of focus and vividness, the degree to which something stands as figure against ground, and *focus* should be added to our matrix as a general category. I am unsure of the fulfillment or *telos* of focus, of being etched as figure; perhaps it is individuality in demarcation from background and from others. If so, the ideal limit might be absolute specificity and absolute uniqueness, being *sui generis*. Another category of dimensions seemed to deal with fullness, abundance, richness, wholeness. The ideal limit of these might be being all-encompassing. However, their precise placement is unclear. Let us try *fullness* as the general category, with wholeness as its fulfillment, richness as its relational aspect; its inherent aspect, perhaps, would be structure or texture. Thus, we have arrived at—or stumbled onto—the following matrix:

	Inherent	*Relational*	*Fulfillment or* Telos	*Ideal Limit*
Integration	Value	Meaning	Completeness	Perfection
Substance	Weight	Importance	Greatness	Omnipotence
Light	Truth	Goodness	Beauty	Holiness
Scope	Depth	Amplitude	Height	Infinitude
Energy	Intensity	Vitality	Creativity	Infinite Energy
Focus	Sharpness	Vividness	Individuality	Sui Generis
Fullness	Texture	Richness	Wholeness	All-Encompassing

To the diversity of the unordered list of dimensions of reality, this matrix, fragile though it may be, does bring some unity.

There are still further rows we might add to encompass some of the other dimensions that have been mentioned. We might have a row labeled *independence* with entries of self-directing, free, autonomous, and self-choosing, respectively. (These, and the rows to follow, are listed in the now-standard order of the columns: inherent, relational, fulfillment or *telos,* and ideal limit.) We might have a row labeled *peacefulness* which encompasses serenity, being pacific (or at one with the outside), harmony, and that ideal limit which passeth understanding. We might have a row labeled *development* which encompasses (inner) maturation, growth (outward), purpose, and destiny. Finally, we might have a row labeled *existence* which encompasses temporal existence as its inherent aspect, spatial existence as its relational aspect, causal interaction as its *telos* or fulfillment, and, as its ideal limit, being a necessary being or *causa sui.* These four additional rows are charted as follows:

	Inherent	*Relational*	*Fulfillment or* Telos	*Ideal Limit*
Independence	Self-Directing	Free	Autonomous	Self-Choosing
Peacefulness	Serenity	Being Pacific	Harmony	Peace That Passeth . . .
Development	Maturation	Growth	Purpose	Destiny
Existence	Temporal Existence	Spatial Existence	Causal Interaction	Causa Sui

Adding these four rows (containing their sixteen additional dimensions) to our first chart would produce an expanded chart of eleven rows and four columns. Eleven is a considerable number simply to list without further structuring; perhaps seven was also. We can take the process one stage further, though. If we found an additional row entry (of four further dimensions) which when added to the expanded chart yields a four-by-twelve matrix, then perhaps the resulting twelve rows could themselves be arranged within a further four-by-three matrix. That would provide a better understanding of how those twelve were interrelated, and it would transform the two-dimensional four-by-twelve matrix into a three-dimensional structure, a four-by-four-by-three rectangular poly-hedron. Such a polyhedron would contain and tightly interrelate forty-eight component dimensions.

Let us investigate how this might work, acknowledging that these speculations are indeed tenuous. The labels of the eleven rows which (with a twelfth thus far unnamed one added) we need to structure into a four-by-three array are: integration, substance, light, scope, energy, focus, fullness, independence, peacefulness, development, and existence. How can these be illuminatingly grouped? The rows of scope, integration, fullness, and substance fall into the more general category of *structural composition* or organization; whereas the rows of light, energy, and focus all involve a concentrated movement or a *vectorial direction,* a kind of action. Moreover, some pairings seem natural within this organization. Energy as a vectorial direction pairs with fullness as a structural composition; one can check that by seeing how along each of the four columns of the chart the rows of energy and fullness correspond, how the energy dimension is a concentrated form of what the fullness dimension is as a spread-out structural organization. Similarly for the pairings of focus and integration, and light and scope. Paired with substance will be the unnamed twelfth category. A third grouping of the labels of the rows has to do with manner or style, or *mode.* Into this group we might put (in an order coordinate with that above) independence, de-velopment, and peacefulness, while existence is grouped with substance and the unnamed category.

We thus get this kernel of a further matrix:

Vectorial Direction	*Structural Composition*	*Mode*
Energy	Fullness	Independence
Focus	Integration	Development
[Unnamed]	Substance	Existence
Light	Scope	Peacefulness

This new group of three headings—structural composition, vectorial direction, and mode—seems to specify the nature of something's functioning, how it *operates*. It specifies functioning's structural basis and kind of action (in direction and mode); we might therefore also say it specifies something's *functioning nature*. The four columns of our chart (inherent, relational, *telos,* and ideal limit), on the other hand, seem to specify an intentionality (to use the philosopher's term), an outward-moving narrative. This unfolding need not be in time, however, so we might think of it as something's *potentiality*. More neutrally, we can think of it as a kind of *towardness*. We now have two of the three sides of our polyhedron: the Functioning Nature and the Towardness (or potentiality).

What then is the polyhedron's third side? We can discover this by regrouping the twelve row headings of our expanded matrix, this time into four groups (which will cross with the three of structural composition, vectorial direction, and mode). Independence, energy, and fullness seem to fit together into a group we might term *liveliness;* light, scope, and peacefulness seem to fit together into a group we might term *spirit;* focus and integration seem to fit together into a group we might term *concentratedness,* and perhaps we should place development here too, as a kind of concentratedness in time; finally, existence and substance seem to fit together into a group we might call, for lack of a better term, *thereness*. These four more general categories—spirit, concentratedness, liveliness, and thereness—together describe (let us reach for a big word) something's *being*. Being, then, becomes the polyhedron's third side.

Figure 2 shows what our (rectangular) polyhedron looks like, arrayed along its three axes of Towardness, Functioning Nature, and Being. Within this four-by-three-by-four polyhedron are arrayed forty-eight dimensions of reality. Figures 3 through 6 segment the polyhedron so that all the dimensions can be seen.

The English philosopher J. L. Austin has argued that it is a mistake to speak in the very general way we have about the notion of reality, even if we make it less general by specifying its dimensional aspects. Look at the more modest word *real,* he says. We speak of something's being real of a kind, such as a real watch or a real duck. According to Austin, *real* is used simply to mark a contrast with other negative states, with being a decoy or a toy or artificial or dyed or

The Matrix of Reality

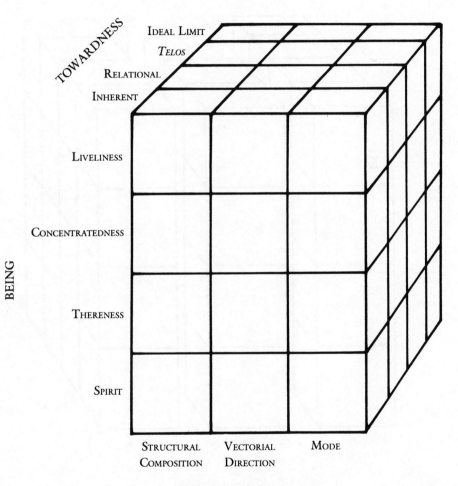

FIGURE 2. The polyhedron of reality.

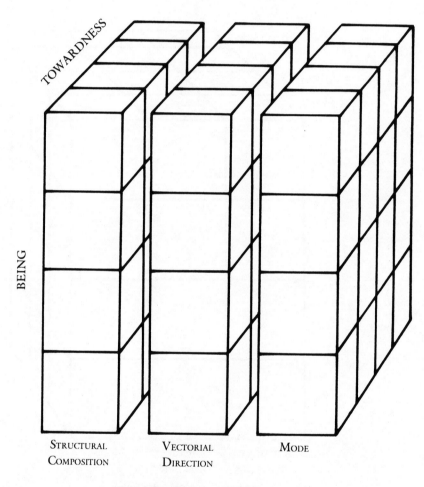

FIGURE 3. The polyhedron broken apart to show all the constituents.

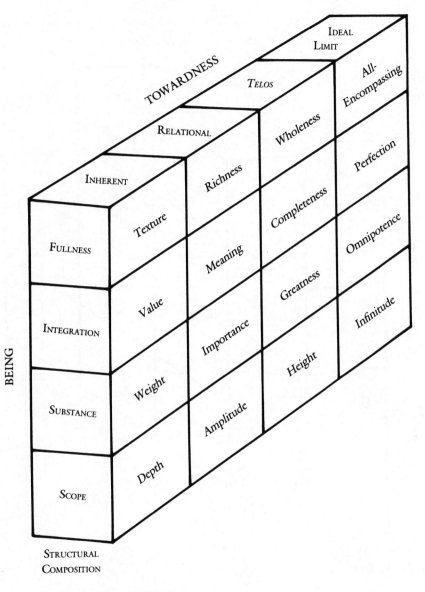

FIGURE 4. The complete structural composition segment of the polyhedron.

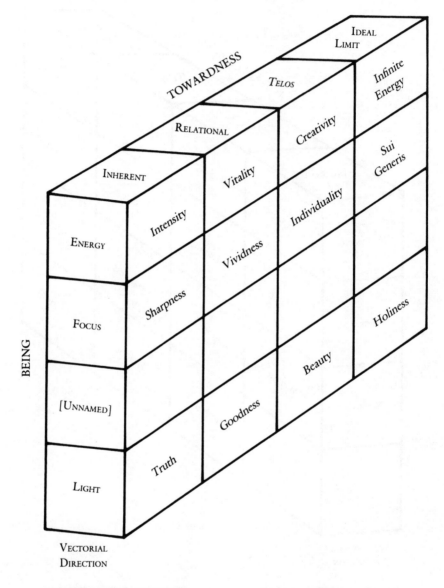

FUNCTIONING NATURE

FIGURE 5. The vectorial direction segment of the polyhedron.

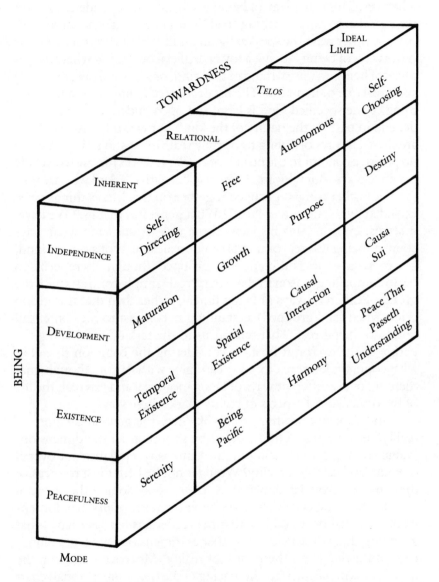

FUNCTIONING NATURE

FIGURE 6. The complete mode segment of the polyhedron.

whatever. This other way of being is what has independent content; for a speaker to call something "real" is just to exclude one (or several) of these other ways the speaker has in mind.* However, each of these other ways of being—being a toy or artificial or dyed or whatever—is a way of being an unreal thing of that kind, or a less real one, or simply not a real one of that kind. The list of ways of failing to be a fully real thing of the specified kind is large and open-ended. Its content will depend in part on the nature of the kind, but we still must ask: Why are these all ways of failing to be fully real? In Austin's view, there is no positive content to the notion of "real"; it serves merely to exclude negative ways. But why are these ways "negative"? And why are they (and not other things) grouped together on this list, as things to be excluded by the notion of "real"? What generates that list? We have, it seems, even in Austin's view, some way of knowing what ways count as being less real or unreal or not real, at least of a certain kind. Once we have these different ways grouped, though, there seems to be no compelling reason to claim that "real" simply contrasts with the group of different ways of being unreal, rather than that this group is identified (and grouped) as standing in contrast to the contentful notion of being real. That returns us to the task of considering the nature of reality (or at least, to considering the common thread in what counts as lesser reality). We can agree with Austin, though, that there are many different ways of being more real and less real; the list of the dimensional aspects of reality marks these ways.

Still, is it not arbitrary to invoke here the general category of reality? Is anything definite added by grouping all the dimensions (value, meaning, weight, importance, intensity, etc.) into one overall category and calling it reality? Would it not be better just to speak of these more particular dimensions, or to apply some other general term to them, especially since applying the term *reality* here loosens its tie to actuality? I do hope that the reader has felt (as I have) that grouping these dimensions together as dimensions of reality illuminates both them and the nature of reality. Moreover, arraying the dimensions in the intricate interlacing of the (two-dimensional) chart does not leave them a disconnected list; unrelated things could not

* J. L. Austin, *Sense and Sensibilia* (Oxford, England: Clarendon Press, 1962), Chapter VII.

dovetail so well, and it seems reasonable to think they therefore form interrelated aspects of some *one* notion. Why else would they fit together that well? (This point holds even when we admit that some of the placing in the matrix depended to a great extent upon "feel"; perhaps the point has less weight, though, in the case of the more tenuous polyhedron.) It would help to put the interrelated structure of the matrix or the polyhedron (how the dimensions get arrayed, the labels of the rows and columns, and the general categories they fall into) to some further theoretical use, perhaps on the fact/value question or in empirical applications—for example, in dealing with what leaves lasting effects in memory, or in understanding psychiatric patients who report that they or the world feel unreal. It is a task for metaphysics to apply it elsewhere too.

Still, even if because of their interlacing it be granted that the dimensions comprise aspects of some one notion, why call this the notion of reality? A fuller answer might fruitfully begin by listing the traditional criteria of reality, criteria such as being invariant (or less variant) under certain transformations, having a stable equilibrium, being an object of value or veneration, being more permanent, specifying a goal toward which things move, underlying other phenomena, making other things seem in contrast somehow lesser, or whatever.*

However, I do not know of a satisfactory way to unite these into one sharp and satisfying picture or to explain why these are criteria of *reality,* why it is *these* criteria that reality exemplifies. So I would do well again to emphasize the very tentative nature of what has been presented in this section. There is a need to develop a more adequate chart, a better structuring of reality's dimensions, and especially a better understanding of the underlying story the chart tells and hence of the reality it depicts and of our place within that. Some few further thoughts on the underlying nature of reality I relegate to the appendix to this section.

* See the illuminating discussion of Plato's degrees-of-reality theory in Gregory Vlastos, *Platonic Studies* (Princeton, N.J.: Princeton University Press, 1973), Essays 2 and 3.

Appendix: The Metaphysics of Reality

What nature of ultimate reality gives rise to the particular order we have sketched? No theory I know of, whether scientific naturalism, Western theism, Vedanta, Madhyamika Buddhism, or the metaphysical systems propounded by philosophers, accounts for the matrix or polyhedron just developed; no such theory explains why reality includes those dimensions, why it is organized according to those categories labeling the columns and rows. (So much the worse for the matrix?) I want to speculate about the nature of the reality ensconced in the matrix; however, what I have been able to arrive at is less illuminating and less incisive than I would like.

The notion of ultimate reality can refer to different things in the theories mentioned: the ground-floor stuff out of which everything is composed; the fundamental explanatory level which explains all current happenings; the factor out of which everything else originated; the goal toward which everything develops; what is most real. These different modes of ultimacy do share a common feature, though. Ultimacy always marks the extreme end of an ordering. This ordering can be based upon a chain of explanation, a chain of origination, a chain of further and further goals, etc. In each case, what is ultimate comes at the extreme end of an ordering, an important and extremely lengthy, perhaps even infinite, ordering—its position there is what makes it ultimate. It is the better or more important end of the ordering that constitutes its ultimate side. Ultimate reality resides at the deepest end of the ordering, not the most superficial. The German philosopher Heinrich Rickert held that the word *real* "is identified with the highest, deepest, inmost, most essential, or other superlatives beyond which nothing more is thinkable."*

Ultimate reality marks the better extreme end of an important, lengthy ordering. The dimensional aspects of reality (such as value,

---

* Quoted in W. M. Urban, *The Intelligible World* (London: Allen and Unwin, 1929), p. 152.

meaning, weight, intensity, etc.) are themselves dimensions along which things can be arrayed and ordered. Along each of these dimensions, more is better and is also more real. Most is most real. The dimensions of reality differ from Aristotelian virtues, where the best position lies at the (golden) mean, not at either extreme. Courage, Aristotle held, lies in the best place *between* cowardice and foolhardiness, whereas on the basic evaluative dimensions, more continues to be better. These evaluative dimensions also are the basic dimensions of (increasing) reality; a higher score along them continues to bring greater reality. The basic dimensions of reality and of evaluation continually ascend, without a downturn. An adequate theory of the nature of reality will explain why this is so.

Reality is without limit, infinite. There is no stopping point, no satiation point, along its dimensions. There is no limit to how sharply reality can emerge, to its energy or fullness or focus or integration or . . . ; there is no final or fundamental level or stopping place. (Is what is ultimate about reality that there is no ultimacy?) The last column, headed *ideal limit,* should not be seen as marking a stopping point; there can be degrees there too. Some mystics report new enlightenment experiences which they maintain far transcend their previous ones, ones they had sincerely seen as infinite and unsurpassable. These earlier experiences are now seen as delimited, even though it was appropriate to describe them in the most intense terms in comparison to ordinary experience. An infinite reality would encompass different levels or orders of infinity. If the basic fact about reality is that it is infinite, then its coming in degrees will not be surprising. Its component aspects will therefore be dimensions, aspects that have gradations.

Still, we want to understand why reality arrays itself into that particular matrix or polyhedron, its dimensions into precisely those rows and columns. Is there some general description or narrative account we can offer of the labels of these rows and columns?

The four columns of the matrix provide a profile specifying the potentiality of a thing. If you know something's inherent character or nature, its relational nature, what constitutes its fulfillment and what its ideal limit, then you know its directional potential, its career, what it is *toward*. The columns are listed in an order: inherent, relational, fulfillment, ideal limit. Is the direction here simply that of enlargement outward or is a more complicated narrative embedded?

The labels of the eleven rows of the matrix (before these are arranged in the polyhedron)—integration, substance, light, scope, energy, etc.—provide (in their degrees) a description of something's state, a latitudinal cross section of its mode(s) of being, its metaphysical *constitution*. After reforming the matrix into the polyhedron, we can say further that this state-description divides into two parts or aspects: a description of something's functioning nature, how it operates, and also a description of its being.

The three most general axes, being, operating, and towardness, can be put together coherently. Being has a mode of functioning and operation that is directed, a pointing toward. *Being operates toward.* We have a subject, *being,* a verb, *operates,* and a preposition (a directionality), *toward.* But what about an object? Toward *what* does being operate?

Here it is worth listing four possibilities. The first is that the basic nature of reality consists in being's pointed operating, its operating intentionality. That is the basic metaphysical fact, that there is being that somehow is moving or growing or transforming or operating not at random but in a direction, toward. (That would be analogous to, but not the same as, a person's acting toward a goal.) In this operating toward, there is an immanent teleology. Within this fundamental metaphysical fact about reality, that being operates toward, value might get born. (Here *value* is used not as degree of organic unity but in its most general sense of whatever is evaluatively valid.) For we might say: Value is what being operates toward. Value is given rise to by being's having a directional operation; if being were static or its motion were random, there would be no value. It is not that being moves toward something *because* there is value preexisting in that direction. There is value because being moves towards. *That* way. All these three components are so fundamental—being, its operating, its towardness—that there is no way to ask whether being might not be operating in a *wrong* direction; there is no level deeper to stand on in asking this question. Such a picture is appealing on an abstract level, perhaps, yet still we want to make an objection: If the largest thing we know, the universe, were moving toward a heat death and disintegration, would *this* direction specify or determine the nature of value in the universe? Why then should it be different if it is reality or being that is moving toward something?

The second possibility gives more specific content to what being operates toward. The direction of the towardness is from internal to relational to *telos* to ideal limit, so the standard is fixed by the ideal limit at the endpoint. That column, we recall, contained the dimensions of perfection, omnipotence, holiness, infinitude, infinite energy, *sui generis,* all-encompassing, self-choosing, the peace which passeth understanding, destiny, and being *causa sui.* These are, of course, many of the traditional attributes of God. What being is moving toward, then, according to this second possibility, is becoming God. Not the origin of being or its earlier cause, God is rather its *goal,* what it is moving and operating toward. What being is up to is becoming God! (Very inspiring—but couldn't we have arranged those very columns in the reverse order?)

The third possibility, more traditionally theological, sees God as the origin of being. Nevertheless, being still can be moving toward becoming Godlike, toward having (almost) all the ideal limit qualities of God, perhaps in order to form a new joint identity with God, one which possesses a degree of reality unavailable to God alone. (And might this *we* then create something new as *its* "offspring"?)

An earlier meditation on God and faith ended by saying it had described the concept of God but not God's nature. Can metaphysical speculation help? If God is the ideal limit of being's functioning nature, then God's nature is given determinate content in the particular dimensions that stand at this ideal limit. However, the very concept of God—we saw earlier—does not require the greatest possible perfection; for a metaphysical theory to specify content to God's nature, then, there would have to be reason—perhaps provided in people's highest or deepest experiences—for thinking God did reside at that ideal limit.

The fourth possibility sees being's movement toward as a process that is iterative or recursive. The cross section of reality that is at the level of ideal limit itself can be conceived as something occupying the *first* column of a *new* matrix, about which we can ask in turn: What is *its* relational nature, *telos,* and ideal limit? This may be something different. The notion of "ideal limit" need not be transitive; the ideal limit of the ideal limit of something need not itself be that thing's ideal limit. Here is an example: The ideal limit of the sequence of finite positive integers might be the smallest infinite number, but the ideal limit of different infinite numbers constructible from this one, whatever that is, is not itself the ideal limit of the positive integers. The first infinite number has jumped up a category from the finite, and the ideal limit of that new category is too distant from the finite to be its ideal limit too. The sequence of the columns of the matrix or polyhedron of reality then might describe an iterative process. It stimulates the imagination to contemplate such a possibility. Yet, although generalizing a problem does frequently point to its solution, this iterative possibility does not seem to help us to a more adequate understanding of what being is moving toward, as described in the matrix or polyhedron we have been considering thus far, the very first not yet iterated one.

The theme of being operating toward is an evocative one, but murky. We have yet to arrive at a deeper and more adequate understanding of reality's nature and array.

18

Darkness and Light

REALITY AS limned here is not wholly rosy; it can be increased along particular dimensions in painful or immoral ways. Evil can be encompassing, pain can be intense. Isn't it dangerous, then, to commend connecting deeply with reality and becoming more real? This danger is lessened by the general combined stance, yet mightn't even it allow our relating to reality to be increased by following a negative direction?

Note that giving "the positive" itself the status of a dimension of reality, entering it within the matrix, would not eliminate the problem of the negative path. The more positive something is, the more real it would be—all other things being equal—so that going in a positive direction would be a way of becoming more real. However, this still leaves the positive in a precarious position; as just one dimension among others, it could be outweighed by opportunities along these other dimensions, so someone's route to greatest reality might be a negative one nevertheless.

Some dimensions of reality have a decidedly positive cast—for instance, value and meaning, goodness and holiness. These all occur in the row of light. (There are other positive ones also, and some dimensions in the matrix appear morally neutral.) Might there also be another category of dimensions, a row of *darkness* which, while not focusing especially on moral issues, includes explicitly some things we term negative—for instance, suffering and tragedy? (Could darkness be charted with suffering as its inherent aspect, existential despair and angst as its relational, and tragedy as its fulfillment? What then would be at its limit?) Are not these equally aspects or dimensions not simply of actuality but of reality, along with strife, opposition and conflict?

Nietzsche viewed the vigorous play and struggle among such forces as crucial to life, often as life-enhancing. A focus only on the positive and upon goodness, he thought, truncates man: "It is with the man as it is with the tree. The more he aspires to the height and light, the more strongly do his roots strive earthward, downward, into the dark, the deep—into evil."* Darkness should not be conflated with evil, which is just one form of it: "It is out of the deepest depth that the highest must come to its height." Finally: "I believe that it is precisely through the presence of opposites and the feelings they occasion that the great man, the bow with the great tension, develops."† Nietzsche means not simply that the negative is a necessary instrumental means to the positive but that the two together form a dynamic whole in continuing tension; it is this whole and its tension that he prized, the obstacles as well as their overcoming.

Rilke wrote in a letter:

> Whoever does not, sometime or other, give his full consent, his full and *joyous* consent, to the dreadfulness of life, can never take possession of the unutterable abundance and power of our existence; can only walk on its edge, and one day, when the judgment is given, will have been neither alive nor dead. To show the *identity* of dreadfulness and bliss, these two faces on the same divine head, indeed this one *single* face, which just presents itself this way or that,

* Friedrich Nietzsche, *The Will to Power* (New York: Vintage Books, 1968), p. 967.
† Friedrich Nietzsche, *Thus Spoke Zarathustra*, in Walter Kaufmann, ed., *The Portable Nietzsche* (New York: Viking, 1954), pp. 154, 266.

according to our distance from it or the state of mind in which we perceive it—; this is the true significance and purpose of the Elegies and the Sonnets to Orpheus.*

I find I cannot take the step—one that no doubt feels exhilarating and liberating—of placing the negative on a par with the positive. There are two other routes to follow; one starts with reality in general and gives the negative its subordinate due within that, the other builds from the very beginning upon the positive. I begin with the first, more formalistic attempt to contain the negative.

Tragedy and suffering can be a means to greater reality when they do not completely overcome or destroy someone, and they have their own intensity. However, the negative is limited, I want to claim. This is not simply because it tends to interfere greatly with other dimensions of reality (including ones not in the row of light), so that the negative is a poor trade-off, one that diminishes the reality score overall even if it raises it in particular respects. The negative is more limited due to its own nature. If there *were* some row on the matrix appropriately labeled darkness, then the scores for that row would be less than for light's row. On some appropriate scale of measurement, the highest possible reality scores for the negative fall short of what the positive can reach. The standard of reality does not aim us equally toward the negative.

Moving to a higher place along any dimension of reality in the matrix—value, for example—itself makes something more real, whereas an increase in darkness—suffering or evil, for example—in itself does not make something more real; it does so only by riding on the back of another already given dimension of reality such as intensity or depth, and increasing a thing's score along that dimension. Evil *qua* evil does not make something more real; value *qua* value does. Moreover, some negative aspects do not merely differ from but are the *opposite* of one of the (positive) dimensions. Hence, increasing reality through evil, say, does not merely also lower the reality score along some other dimension by chance; it does directly the opposite and is defined in part by how it moves downward along

* Letter to Countess Margot Sizzo-Notis-Crouy, April 12, 1923, quoted in Stephen Mitchell, ed., *The Selected Poetry of Rainer Maria Rilke* (New York: Random House, 1982), p. 317.

that dimension. The negative, which can increase something's reality only by also raising that thing's position along some positive dimension, operates directly itself—at least a portion of it does—to oppose and enfeeble still another positive dimension. It seems a plausible principle to exclude any such attempt to increase the degree of reality through a direct opposition to any of reality's dimensions. (The state of *understanding* the negative may itself be something positive and deep, though, with a profile along reality's dimensions.)

The dark or negative side also includes what is not (morally) evil itself or the direct *opposite* of a reality dimension—for instance, suffering and tragedy. It is with a somewhat divided mind that I say these things can increase reality only by moving a thing further along *another* dimension, for one part of me wants to acknowledge that *these* components of darkness are themselves separate and independent aspects of reality, not subordinate. Isn't that a more profound and less truncated view of reality? I worry.

However, the negative's subordinate status is reinforced by the character of the connection to reality that is intended. Conflict and strife, antagonism and destruction, also are connections, but not the kind *to* reality that anyone intends. But if what is desired is a positive connection, that can happen more fully and completely with reality that itself is positive. Even if the negative side of reality were equally deep and great—something we denied before—that side could not be connected to as deeply and fully, through a negative connection or a positive one either. The type of connection with reality we aim for affects the character of reality we connect with as well as the kind we have ourselves. Moreover, the general combined stance will not point toward the negative. Acting negatively upon someone diminishes his overall relating to reality (even if it increases his reality in *some* ways) and hence is excluded by the combined stance's concern with (all of) our relating to reality.

Perhaps the very greatest reality we can have or connect with is positive—the positive is a global optimum—yet might not small changes toward the negative improve our (connection to) reality somewhat? Here too I would like to maintain the optimistic position, though with somewhat more hesitation. Although dark steps might enable someone to reach greater reality than he currently has or knows, they do not bring him to the greatest reality he can reach through equally small steps that accord with the combined stance.

What is the basis of the categories of the positive and the negative themselves; does that distinction exist *at* the most fundamental level or does it arise later? Rather than having these categories arise from the interplay of the entries *within* the matrix of reality, it would be more satisfying theoretically to have them connected to the labels of the rows and columns which structure that matrix. When we manage to find the narrative implicit in the labels of these particular rows and columns, perhaps then will the basic distinction between the positive and the negative be grounded.

Movement toward greater reality need not follow dark paths, yet it can lead away from the happiness principle. (It is hard to see the individuals we think of as most real—Socrates, Gandhi, Einstein, Jesus, Napoleon, and Lincoln—as *happier* than other people.) Happiness has a more interesting relation to the notion of reality than that of possible conflict, however. Moments of happiness are times when we feel especially real; happiness that is intense, focused, enduring, and fitting is itself very real and makes us feel very real too. Perhaps, then, feelings of happiness are desired not solely because they feel *good* but also because they constitute a clear way of feeling real. But if part of the appeal and rationale of happiness is its connection to being and feeling more real, then when another route carries more reality but less happiness the conflict will not be so pointed, for this other route will then carry more of what we (in part) want happiness *for*. Trading some happiness for other dimensions of reality different from the ones happiness exhibits will not constitute such a sacrifice. However, I do not mean to laud *feeling* real above all, even though it is valuable. It is *being* real that is primary; the feeling without the being could be provided by the experience machine.

Earlier we placed existence (or actuality) as a row of the expanded matrix (with entries of temporal, spatial, causal interaction, and *causa sui*). The very first reality principles that we formulated were actuality principles, recommending connection to actuality as a means to pleasure (Freud's principle) and as important and valuable in itself. Since actuality is a row of the (expanded) matrix, connection to actuality is itself a way of being more real. Can we dispense, therefore, with those early reality principles? However, while actuality is involved in *some* dimensions of reality, the matrix leaves open the possibility of achieving greater reality through other dimensions, without any connecting to actuality. This issue could be sidestepped or at least minimized if the actuality row received especially great *weight* within the reality matrix.

Arraying the dimensions of reality in a matrix gives us an idea of their mutual structure and interrelations but does not give any ranking of these dimensions. There is no way specified to tell which of two things has greater reality, unless one of them ranks higher than the other along *all* the dimensions of reality. This is a long way from knowing how to begin to utilize the economist's formal apparatus of ranking, indifference curves, and tradeoffs. And if we think that things are more real when they have significant scores along *many* of the dimensions, so that well-roundedness counts, an overall formula for assessing reality will have to take this into account (for instance, by incorporating a term for the primary bulk of the exhibited, perhaps weighted, dimensions).

I myself would want to give the whole of the light row, with its entries of truth, goodness, beauty, and holiness, especially great weight for people's lives. We are far from a complete linear ranking of the dimensions, however, and that may just be impossible. Yet even a mere listing of dimensions may be helpful, reminding one of what to take into account, what *may* be relevant. The matrix adds structure to the initial listing of component dimensions; it provides an evocative model of reality, to stand in for the correct interrelated theory, and a model of the self's integration as well.

It would be nice to think that the realm of reality itself is not already prefixed in a hierarchical order but is open to new ways to combine and integrate its dimensions. Not knowing the complete ordering, in any case room is left for creative endeavor from us. We become most real not by moving up a prefixed scale but by finding and inventing our own new way of combining and exhibiting reality's dimensions. Utilizing our own special characteristics and opportunities, we configure ourselves and our lives as a particular trajectory through the dimensions of reality, one others would not have formulated beforehand but which, once before them, they can recognize and receive as our particular way of living reality.

Free will (in a not completely deterministic world), in one view, resides in our giving weight to reasons.* Whether something is a reason for or against doing an action is not up to us—that might be determined by the nature of the consideration, and which considerations are available to us might be shaped by social factors, but the weight any particular one of those reasons gets is not prefixed by any external factor. In deciding to do an action, we mull these reasons over and decide which have the greatest weight—that is, we *give* those reasons greater weight; and we continue to adhere to that greater weighting, rather as the law adheres to precedent. After the choice, others (and we too) may say we did that act because the reasons in its favor were more weighty, but had we done another act (which we *could* have done), its performance too would be said to be caused by the different reasons in *its* favor. Our doing the act elevates the background considerations in its favor to causal status; we might say the action was caused but not causally determined. Within some range, what we do is up to us because the weight of the reasons that move us is something we bestow. Hence, the fact that the (evaluative) dimensions of reality are not preordered in some fixed hierarchy, rather than being something to bemoan, is precisely what allows and enable us to act in freedom.

Perhaps, more extreme even than finding our own way of weighting and exhibiting reality's dimensions, we each must make our own charts, at least implicitly, living our own understanding of reality's interconnected nature, discerning new dimensions to be added to the chart, to be explored, responded to, and incorporated within our lives. (Should purity be placed on the chart? Grace?) No particular matrix we arrive at need be considered final; we each contemplate and live the widest and best-structured matrix we've been able to understand thus far, even as we are ready to transform it.†

* This view is elaborated further in my *Philosophical Explanations,* pp. 294–316. That books also presents a conception of what might constitute free will in a completely deterministic world; see pp. 317–362.

† We can note that wide and inclusive as the whole category of reality is, traditions speak of another realm we have not yet touched, which they call the Void, or Silence, or Emptiness; specific meditative practices are said to enable us to reach and live within this realm within us. What new standard might emerge then?

We began this section with the worry that a concern for greater reality might lead someone in a negative or unethical direction; it will help to look directly at ethics itself. Ethics is not one single structure; it is built in four layers. The first layer, the ethic of respect, mandates respecting another adult person's life and autonomy (as well as a younger person's potential adulthood); its rules and principles restrict interference with the person's domain of choice, forbid murder or enslavement, and issue in a more general list of rights to be respected. The second layer, the ethic of responsiveness, mandates acting in a way that is responsive to other people's reality and value, a way that takes account of their reality and is intricately contoured to it. Its guiding principle is to treat reality *as* real, and it too issues in guidelines: Do not destroy another person's reality or diminish it, and be responsive to another's reality and act so as to enhance it.*

Which takes precedence, respect or responsiveness? Which is to be followed when the two diverge? Responsiveness is the higher layer, yet it rests upon the layer of respect. By this I mean that respect is mandated along with its principles and rules; when in some particular situation responsiveness calls for something different, that indeed is to be done, but in a way that involves the *minimum* divergence or deviation from those rules of respect. The layers are related by a principle of minimum mutilation: Follow the principles of respect, and when it is necessary to deviate from them in order to achieve responsiveness, do this in a way that involves the minimum violation or perturbation of the norms of respect.

Notice how this structure differs from another that would place the maximization of responsiveness first, and among those policies or actions that tie in maximizing this, then pick the one that best satisfies the principles of respect. The principle of minimum mutilation countenances deviations from the rules of respect in order to achieve responsiveness, but it is not committed to achieving maximum responsiveness no matter at what cost to respect. Any additional responsiveness gained would have to outweigh the additional cost in respect. It could sometimes turn out that a responsive action is selected that somewhat rends the fabric of the rules of respect, but the very most responsive action does not get selected because its rending

* The ethic of respect—or one version of it—is presented in my book *Anarchy, State and Utopia;* the ethic of responsiveness is presented in my *Philosophical Explanations,* Chapter 5.

would be too massive.* This then is not a structure that maximizes responsiveness or one that undeviatingly mandates respect. It allows divergence from respect for the sake of greater responsiveness, but only when this is *enough* greater to outweigh the loss in adhering completely to the norms of respect. The divergences it countenances involve the minimum mutilation necessary.

The third layer is the ethic of caring. The attitude of caring can range from caring and concern to tenderness to deeper compassion to love. Responsiveness too might sometimes involve or mandate this—it depends upon the particular nature of the reality being responded to—but these attitudes are distinctive enough to warrant independent consideration. This layer too has its values and principles; at its more intense it mandates *ahimsa,* nonharm to all people (and perhaps to all living things), and love ("Do unto others as you would do unto those you love"). Here we often find religious bases for these attitudes—Buddhist compassion, Jewish *tsedaka,* Christian love—and nonreligious forms too are possible. The ethic of caring stands to the previous ones as responsiveness does to respect; it is to be followed when its recommendation diverges from the others, but only in accordance with the principle of minimum mutilation.

In one sense the succeeding layers are *higher* ones; they can justify deviations from the earlier ones and their standards seem more

---

* Suppose we could measure by how much an action—call this action A—fulfills what respect requires—call this Respect (A)—and the amount by which action A fulfills what responsiveness to reality calls for—call this Responsiveness (A). Let us denote full adherence to the rules and principles of respect by R*. Then if A deviates from what respect requires in order to achieve more responsiveness, R* − Respect (A) will measure the amount of this deviation, and the principle of minimum mutilation calls for trying to reduce or minimize this particular difference. In deciding whether to do A rather than an act B more in accord with the norms of respect—B may be completely in accord or involve less mutilation of the fabric of respect than A does—we need to be able to measure the gain in amount of responsiveness of A over B, Responsiveness (A) − Responsiveness (B), the loss of adherence to respect of A over B, Respect (B) − Respect (A), and then, most importantly, to decide when one of these outweighs the other. This is a matter not simply of comparing the two sums (for much will depend upon the two different scales of measurement for Responsiveness and Respect) but of a moral judgment. A will be recommended only when it is judged that Responsiveness (A) − Responsiveness (B) outweighs Respect (B) − Respect (A). Otherwise B will have to be done, or another action, C, even more in accord with the norms of respect whose greater respect is not outweighed by B's greater responsiveness. (For further elaboration of detail relevant to specifying this structure with its feature of minimum mutilation, see my *Philosophical Explanations,* pp. 485–494.)

inspired. Yet the earlier standards are the more basic ones; they are to be satisfied first and they exert a strong gravitational force upon any deviations, pulling these toward conformity in accordance with the principle of minimum mutilation. Within one layer, the action called for by respect (or responsiveness or caring) for one person might be different from the action called for by that attitude toward another, and even toward the same person the very same attitude might seem to mandate different actions. These differences might be resolved by moving up a layer—if it arises at the layer of respect, look to see if the issue is resolved by the layer of responsiveness, and if not, look to the layer of caring; and if moving up layers does not resolve it, moving down one (or two) might.

There is a further layer, the ethic of Light. (I capitalize the term *Light* this once to remind the reader of the special sense given it.) The category of light appeared as a row in the matrix of reality; its entries were truth, goodness, beauty, and holiness. At this layer does one have the attitude of enhancing the light of those we are able to affect or of increasing our own? When an attitude (and mode of behavior) toward others is distinguishable from a way of one's own being, the problem arises of linking ethical behavior toward others with the best way to be. The layer of light dissolves that distinction.

The ethic of light calls for a being to be its vessel. To be a being of light is to be its transmitter. The divergence between self and other is overcome; light cannot be separated from its shining, its being from its manifesting.

To be a vehicle of light is to be its *impersonal* vehicle. To try to put a personal stamp on it would distort it, warping it to your confines. The *Bhagavad-Gita* speaks of motiveless action, by which I think it means making oneself a pure and impersonal vehicle through which something else can act and be transmitted. An opera singer might view herself as a vehicle to transmit the music, using the full resources and resonances of her body to let that music flow purely through her. There is a difference between someone who *tries* to give an interpretation of the music, putting her personal stamp upon a performance, and someone who tries to allow it to happen purely, although, of course, the latter too is a particular person whose singing we hear as bearing her mark. Perhaps the difference is that *she* does not hear it that way or contour it so that she or we can.

A vehicle of light will bring to it his or her central focus of alertness and openness, noticing exemplifications or instances of truth, goodness, beauty, holiness, nurturing them, allowing them full latitude to do their transforming work, and then acting with spontaneity. The way truth, goodness, beauty, and holiness act through and transform you becomes *your* way of light. We now can formulate a further reality principle, the sixth: Become a vessel of light.

Earlier, we attempted to combine the three stances toward value—the egoistic, relational, and absolute—by a multiplicative formula, but this was an artificial merging, really, with no distinctive rationale other than the need somehow to combine the stances. Being a vessel of light, however, *does* integrate the stances even as it further specifies them.

In the theory of reality presented thus far, most of the dimensions (intensity and vividness, for example, importance and even value as degree of organic unity) admit just about anything as constituting the content of reality. With such a formalistic theory, the problem arose of whether evil, pain, brutal power or mere wealth might not increase reality—for reality itself was described as requiring no particular content. This led to attempts, somewhat unconvincing, to show how that formalistic theory of reality could point away from dark content. Instead, we can make the row of light—that is, truth, goodness, beauty, and holiness—the content of reality, while all the other dimensions of reality increase reality when (and only when) they enfold *this* content. Intensity or vividness increase reality when they intensify or make more vivid truth, goodness, beauty, or holiness; value is a unification of the diversity of some portions of truth, goodness, beauty, or holiness; depth makes for more reality when it is the depth of these; and so on. Or perhaps, rather than requiring these other dimensions to be filled by the content of light, we can see them in general as increasing reality provided they are not filled with the *opposite* of light; neutral content will serve within them.

No longer, however, would we try to justify the good from within a largely neutral theory of reality; reality gets built upon truth, goodness, beauty, and holiness from the beginning. But why did we want to provide some neutral rationale for the good, anyway? Why not just admit that we are committed to the good and to light? After all, if we told some neutral story that turned out *not* to lead to the good—for instance, so far as we know, deductive logic all by itself does not point that way—then we would say this was not the appro-

215

priate neutral story. Perhaps we desire a neutral story in order to convince someone else, but history reveals scant success along that route, and if that story *did* lead to the good, a sufficiently probing critic would uncover its initial nonneutral tinge or the place where nonneutrality got slipped in—after all, if it were neutral through and through, then it would not be able always to lead to the good rather than the bad.

Kant wanted duty to be based upon something other than a good inclination, in order to bind inclination. He wanted a more *secure* basis for morality—for what if the good inclination were absent or not strong enough?* Many constructions of theoretical ethics are based upon a fear or distrust of our own inclinations and are meant to bind them. A basis is sought for the good, a factual *existence* to undergird it, because the *allure* of goodness is presumed not to be strong enough without some additional authority. Similarly, those who try to root goodness in rationality presume that rationality is the more secure of the two.

How would we view ethics if we *did* trust our inclinations? We then might see it as an amplification of our good inclinations, as enlarging, regularizing, and channeling them, as telling how to become light's vessel and transmitter. If the theoretical building of foundations for ethics is born of distrust of light's allure—that is, distrust of our configuration of desires—then the task is not to buttress that light by argument but to turn ourselves into beings who then can trust our inclinations.

It would be desirable to say something illuminating about the dimensions of light, about inner truth (and its clarity and transparency), about goodness, about inward beauty and Keats's equation of beauty and truth, about holiness, and to say why light seems their appropriate constituent or metaphor. How can a person's face seem to shine with goodness, why did halos seem appropriate in religious art, why have the Quakers spoken of "an inner light?" One day, perhaps, we will be able to understand being ethical—not its foundations or its consequences, but what being ethical *means*.

* In *Neurotic Styles,* David Shapiro depicts the obsessive-compulsive person's concern to direct his slightest action by general maxims and principles as he replaces the need to reach his own overall decision by the technical problem of applying general principles to the given details.

19

Theological Explanations

NOT JUST METAPHYSICS but theology too has wrestled with darkness. A traditional theological question asks why God allows there to be evil in the world. I want to consider some untraditional answers. While for the religious this problem is a pressing one, the nonreligious too can find it interesting, or at least a challenging intellectual exercise.*

"The problem of evil" is set up by the fact that God, as traditionally conceived, has certain attributes: omnipotence, omniscience, and goodness. Yet, evil exists. Eliminate one of those attributes and there remains no hard intellectual conflict. If God weren't omnipotent, then evil might exist because he (or she) could not prevent it. If God weren't omniscient, then evil might exist because God didn't know he was creating it in creating the world. If God weren't good, if God didn't mind there being evil (at least as we conceive it), or if

* An earlier version of this section appeared in *Ploughshares,* Vol. 11, No. 4, pp. 151–166.

God were malicious, then similarly evil might exist and there would be no (intellectual) problem. There seems to be no way to reconcile those characteristics of omnipotence, omniscience, and goodness with the existence of evil in the world, whether it is in people doing evil to others or in events—the standard example is earthquakes—causing great suffering to people who do not deserve it. There seems to be no religious explanation that can be offered for a world containing evil. At any rate, no adequate and internally satisfactory religious explanation (or theodicy) has yet been offered.

One path has been to deny that evil exists at all. According to some views, evil isn't a positive thing, it is a privation. What (and all) evil is is the lack of goodness. It is not that God made evil—he just didn't fit in enough good everywhere, he didn't fill up everything with goodness. (These theorists must have thought that if God didn't create evil but merely failed to create enough goodness to constitute goodness enough, then God would be less responsible morally for what evil exists.)

The view that evil is merely a lack of goodness has never seemed very plausible, especially to those who have undergone or suffered it. If goodness is a score above zero, then evil is not zero, not merely a lack of goodness, but a score below zero. It is something in its own right, something negative. One doctrine has seen evil as having a role in the world, to educate us. The world is a big school, what Keats called a vale of soul-making. We undergo evil and gain wisdom through suffering. Thus, a divine being has kindly provided for our education.

That raises a very serious question about why we weren't skipped in certain grades. Why weren't we made prefabricated or made with a more advanced status so that we didn't actually have to go through this complete learning process?

Another traditional doctrine sees evil as stemming from free will. A divine being created human beings with free will, realizing they sometimes would use it to do evil. Yet not all bad things occur to human beings as a result of the action of other human beings; there are natural disasters, earthquakes, storms, etc. The free-will theorist might in principle ascribe these events to the actions of other beings to whom God gave free will—(fallen) angels or demons; thereby, in one way or another, all evil would be accounted for by the actions of free agents.

But if God wanted to create beings with free will, couldn't he have predicted in advance which ones were going to (mis)use their free will by doing bad, and then just have left them out of the creation? (A large and delicate literature debates whether this is really a possibility.) Free will is valuable; only autonomous agents have moral virtue when they choose good rather than evil. But a theorist who explains evil via free will has to hold not only that free will is good and worthwhile, but that it is far and away more valuable than the next best alternative. Suppose the next best alternative to free will is beings who have goodness ingrained in them, so that they naturally and inevitably choose the good. Maybe that's not *as* good as beings with free will who face temptation and autonomously choose the good. But how much worse is it? Is the difference so great and important that it would justify having all of the evil and suffering this world contains? Is the extra value gained by having beings with free will, as compared to the next best alternative, enough to outweigh all the evil and suffering that (by hypothesis) free will brings in its wake? To say the least, it is unclear.*

Let us recall some other positions taken about this problem. There's the view that the world was created out of preexistent material, not *ex nihilo* (as standardly interpreted). Plato (in the *Timaeus*) takes the view that a divine artificer acts in this way. One Kabbalist view, in the Jewish mystical tradition, holds that there were previous creations; shards left over from these earlier creations interact negatively with the current one. So God really isn't to blame for any evil or defect in creation, because such things are due to the character of the previous material left over. What could you expect given what he had to work with? However, this view places a limitation on the power of God. Even if preexistent material was utilized, why couldn't God have transformed it so as not leave the later residue of evil?

According to Plotinus and the neo-Platonists, a divine being (the One) emanates lower levels. It involuntarily gives forth these levels but doesn't know about them—you might say it secretes them. Since the divine being doesn't know about these lower levels, it doesn't do anything to prevent them. More and more levels are

* Religious explanations need not assume that free will's purpose lies in its intrinsic value for *us*. Suppose God created beings with free will in order to make them unpredictable, so that he could follow their story with interest and surprise—they would be God's television serial.

produced, each level giving forth another. When you get far enough away from the divine, you reach the level that evil exists in. And unfortunately, that is the level *we* inhabit, or at least our material natures do. Whether or not the neo-Platonic view is theoretically appropriate, it does not leave a God worth worshiping. We are presented with a being that doesn't know what it's doing, that involuntarily gives forth things, that doesn't know what is going on. Such a theory might conceivably serve as metaphysics, but it won't do as a religion.

The Gnostics (whose doctrines, along with neo-Platonism, fed into Kabbalah) held that the divinity that created our world wasn't all-perfect and all-wise; it also wasn't the top divinity there was. A God higher than our creator exists who is more distant from our world. Our world was created by a helper or a rebellious divine spirit—at any rate, by somebody who botched the job in some way. This led Gnostic theorists to think their task was to escape this world, moving beyond the reign of the local lord to somehow make contact with the higher all-good divinity.

Dualist views of one kind or another have been frequent in the history of thought. Having more than one God enables you to say that there is one who is all-good—he's just not the one you're dealing with, who is responsible for all of this. But that merely postpones the problem; it pushes the same problem to another level. If the higher God really is a top divinity (let's stop with two, and not worry about three levels or an infinite number), then why does that higher being allow the one who's dominating our world to mess around with it in the way he has? If that topmost divine being is all-good and doesn't want suffering or evil to take place, then why does he allow this lesser divinity to make such a mess over here? (Doesn't he have the power to stop him?) If the higher being created the lesser one, why didn't he create him as one who wouldn't act wrongly? It is clear that Gnostic doctrines only postpone the questions, though no doubt it is satisfying to think for a while that *somewhere* there is a God who is not to be blamed for anything.

One strand of the Jewish tradition, Kabbalah, holds—I follow the descriptions of the great scholar Gershom Scholem—that within the divine being, within *einsof* (translated as without limits), there are attributes, realms (*sefirot*). Evil in the world results, in the standard

Kabbalist view, through a tension between various divine attributes. These attributes each are good in themselves. No attribute is bad or evil or blameworthy. Only somehow in their interaction things don't work out so well. It is not an accident, I think, that for the two attributes which didn't work out so well, the Kabbalist writers focused on judgment (*din*) and loving kindness or mercy (*chesed*). These were in tension, they somehow couldn't reach the right balance; because of their tension and imbalance, trouble occurs in the created world.

You might ask: Why couldn't the divine being get them into the right balance? Isn't that an imperfection in the divine being? But between judgment and loving kindness, between justice and mercy, who knows what the right balance should be? These things are always in tension. (In certain views, it's hard to see how there would be room for mercy at all, if there's justice. If mercy means giving people less than they deserve—that is, less punishment that they deserve—then can that be just at all if they do deserve something bad? I ask this not to endorse the incompatibility of mercy and justice but to exhibit the tension, a tension that remains when they are given separate spheres: justice seeking to make right the past, mercy seeking to heal the future.)

Since there always has been a tension in the history of thought between justice and mercy, the Kabbalist thinkers did well to pick out these as the two in imbalance. That wouldn't indicate any flaw in the divine nature; those very attributes themselves, given *their* natures, couldn't fit together easily. Nevertheless, a divine being should contain both.

Still, why didn't the divine being work out the perfect balance? One might hold that there simply is no single right balance, even for God to work out, but the standard Kabbalist theory was that *din*, justice or judgment, overstepped its bounds in the right balance. In the view of Isaac Luria, when, in order to create the world, there is a contraction of the divine being into itself, some of the *din* coagulates or concentrates and is left out, a little speck that eventually produces whatever bad things we encounter. Later, Nathan of Gaza, a follower of the discredited purported messiah Sabbatai Zevi, claimed that there were different components to God. There was God who was completely self-satisfied, and in no way wanted to create the world—

he just wanted to be busy in contemplation, as a good Aristotelian. Another part of God, however, wanted to create the world. It is because the self-satisfied aspect of God resisted the creation of the world that there is evil in it.

All of these Kabbalist theories possess the following virtue: They try to explain evil's existence in the world in terms of some tension, conflict, or interactive process within the divine nature. In this way, they are, as Scholem pointed out, theosophical views in that they talk about the internal nature and life—"psyche" isn't quite right—and ongoing existence of a divine being. Within this realm, they find much room to maneuver, utilizing mystical experiences and interpretations, often esoteric, of traditional texts. Such theories are especially profound.

With their expulsion from Spain in 1492, the Jewish people underwent an enormous trauma. The Kabbalist picture of the *Shechinah* (an aspect of the divine presence) as displaced, in exile and having to return, mirrored the earthly situation of the Jewish people in exile from Jerusalem and their holy land. When suffering of the most traumatic sort beset the Jewish people on earth, the Kabbalists held that everything was not harmonious in the divine realm either. (A large part of Kabbalah's appeal to the Jewish people then, Scholem maintains, was due to this parallelism.) Unlike the standard views wherein God for his own reasons has created evil here (he wanted to create beings with free will or whatever) and is just whistling along happily, the Kabbalists said there was trouble up there as well. There was a parallel between the human realm, in which bad things were happening, and events in the divine realm, which didn't leave that realm untouched. A divine trauma corresponded to the exile of the Jewish people; an aspect of God was in exile and not in its proper place. It was thought that the Jewish people had a particular function to perform, that by so doing they could help the divine *Shechinah* return to its proper place. We shall return to some features of the Kabbalist view later.

Leibniz's view of the problem of evil is best known from Voltaire's satire in *Candide*. Leibniz said that God created the best of all possible worlds. Voltaire presents us with a character encountering one disaster after another and saying, ridiculously, "Yes, it is the best of all possible worlds." How could somebody as smart as Leibniz, the coinventor of calculus, say something as dumb as what Voltaire attributes to him? (Recall the joke: The optimist thinks this is the best of all possible worlds and the pessimist agrees.)

What did Leibniz actually mean? Leibniz thought that God was going to create the most perfect of the possible worlds. The possible worlds are those that don't involve a contradiction; a world in which you're both reading now and not reading right now is not a possible world. Within the realm of logical possibility, God picked, according to Leibniz, the best and most perfect—but best and most perfect in what respect?

Leibniz's idea of the perfection of the world was one whereby a simple set of principles and laws gave rise to the wealth of the world's detail. The most perfect world would have the greatest diversity given rise to in the simplest possible way—that is, would have the greatest organic unity. In setting up a world you will want simple, natural laws, yet through their operation, occasionally, there will be earthquakes and natural accidents, sometimes with people wandering into them. However, God could have avoided that. He could have sprinkled in miracles—like raisins in a raisin cake—that would have intervened at just the right moments. (Maimonides discusses whether miracles are built in, preprogrammed, or popped in later.) Each disaster is avoided by a separate little wrinkle, if not by a miracle then by a separate little complication in the original natural laws. Although that could have been done, in Leibniz's view it would have resulted in a highly imperfect and unaesthetic world. A raisin-filled world would not have been perfect or desirable. So in Leibniz's view, in creation God was creating the most perfect of all possible worlds; he—Leibniz and God both—viewed as best a world in which the greatest wealth and variety of facts (including a lot of good things) would be given rise to in a very simple way.

Clearly, this is not the notion Voltaire satirized. Still, we might wonder why we should worship a divine being who cares only about so aesthetic a perfection. If bad things occur, morally bad things, that being won't care about them at all except insofar as they mar the world's aesthetic perfection. (He might care to this extent: If two worlds were tied in having the most aesthetic perfection, he would prefer and pick the one that causes the least suffering for us.)

However, we can modify Leibniz's view to involve (as the

economists say) trade-offs. In this altered view, God does not create the most perfect of all possible worlds (the one giving rise to the greatest diversity in the simplest possible way), but he creates the seventeenth most perfect of all the possible worlds. He sacrifices some metaphysical perfection in order to alleviate a large amount of suffering that otherwise would go on. Such a God cares about us; he hasn't just chosen that most perfect world growing out of the simplest possible laws. He has thrown in a few raisins here and there, complicating things. To be sure, he has not created the morally best world for us. This would involve very many little miracles and raisins dropped in, and that world, the 1695th most perfect, is *too* unaesthetic and imperfect for him. Yet he hasn't created the best world from his point of view, either. He has made some sacrifices, creating a world lower on his hierarchy of perfection in order to enhance moral goodness here. Such a being shouldn't be scorned for not caring at all about human welfare—he's made important sacrifices for our sake, although he doesn't care about it solely. However, I do not believe that even this modified Leibnizean view can provide an adequate religious explanation for the existence of evil, for a reason I shall come to soon.

Since the time of Leibniz, many philosophers have discussed possible worlds, even if not always the best. One recent philosopher, George Schlesinger, has claimed there is no such thing as the best of all possible worlds. The only thing that could be best would be a world of infinite value, but the only thing that has infinite value is a divine being, God. (God, for reasons we needn't go into now, isn't going to create another being with infinite value just like himself.) So all God can do in creating a world is to create one of finite value.

But why does God want to create a world anyway? (We are aware of the warnings that one shouldn't speculate about certain things, and how those people who do will realize it would have been better had they not been born.) Usually theological discussions of creation are carried on apart from discussions of evil. People assume there are separate questions: Why create a world? Why create one with evil in it? But perhaps, if we understood the reasons for creation, why a perfect divine being would create any world at all rather than simply resting content all by itself, then we would understand why this world has the character it does, including evil.

God doesn't want to create a world to add to his or her own value (being already perfectly self-satisfied and infinitely valuable) or out of need (though the Jewish tradition often describes functions that individual human beings, or the Jewish people as a whole, can perform). A divine being is trying not to add to the total value there is—that's already infinite due to God's own presence—but to create other value for its own sake, and any created world can only have finite value.

God, in creating the world, is bringing about a certain magnitude of value, a finite magnitude. It's as if God is picking a number. God picks a number—suppose, 1,000,563—and that's the amount of value, merit, and goodness in the world. Then we ask God, "Why didn't you pick a higher number?" He asks what number he should have picked. We say, "Why not 5,000,222?" He says, "If I had picked that one, you'd say, 'Why didn't you pick a higher number?' Given that a world I create can't have infinite value, it will be of finite value. So any world I created would be criticizable in the same way for not being better." In theory, there's no best of all possible worlds—just as there's no highest positive integer. For any world that God creates, there could always be a better one. God had to pick some world or other if he was going to create a world, and he picked this one.

Thus, Schlesinger's reply to the problem of evil asks (it feels like a technical trick): What are we complaining about? Why are we complaining about this world, asking why God didn't make it better, why there is evil in it? For any world he would have created, wouldn't we have said the same thing?*

We want to reply that we wouldn't, because there is one natural line we can draw and ask why God didn't at least make the world better than that. We could draw a line at the existence of evil. Maybe that world without evil isn't as splendiferous a world as one can imagine; maybe there's no limit to how splendiferous a world can be. (Maybe if God really was making it splendiferous, the world wouldn't include us at all!) But at least God could have created a world without all the immense pain and suffering that now exist.

There is one line, marked by the existence of evil, yet the world

---

* See George Schlesinger, "The Problem of Evil and the Problem of Suffering," *American Philosophical Quarterly,* Vol. 1 (1964), pp. 244–247; *Religion and Scientific Method* (Dordrecht, Holland: D. Reidl, 1977).

is below that line in its score and value. Why didn't God cross that line at least? The counterreply to this, in Schlesinger's line of argument, is that there are an indefinite number of lines. We are noticing just one line, involving no evil, and asking why God didn't cross that line. But he has crossed a lot of other lines. There are many disastrous ways the world could have been that it isn't—it wasn't created that way. He did cross those lines. If he also had crossed this line (involving no evil) we would notice another line up ahead and ask why he didn't cross that one. The argument now has moved one level up, only this time with lines that can be drawn, instead of varying the amount of value to creation.

Someone might ask why God didn't at least prevent enormous magnitudes of evil. The answer similarly might be that he *did* prevent the most enormous magnitudes; for example, perhaps he has acted to avoid events and wars that would have killed 100,000,000 people. Whatever are the greatest of the evils remaining after God eliminated the most enormous will seem enormous to us since they are at the top of the scale with which we actually are acquainted; so we will, mistakenly, then ask why God didn't at least remove the most enormous evils. He did.

Perhaps this theory satisfies the intellectual criteria we would have listed, at first, in thinking about a satisfactory solution to the problem of evil. We might only have wanted something that would logically reconcile divine omniscience, omnipotence, and goodness with the existence of evil in the world. We might have thought any theory that reconciled these would be a satisfactory solution. Except that this one isn't.

One condition to impose on an adequate religious view of the existence of evil is that it provide something to say to somebody who is actually undergoing suffering or pain or evil. That doesn't mean that what is said would necessarily have to comfort the sufferer. Perhaps the true story isn't a comforting one. But it cannot be something to make one shrink in embarrassment. What the theory we have considered provides is not a possible, not a decent thing to say to somebody.

Another view of the existence of evil has the same defect, yet is worth describing. Consider the reason why God wants to create a world at all, rather than continuing alone in whatever situation he is in. Is this a reason for creating just *one* world? Recall the stories of a sequence of creations that were inadequate, and also the science fiction themes of parallel noninteracting universes.*

God isn't going to create a world in order to increase his own value or goodness, or whatever—that's already infinite. Neither is the total amount of value there is going to be increased; adding a finite amount to an already infinite amount doesn't make that any bigger. The reason has to be to create that world, of finite value, for its own sake and value. But, then, why create just *one*? Why not create many worlds, many noninteracting universes?

If a divine being were going to do that, what would these worlds be like? Would he create the same one with the same details over and over and over again? Maybe there's no point to that, or maybe he would do so five times or twelve times or a million times. Still, adding a different world also would introduce some variety, some value of its own, without subtracting from what already had been created. Perhaps, then, a divine being would create all worlds of net positive value. (A world has net positive value if when that world's amount of goodness or value or whatever is assessed and its amount of badness is subtracted, then the result is still a plus.) A world would get created if that world's existing was better than its not existing. Thus, we can imagine a divine being setting out to create multiple universes, all of which are valuable.

You say you see a lot of defects over here in this universe, and ask why God didn't make the universe better. He did make a better one; he made another one that was better, in just the ways you are imagining. He made that one *and* he made this one too. "Well, why didn't he make *only* that one?" Would it have been better if he had made only that one, instead of both that one plus this one? No, not if this one is worth existing also. "But why didn't he put me in that one rather than this one?" Of course, anybody he placed in this one

* David Lewis states the position that all possible worlds exist in *Counterfactuals* (Oxford: Basil Blackwell, 1973), and elaborates this position, defending it against objections, in *Plurality of Worlds* (Oxford: Basil Blackwell, 1986). In my *Philosophical Explanations,* I discussed how this position, or a truncated version, might help in answering the question: Why is there something rather than nothing? The application of it to the problem of evil that is presented here was developed in discussions with Stephen Phillips.

would ask the same question. (Moreover, this universe or you yourself may be so structured that you could exist only in it or in similar ones.)

In this picture, there is a good, divine being that is creating all worlds of net positive value, and our world, although it contains some evil, is one of those. It is better that our world exist than that it not, and the answer to the question of why a good God didn't make the world better is that he did make a better world *also*. He created all possible good worlds, not only the best of all possible worlds (as Leibniz thought), not only any *one* world. He created a multitude of possible (good) worlds. Indeed, if he created an infinite number, then this might be his route to a creation of infinite value. For though the value of each individual created world is finite (and positive), the infinite summation of these finite values can itself be infinite.

While this theory, perhaps, is somewhat easier to present to someone who suffers evil, it is not clear that it ascribes a morally acceptable pattern of behavior to the deity. Because a world is of net positive value, is it automatically all right and morally permissible to create it? Consider how the comparable principle applies to creating children. Suppose there were a couple who otherwise didn't want to have a child but thought it would be handy to have a little servant around the house. They think, "We otherwise wouldn't create this child, being busy with careers or amusements, but if we had the child and then kept it semi-enslaved to serve us, even then its existence would be of net positive value. Nobody could criticize us for bringing it into existence, for it would be better off living, even that way, than not existing at all. So it's perfectly all right to have that child and keep it permanently as a servant. We are just following the policy of creating something so long as its existence is more valuable than not."

But clearly, it is not all right for the couple to have the child that way. Whatever explanation we ultimately give of why not, they cannot bring a child into such an existence and then repel criticism by saying, "But otherwise we wouldn't have made it exist at all. Its existence has net positive value, so what is it complaining about?" Once the child exists, it has a certain moral status. Others, including the parents, cannot just treat it any way they want compatible with its existence being a net plus.

Choices that affect the size of future populations raise these issues in an acute form. And moral theorists do not find it easy to delineate the correct moral principles to apply there.* Even if each person in the growing population of India thinks his or her life better than not existing at all, we believe it would be better for the population there to be smaller, with fewer people living better. We don't think the total amount of happiness should be maximized if that would involve continuing to add massive numbers of people who each are barely positively happy or barely better off existing rather than not. That would lower the average happiness by too much. Yet neither do we think a situation desirable merely because the average happiness is at a maximum—that might occur because only one or two people existed at all, *extremely* happy people!

Parallel to issues about bringing new people, thus far nonexistent, into the world are issues (this time faced by a deity) about creating new universes. The question, How good does a universe have to be to make it worth creating? is parallel to the question, What does a person's life have to be like for us to think beforehand that it would be better if that person were here? (Afterward, though, the question is different; we won't say of each person outside the pale of the first answer that it would be better if that particular person weren't here.)

The topics are different, one involving people thinking about creating new people, the other involving a divine being thinking about creating universes, yet the problems have a similar structure. It's very difficult to figure out what the appropriate moral principles should be for such situations. But it seems the following is *not* an acceptable principle: It is always morally permissible to create something when its existence is of net positive value. So we cannot solve the problem of evil by saying that God created all universes of net positive value, and ours, though it contains much evil, is one of those.

Perhaps it would be acceptable, though, to create all universes that have a net value greater than a certain significantly large quantity. It is not sufficient merely if the net value of a universe is greater than zero; it must also be a certain substantial level above zero. It is difficult to know exactly what that threshold quantity should be. But

* See Derek Parfit, *Reasons and Persons* (Oxford, England: Oxford University Press, 1984), Part IV.

plausibly our universe meets this more stringent condition and scores above the cutoff quantity.

When we're not sure what principles should govern choices about population numbers, can we do moral philosophy by turning to theology? To find the right population policy, should we formulate a general moral principle such that if God were following it in creating universes, he would have created this one? Can we test a moral principle for a structurally parallel realm by seeing whether it's a principle that God could have followed in creating our world? That would give religion a role in ethical theory, based upon the religious premise that God acted acceptably in creating this universe. An ethical theory then could be tested by whether it had this consequence, and only those passing this test would be candidates for use in deciding other hard moral questions.

Can we solve the problem of evil, then, by saying that God created all possible worlds of very significant net positive value, and ours is one of those? (Why didn't he create a world that was better? He did that too.) It seems to me that this too would be hard to say to people who are undergoing suffering. ("This is one of a basketful of worlds that God created. Don't complain that he didn't make a better one. He did. He created a lot of better ones, and some worse ones as well. You and your suffering are just somewhere along the line.") We might consider, too, the view that God creates not all worlds whose *value* is above a certain threshold, but rather all worlds whose *reality* is. That might, of course, leave more room for evil to enter in, but it is not clear whether it would leave God a fit object of our worship.

Other ethical distinctions might be used to get some leeway here: There is the distinction between doing something and letting it happen (or not preventing it); and the distinction between trying to maximize the best end result and just following certain moral restrictions. Someone might say that God isn't really obligated to maximize and create the best of all possible worlds or the best universe for us; so long as he doesn't *do* anything too terrible, and refrains from various things, then he's off the moral hook, even if he *allows* certain bad things to happen. However, the distinction between making something happen and merely standing by isn't a clear one when the Creator of the whole universe is involved.

What criteria then, must any satisfactory answer to the problem of evil meet? First, the obvious one that it must somehow reconcile those three attributes of God—omniscience, omnipotence, and goodness—with the existence of evil in the world. An answer has to intellectually fit those things together.

Second, the answer has to be something we can actually utter and bring ourselves to say to somebody who is undergoing suffering, or who has a loved one who is, or who has experienced and knows of suffering in the world.

I feel less certain about the third criterion, which involves a psychological speculation. It seems to me that we actually won't find a religious explanation satisfying unless something analogous to it also would serve to answer the more personal question of why our parents, who once seemed to us omnipotent, weren't better to us or even perfect. (I am not claiming that religious beliefs are merely family life projected large.) An answer is being sought, I think, that would satisfy at that level as well.

Fourth—and here I draw from the Kabbalist tradition—the explanation of evil should not leave a divine being untouched. It won't do to say that he or she is just proceeding along merrily doing what's best (maximizing some good function, creating the best of all possible worlds, giving us free will, or whatever), and it so happens that a consequence of its doing what's best is that things are sometimes pretty terrible for us down here. God cannot just proceed merrily along. For an explanation to be satisfying, at least concerning the traumatic evils that occur, it has to in some way show that flaw reflected up in the divine realm.

This condition is not satisfied by Leibniz's view that God creates the best of all possible worlds, or by various gimmicky modifications such as the view that God creates not just one universe but *all* the sufficiently good universes, including this one (hence jauntily replying to the question of why he didn't create a better one: He did that too). These theories all leave the divine being too detached from our plight and situation.

Fifth, a satisfactory explanation must talk about a divine being worth worshiping, a divine being that you can have a religion about. (Plotinus's theory that this realm is a lower one somehow emanated by a God that doesn't even know of it fails this test.) It cannot just be a detached metaphysical theory. Not only must God not be detached from what's happening here, the explanation must leave us attached to God in certain sorts of ways, not simply created by him. The "object relations" have to work well in both directions.

One other condition on an answer to the problem of evil is thrust upon us by the Holocaust. In theory, every and any evil, however slight—the suffering of one child—raises the theological question of why an all-powerful, all-knowing, and good God allows it. However, although the intellectual problem is the same when the evil has the traumatic magnitude of the Holocaust, the emotional problem is not. That raises a special problem.

It is, moreover, especially a problem for Jewish tradition, which holds that the Jewish people stand in a special relationship with the divine being. It is not enough for Jewish theology somehow to offer some story or explanation that reconciles a divine being with the existence of evil; it is this particular stupendous evil to the Jewish people that must be fitted within a religious picture. Some have wondered whether the creation of the State of Israel, so close in time afterward, might not redeem all, but (although these are not easy matters to speak of) this does not seem an acceptable answer, nor has it seemed so to Holocaust survivors living in Israel.

The Jewish theology of the future, I think, will have to do for the Holocaust what Kabbalah did for the Expulsion from Spain, where the situation of the *Shechinah* in exile mirrored and was mirrored by the situation of the Jewish people.

The Holocaust constitutes some kind of rift in the universe. This must be echoed by some rift in the divine life or realm. There must be some kind of trauma there as well. God is not left untouched.

We can mention three possibilities which, though not completely satisfactory, begin to get the flavor of the kind of explanation that is needed. Since the Holocaust *almost* ended the existence of the Jewish people, a theological view might hold that it corresponds to an event of that magnitude in God, to something that almost ended the divine existence. For instance—and I don't mean to say something offensive—an attempt at self-destruction on the part of God.

Why would something like that happen? Could something like that happen? Could the divine being choose to end its own existence? Does it have the power to do that? In the philosophical literature there is a somewhat gimmicky question known as the paradox of omnipotence: Could God create a stone so heavy that God could not lift it? If God couldn't create the stone, then there's something he or she couldn't do, so God isn't omnipotent. If God could create that stone, then there's something else God cannot do, namely, lift it. In either case, then, it seems that God is not omnipotent. Since the problem is a gimmicky one, I won't stop here to survey the attempts that have been made to work it through.

It is not very clear whether a divine being could end its own omnipotent powers. (I don't mean to conclude quickly—*à la* the paradox of omnipotence—that if it can't then it's not omnipotent.) As for those traits we think God has, could God stop having them? Could God stop being omnipotent? Could God stop existing, if he or she chose? Not only isn't the answer clear to us, it also might not be clear to the divine being himself or herself. Don't just *define* the divine being as omniscient; there might be certain facts about the limits of its own powers at that level that it doesn't know. Whether it could end its whole existence or not might be the last thing it didn't know about itself. It might be something, though, that it had to know, or to attempt, in order to accomplish some other task.

An attempt by God to end his own existence, then, is not excluded by the very concept of God, and it does have the right order of magnitude to correspond to an unparalleled rift in our universe. Although it has the right magnitude, nevertheless this theory is inadequate. If God's attempt at self-destruction is an experiment, done from intellectual curiosity about his own possible limits, then the event so motivated, however momentous, is not of the right sort to parallel the Holocaust, which fell upon the Jewish people involuntarily. Perhaps some other egodystonic motive might lead God to attempt self-destruction, but I have nothing appropriate to suggest.

Here is a second attempt, also inadequate. God, as traditionally conceived, has infinite power to do anything he chooses; he is omniscient and so knows every fact that there is and every fact that there will be. But although God has infinite knowledge of all truths, perhaps he doesn't have infinite wisdom. Wisdom is another kind of thing, not the same as (ordinary) knowledge. Think of the kinds of situations where people say, "If you haven't been in a war, you don't really know what it's like." You can read about it, you can see films, you can have it described to you, but there's still something that you don't know. There's a kind of knowledge you don't have, experiential knowledge, what the philosophical tradition sometimes calls "knowledge by acquaintance."

Are there some things which God can know only by undergoing them himself (or herself) or by experiencing what his creations undergo? Wisdom, the Greeks held, might be attainable only by undergoing certain experiences of suffering. Might a divine being need to gain wisdom in a similar way? In gaining this experience, God wouldn't be left untouched; the sufferings people experience here would in some way also be affecting the divine being. He too is undergoing these experiences, to gain a kind of knowledge not obtainable in any other way, knowledge he might need for some other important task. Does it make a divine being imperfect if it doesn't start out all-wise? Maybe it's better for a divine being to gain wisdom than to start out with it fully; maybe it's better for it to earn wisdom, in a certain way.

A third view would hold that God created (not man but) the world in his own image as a material representation of himself, perhaps as an act of self-expression. (Is the whole of the material world a representation of the divine being's emotions; are we living in, and part of, God's emotional life?) Without his goodness being diminished, God might have subsidiary parts whose tendency goes against the whole but which are well-controlled, just as good men can have under control passions or unconscious desires that are unexpressed or expressed only in acceptable ways. What then will be the character of a universe created in this God's image? This vast universe will contain small dissonant parts which do not prevent it from being excellent overall. God does not attempt, in this third view, to create the most perfect possible world but rather to create a world in his own image. (Or perhaps he creates many such worlds, all differently apt representations of himself.) Although the small parts God keeps under control do not make him imperfect, their representation in this universe does constitute a (moral) imperfection here. This universe is not a perfect likeness; it is only one possible image of God, capturing many but not all salient aspects. The mapping that makes our universe a representation of God does not preserve perfection. (Nonetheless, perhaps we can feel exalted in contributing to a representation of God, being a dab in his portrait, a vowel in his name.)

This third view does correlate something within the divine realm to evil here. However, that something may not be sufficiently upsetting there. A satisfying solution to the problem of evil, it seems, must place us in a universe where the image of the representational mapping preserves (but doesn't augment) upsettingness. Moreover, what is to be preserved is how upset *we* feel—the universe as a whole may not be terribly upset at the evil within it. (At this point, though, hasn't our demand for a satisfying solution to the problem of evil become too humanocentric?)

These three alternatives, concerning self-destruction, wisdom, and creation of the world in God's image, are not satisfactory theories of the internal life and motivation of the divine being. The concept of God, we already have seen, is not (restricted to) the most perfect possible being. Earlier we formulated the concept as: the most perfect actual being, far superior to the next most perfect, who also stands in a most significant relation to this world (such as being its creator). A slightly different definition would replace the notion of "most perfect" by "most real." God would then be the most real actual being, whose reality far surpasses that of the next most real being, who stands in a most significant relation to this world, etc. Apparent defects in God's perfection or goodness might then contribute to his greater *reality* overall. In any case, the next task of theology (especially of a Jewish theology) is to dare to speculate, as the Kabbalists did before, about a divine being's internal existence. A daring theory is needed to drive issues about evil deep within the divine realm or nature in some way, leaving it deeply affected yet not itself evil.

20

The Holocaust

THE MURDER of two thirds of European Jewry during the Second World War as part of the determined attempt to annihilate it completely—now known as the Holocaust—is so momentous an event that we cannot yet grasp its full significance. It is difficult enough even to chronicle what occurred—knowledge of much of the suffering and bestial cruelty has disappeared along with its victims—and simply reading the details staggers and numbs the mind: the wanton cruelty of the German perpetrators in continual beatings, the forcible herding of people into synagogues then set on fire to burn them alive there, dousing gasoline on men in prayer shawls and then burning them, dashing children's brains against walls while their parents were forced to watch, so-called "medical experiments", machine-gunning people into graves they were forced to dig themselves, ripping beards off old men, mocking people while inflicting horrors on them, the inexorable and unrelenting organized process that sought to destroy each and every Jew and to degrade them completely in this process, the lies about resettlement in the east in order to maintain some hope and partial cooperation, calling the street from the Treblinka railroad station to the gas chambers through which the Jews were forced to walk naked *Himmelfahrstrasse,* the street to heaven—the list is endless, and it is impossible to find one particular event or a few to encapsulate and symbolize all that happened.*

How are we to understand these events? Social scientists and historians can try to trace their causes, to learn how it could happen that a country occupying the height of Western civilization—the land, as everyone says, of Goethe, Kant, and Beethoven—could pluck a people from its midst for extermination and stick to this task so ferociously, could consent to be led by a man of such festering hatreds so openly expressed. Other phenomena now unavoidably will be seen in its light, such as earlier antisemitism or feelings of racial superiority in any culture. And we can trace the further consequences of the event in the denuding of Eastern and Central Europe of Jews, the bringing of nuclear weapons into being; and trace also the disheartening consequences in how we now think about Western civilization and about the line of hope from Greece through the Renaissance and the Enlightenment until just recently.

The Holocaust is something we have to respond to in some significant way. Yet it is not clear what responses would serve: remembering it, constantly being haunted, working to prevent its like from ever occurring again, a sea of tears?

The significance of the Holocaust is more momentous even than these tracings can know and these responses can encompass. I believe the Holocaust is an event like the Fall in the way traditional Christianity conceived it, something that radically and drastically alters the

---

* Then there is the active participation and aid of others, the Poles, Ukrainians, Roumanians, etc., who indulged their own murderous hatred of the Jews, cooperating in rounding them up and gladly helping themselves to Jewish property and homes left behind (despite the fact that they were themselves being earmarked for subservience to the Germans as their exploited and docile workers); and there is the behavior of still others who stood by knowingly and often approvingly, or who impeded the escape of victims—the British, for instance, in turning back to Germany ships containing people fleeing to Palestine, and pressuring other nations to do the same; the members of the U.S. State and War Departments who obstructed the rescue of European Jews, impeded their immigration, and resisted all urging to bomb Auschwitz's gas chambers and the railroad tracks leading to them.

situation and status of humanity. I myself do not believe that there was actually that Edenic event since which man has been born in original sin, but something like that has occurred now. Mankind has fallen.

I do not claim to understand the full significance of this, but here is one piece, I think: It now would not be a *special* tragedy if humankind ended, if the human species were destroyed in atomic warfare or the earth passed through some cloud that made it impossible for the species to continue reproducing itself. I do not mean that humanity *deserves* this to happen. Such an event would involve a multitude of individual tragedies and suffering, the pain and loss of life, and the loss of continuance and meaning which children provide, so it would be wrong and monstrous for anyone to bring this about. What I mean is that earlier, it would have constituted an *additional* tragedy, one beyond that to the individual people involved, if human history and the human species had ended, but now that history and that species have become stained, its loss would now be no *special* loss above and beyond the losses to the individuals involved. Humanity has lost its claim to continue.

Why say it took the Holocaust to produce this situation, when we know what a developed Western civilization already had countenanced: slavery and the slave trade, Belgians in the Congo, Argentinians exterminating their Indian population, Americans decimating and betraying theirs, European countries grindingly destroying lives in the First World War, not to mention the rest of the world's monstrous record. There is no point in arguing about comparative cruelty and disasters. (China, Russia, Cambodia, Armenia, Tibet . . . will this century become known as the age of atrocity?) Perhaps what occurred is that the Holocaust *sealed* the situation, and made it patently clear.

Yet the Holocaust alone would have been enough, all by itself. Like a relative shaming a family, the Germans, our human relatives, have shamed us all. They have ruined all our reputations, not as individuals—they have ruined the reputation of the human family. Although we are not all responsible for what those who acted and stood by did, we are all stained.

Imagine beings from another galaxy looking at our history. It would not seem unfitting to them, I think, if that story came to an end, if the species they see with that history ended, destroying itself in nuclear warfare or otherwise failing to be able to continue. These observers would see the *individual* tragedies involved, but they would not see—I am saying—any further tragedy in the ending of the species. That species, the one that has committed *that,* has lost its worthy status. Not—let me repeat—that the species deserves to be destroyed; it simply no longer deserves *not* to be. Humanity has desanctified itself. If a being from that other galaxy were to read our history, with all it contains, and that story were then to end in destruction, wouldn't that bring the narrative to a satisfying close, like a chord resolving?

The Holocaust, I said earlier, constitutes a special problem for Jewish theology seeking to understand the actions of God, but it also, I think, affects Christian theology in a radical way. I do not refer here to Christianity's examining its share of responsibility for anti-Jewish teaching over the centuries, or its organized institutions' actual role during the Holocaust, or even the fact that it did not succeed in creating a civilization in which no Holocaust would happen. I mean that the theological situation itself has been transformed.

Christian theology has held that there were two momentous transformations in the situation of humanity, first the Fall and then the crucifixion and resurrection of Christ, which redeemed humanity and provided it with a route out of its fallen state. Whatever changed situation or possibility the crucifixion and resurrection were supposed to bring about has now ended; the Holocaust has shut the door that Christ opened. (I myself am not a Christian, but that is no bar to seeing—perhaps it helps me to see more clearly—what the deepest implications for Christianity are.) The Holocaust is a third momentous transformation. There still remain the ethical teachings and example of the life of Jesus before his end, but there no longer operates the saving message of Christ. In this sense, the Christian era has closed.

It might be thought that what Christ accomplished according to Christian theology, he accomplished forever, once and for all. He died for all our sins, past and future, small and large. But not for *that* one, I think. Recall the theological view that in giving people free will God intentionally limits his omniscience, so that he no longer foresees how people will choose. Perhaps, in sending his only son to redeem humanity, he had nothing like the Holocaust in mind as what humanity was going to need redemption from. But in any case, whatever suffering Jesus underwent, or God the father in watching it, this could not be sufficient to redeem humanity in the face of the Holocaust, I think Christian theology needs to maintain. Or rather, whatever the current situation of individuals one by one, the Holocaust has created a radically new situation and status for humanity as a whole, one the sacrifice of Jesus could not and was not meant to heal. The human species now is desanctified; if it were ended or obliterated now, its end would no longer constitute a special tragedy.

Is humanity permanently reduced to this desanctified status? Is there anything we can do by our behavior over time, so that once again it would be a special and further tragedy if our species were to end or be destroyed? Can we redeem ourselves? No "second coming" could alter our status, not at any rate if it was anything like a repeat performance. Only human action could redeem us, if anything can. But can anything?

Would hundreds of years of peaceful goodness on our collective parts serve, if preceded by a joint repentence for what our history has contained? Perhaps what we need to do is help produce *another*, better species or make way for it; can we regain the status of deserving to continue only by stepping aside?

Perhaps rather we need to change our own nature, transforming ourselves into beings who are unhappy and who suffer when others do, or at least into beings who suffer when we inflict suffering on others or cause them to suffer, or when we stand by and allow the infliction of suffering. This latter change, however it occurred, at least would cut down greatly on the amount of suffering humans inflict. Yet there is so much suffering in the world, if we were unhappy whenever others suffered for whatever reason, we would have to be unhappy all the time; and if we were unhappy always when some people inflicted suffering on others, unless all people were changed in this way, unhappiness would become our constant lot. Or is it that we should be unhappy only when others inflict *massive* suffering, and when we ourselves inflict any at all? Yet if other events such as antisemitism earlier or later, or any group's assertions of racial superiority, must now be seen through the prism of the Holocaust, then—so vast and intense and varied was the suffering inflicted and undergone then—henceforth must not any human suffering anywhere also be seen and *felt* as part of that Holocaust?

Perhaps it is only by suffering ourselves when any suffering is inflicted, or even when any is felt, that we can redeem the species. Before, perhaps, we could be more isolated; now that no longer suffices. Christian doctrine has held that Jesus took humanity's suffering upon himself, redeeming it, and while others were told to imitate Christ, they were not expected similarly to take suffering upon themselves with redemptive effect. If the Christian era has ended, it has been replaced by one in which we each now have to take humanity's suffering upon ourselves. What Jesus was supposed to have done for us, before the Holocaust, humanity must now do for itself.

Hereby also might the rift between Judaism and Christianity be mended. Whatever Christ might once have accomplished—Jews and Christians might agree—now no longer is so; we live in an unredeemed state. The status of the human species can be redeemed, if at all, only through (almost) everyone's now taking the suffering of others upon themselves. Christians could think this a new era that more truly continues and embodies the Christian message; Jews could see others now truly weep over a suffering so momentous and so monstrously inflicted that everyone now must be different henceforth. The Holocaust has thrust the issue of redemption before us anew, except now redemption must come from ourselves, humanity as a whole, with the outcome uncertain.

Someone might think that rather than take others' suffering upon himself, he would prefer to leave humanity as a species unredeemed, letting it remain no tragedy if the human species ended. He might even think this would be better overall, for these thoughts about humanity's ending are, after all, abstract and involve only one hypothetical tragedy, whereas if we all *do* take humanity's suffering upon ourselves, that involves many additional events of actual suffering. So if that were the only way humanity could redeem itself, wouldn't it be better to leave it unredeemed? How much of a tragedy is it if humanity's ending were not to be a further tragedy—and isn't that a tragedy we can learn to live with?

Yet being part of an ongoing human enterprise that is worth

continuing may not be a trivial part of our lives and the meaning we think these have. It was against that background, taken for granted until now, that many activities found their point or significance and many others found a place to permissibly be. One cannot dissolve or shred that context yet leave everything else as it was.

I have outlined here one interpretation of the Holocaust that gives it commensurate weight, but I would not want to exclude other interpretations or insist on this one come what may. The full significance and implications of that trauma—so recent—dwarf a single person's understanding; certainly they dwarf mine.

The Holocaust is a massive cataclysm that distorts everything around it. Physicists sometimes speak of gravitational masses as twistings and distortions of the even geometry of the surrounding physical space; the greater the mass, the larger the distortion. The Holocaust is a massive and continuing distortion of the human space, I want to say. Its vortices and gnarled twistings will extend very far. Hitler too constituted a force that distorted the lives of those around him—his followers, his victims, and those who had to conquer him. The vortex he created has not disappeared. Perhaps every evil of whatever magnitude constitutes some distortion of human space. It has taken a cataclysm to get us to notice.

21

Enlightenment

TO THE QUESTION of what is the very highest goal of human existence, various Eastern traditions reply that it is *enlightenment*. These traditions differ in how they specify this goal (and in the term they use for it, *nirvana, satori,* or *moksha*), but they each hold that it has a fourfold structure. It involves an experience, a contact with deepest reality, a new understanding of the self and also a transformation of it.

Those who describe the enlightenment experience caution that their descriptions are inadequate. The experience (or experiences—we should not assume it is the very same one that everyone has) is said to be blissful, infinite, without boundaries or limit, ecstatic, full of energy, pure, shining, and extremely powerful. Moreover, it feels like an experience *of* something, an experience revelatory of the nature of a deeper reality. This reality can be external, an infinite pure substance constituting the universe; it can be the deeper nature of the self; or, in the case of the Vedanta tradition, which holds that the deepest reality, *Brahman,* is identical to the deepest self, *atman,* the reality can be both. This experience seems to reveal reality to be very different from the way it ordinarily appears. If the experience is not to be dismissed as totally illusory—something those who have it are loath to do, in part because of its other qualities, in part because of its revelatory force—it presents its proponents with a formidable problem: explaining why reality did not previously appear to them as it truly was. It is this task of theoretical explanation that gives rise to particular theories and hypotheses about the ordinary world not rooted in the authority of the experience itself, such as that it is illusion, dream, fictional creation, etc.

That the enlightenment experience feels or seems revelatory of a deeper reality does not guarantee that there is any such reality that exists independently of the experience or whose character is revealed in it. Rarely are the experiences repeatable or exactly replicable, even by the person who has had them, and so this one route to showing their objective validity is closed. Some procedures, however, do make these unusual and revelatory experiences more likely, among them meditation, yogic breathing, etc. Some people see these procedures as producing illusions, while others see them as lifting the veil from reality. It might appear that we should distrust these procedures, and the validity of the unusual experiences they sometimes produce, on evolutionary grounds. Those organisms whose state of consciousness matched reality poorly, managed to leave few or no descendants, so it is our ordinary state of consciousness, nothing unusual, which is well adapted to telling what things really are like. However, the most we can conclude from the evolutionary argument is that our ordinary states of consciousness are reasonably well adapted to detecting those features of reality that are relevant to our survival as organisms until child-rearing age. These will be the usual physical features of moving macroscopic medium-sized physical objects. If there were a deeper spiritual reality, yet knowing its nature was irrelevant to our physical survival and reproduction, which is all evolution "cares about," then there would be no evolutionary selection for states of consciousness that could know or connect with this underlying reality. So the fact that our ordinary modes of consciousness do not reveal this deeper reality is no argument against it.

But are the unusual and extraordinary experiences that people have and report an argument *for* this deeper reality? Whether they are depends upon the answer to the following question: What experiences would people have—what experiences would you expect them to have—when they did those things such as yogic breathing and meditation, but there was no deeper reality? If there were no deeper reality, only the ordinary commonsense one, what would those people experience instead? If they then would experience the very same thing—namely, experiences of (or of being) an infinite pure substance, etc.—then having those experiences does not show that, and is not evidence that, some deeper reality *is* that way. If they would have the very same experiences (doing those things) no matter which way things are, then the experiences cannot show how things are. And there is some reason for thinking the same experiences *might* occur, even in the absence of an underlying extraordinary reality. For when people quiet their thoughts, allowing no idea, concept, or image to enter their consciousness, focusing upon nothing at all, wouldn't we expect them to have an experience that seemed to have no limits? After all, everything that might give it limits or contours or differentiation has been removed or suppressed. To know how much credence to give to the extraordinary experiences, we—and those who have these experiences also—need to be told what the alternative is—that is, what experiences should be expected instead if reality is *not* deep but rather as most people normally think it is. Since no one has yet specified this alternative baseline, it is hard to know what to believe on the basis of the (reports of the) extraordinary enlightenment experiences.

The reality this enlightenment experience seems to reveal is felt to be the very deepest reality, not just a deeper one than ordinarily is experienced. It is difficult to see how the character of the experience itself can guarantee its ultimate depth, though. Could not another hidden level of surprisingly different character underlie the level that is experienced? One Zen master reported a later, deeper enlightenment experience that surpassed, overturned, and placed in a different light his first one; and the twentieth-century Indian philosopher and mystic Aurobindo reported an experience of the vibrant void—an experience Buddhists report as deepest—and said that through it he was able to reach a yet deeper (Vedanta) experience of a full and infinite blissful conscious reality. I do not doubt there are Buddhist sages who also report having both experiences—with the order reversed, the one of the void lying underneath the other of a full infinite reality.

Whether or not the enlightenment experience is an experience of the *very* deepest reality, in part because of the experience's own intense reality (in the special sense of this term) it feels like it reveals one extremely deep. This reality is experienced as wholly positive or—perhaps this is really an inference from the experience—as giving a redeeming place and purpose to whatever in the universe appears negative. The reality principles then constitute a route to the deepest realization of the happiness principle.

The self then is experienced differently, no longer wrapped up in the everyday constituents of consciousness or wholly constituted by it. It may be experienced as a witnessing consciousness out of time, an infinite pure consciousness without beginning or end, a pure mirror and observer of whatever is before it, a void not separate from the larger universe, an infinite space rather than an entity within space, or as identical with the deepest infinite reality itself. In each case, the self's boundaries are extended or dissolved.

This very different character of the self as it is experienced has led some Eastern theories into needless difficulties, I think. If the self is very different and so much more wonderful, then why hadn't we realized this previously? If it is so rich, how come it isn't smart? The explanation offered by the Eastern theories is that the ordinary view, previously held, is something like an illusion or delusion; implausible theories are generated to explain how the illusion arose (or why it has always existed), to explain how something as wonderful as the deep self (the *atman* or *purusha*) could undergo such an illusion, and to explain why, once dispelled, it will not return.

These theorists might do better to propose that the self has been transformed; once it *was* limited and now it no longer is. (The alternative they pursue instead is to say it *always* was unlimited but previously made a mistake about its own nature.) More strikingly, they could say that the self once was not identical to an infinite pure substance (*brahman*) but now has become so.* Picture the waters of

---

* For a theory that allows the truth of identity statements to vary with time, see David Lewis, "Survival and Identity," in Amelie Rorty, ed., *The Identities of Persons* (Berkeley: University of California Press, 1976), pp. 17–40.

a tributary stream flowing into a large and powerful river. After entering, these waters are part of a mighty river; look behind and there is a mighty river as far back as their eye can see. (They hardly notice the insignificant stream.) The waters now have become identical with the river, though previously they were not. The river always was there; these waters now are identical with it (at this downriver or temporal stage), yet before, upstream, these waters were identical only with a tributary, not with the large river. The identity of the waters depends upon the time when we ask. If identity can change with time, this obviates the need for a theory of illusion. Thus these theorists could hold that *brahman* always existed and the self now is identical with it yet was not identical with it before. (No longer must they say the self was identical with *brahman* before also but labored under some illusion that it wasn't.) What would be needed, then, is a theory of transformation, a theory of how a self that is not identical to an infinite pure substance at one time can become identical later, and this theory replaces the illusion theory.

Not only does the person feel during the enlightenment experience that his deepest self is very different, often he is transformed as a result of the experience. The enlightenment experience of a very different mode of self-organization enables him also to encounter the everyday world differently, now less clouded or distorted by the interests of the limited self.

Three things about an enlightenment experience might lead the person to become less ego-centered: first, the experience of the self as less delimited, as an infinite and pure consciousness from whose perspective the ordinary concerns of the separate ego diminish in importance; second, the experience of the deepest reality, from whose perspective too ordinary ego concerns are of small concern; and third, and perhaps most salient, the enlightenment experience itself, experienced as of surpassing value and importance, which thus locates other ego concerns as totally subordinate to its own value and central place in life. That enlightenment experience is felt as being the very most real and valuable. The people who have it, therefore, are unwilling to place other things above it or to dismiss its revelatory character as wholly illusory.

The descriptions of these people—I am thinking especially of the stories about Zen masters and other Eastern teachers—depict them

247

as being absolutely focused, clear, sure, confident, sharply delineated, often breaking established patterns to proceed directly to goals. They know what they are about, their vision is clear and unclouded. They are as real as real can be.

The enlightenment experience not only ends your identifying with the self as a particular delimited entity, it might be an experience of being no entity at all, more like a space. The existentialist slogan held that existence precedes essence; each person then is free to choose his or her own essence. The enlightenment experience is one of being no particular thing; there is no natural kind that you necessarily are. You don't have to possess or choose any essence at all, then; to think you have one is a mistake. Having an essence or identity is for there to be some properties you *necessarily* have, properties you *have to* have, and for there also to be appropriate standards that get invoked for entities of that kind. A prerequisite, then, for feeling totally free is not to have an identity in this sense; no traits of you necessarily hold, there is no kind of thing you necessarily are.* Does this extend to the notions of an "I" and a "self" too? Are not these at least part of the enlightened being's felt identity? If the problem of the meaning of life is created by our limits, and we attempt to gain meaning by connecting up with other things beyond these limits, thereby transcending them, and if the enlightenment experience is one of being without any limits, no particular identity imposing its necessary characteristics and standards, then that will feel most meaningful. More precisely, either it will feel completely (infinitely) meaningful, or it will transcend the very issue of meaning, having obliterated what is the necessary background or presupposition for there to be any issue of meaning at all, namely, the existence of some limits or other.

Is the allure of enlightenment any wonder? The experience is most real, it involves contact with what appears to be the deepest reality, the person is transformed into being more real and completely free—all this and ecstatic bliss too. In addition, the person arrives at a new and more correct view of reality—assuming the experience is veridical—and becomes a more adequate expressive analog of the

---

* One might fit this with the recent philosophical attacks on the notion of necessity by W. V. Quine. See his essay, "Necessary Truth," in his *The Ways of Paradox* (Cambridge, Mass.: Harvard University Press, 1976).

deepest reality.* Enlightenment, however alluring as an end, might not be a goal that can be directly pursued. The means of pursuit, and some of the motives for doing so, might themselves strengthen the very self-structures which enlightenment is to transform. Even if there were no steps to take, if enlightenment *were* the supreme good it would be important to see your life in relation to that.

While many see the purpose of enlightenment as escape into another realm, leaving behind the cycle of rebirth and suffering, some—Aurobindo is one—see it as transforming material existence. It does seem to involve some cost, though, in personal attachment, in love and friendship. "So dazzling is even a glimpse of this supreme existence," says Aurobindo, "and so absorbing its attraction that, once seen, we feel readily justified in neglecting all else for its pursuit."†

A plausible interpretation of Zen also sees enlightenment or *satori* as involving a very different yet particular vision of *this* world, hence a different relation to it, rather than constituting an escape to another realm. Zen *koans* are not meaningless and unanswerable questions designed to get one to realize the limits of rational conceptual thought—why should they do this more than any other evidently meaningless questions?—but have determinate answers that do make sense *given* the very different view of this world they are designed to lead one to. Consider the familiar diagrams of the gestalt psychologists. One diagram we can see as a vase or as two faces

---

* And psychological well-being? It is difficult to know what is the case with enlightenment, but it is reliably reported that serious Western teachers of Buddhist meditation, experienced and dedicated ones who have been through extended training and who themselves do meditate intensively many hours a day, are not above continuing anxieties or attempts to manipulate and dominate others; sometimes they seek professional psychotherapy. (See *Inquiring Mind* [Berkeley, California], Vol. 5, No. 1 [Summer 1988].) Since these teachers—who are to be commended for their forthrightness and seriousness in reporting this—do not, I think, claim to be enlightened, we cannot extrapolate from their cases, but since the written record on enlightenment itself does not speak directly to the question of psychological well-being, some caution is in order in drawing sanguine conclusions.

† *The Synthesis of Yoga* (Pondicherry, India: Sri Aurobindo Ashram, 1955), p. 14. Aurobindo himself retreated for the last twenty-plus years of his life into a three-room suite within his spiritual community, giving occasional audiences, revising his previous books, writing letters to followers, and also composing a long epic poem about spiritual development, *Savitri*.

looking at each other; what is figure in one becomes background in the other. Or the young girl and the old woman, where the old woman's nose is the young girl's chin and cheek. Or the different ways to see a drawn cube; is the bottom right point a front or a rear node? We can get someone who sees the diagram one way to see it differently by fixing upon one feature that can precipitate the different seeing—for example, "Instead of a curve on the right side of a vase, see this part of the line as the profile of a nose turned toward the left." The Zen vision, I suggest, is of this world, not of another realm, yet as different from the usual view as the vase is from the two faces. Indeed, perhaps the usual view precipitates and coagulates around one particular feature, the self. Once we populate the world with an entity, objective or subjective, that is our self, the rest of the world falls into its (perspectival) place. Compare: Once you see that as a nose, the rest of the picture falls into place as two faces. The Zen practices—meditation, koans, sudden sounds, blows—are designed to loosen the hold of the self, to get you to stop identifying with that entity and thereby to see the world *completely* differently. In this interpretation, Zen involves a change in the gestalt of the actual world, shaking your vision loose from the picture organized around the self, not entry into another and wholly separate realm. Given that change, the koans have perfectly clear answers.

A path toward enlightenment also may offer ways to diminish pain and suffering in life, not just by turning away from activities which tend to produce that. Here is one bit of empirical evidence. At first it is painful to sit cross-legged in meditative position for a long period of time. The knees hurt, the ankles hurt, the sensations are intense. Things change, though, when one focuses upon these sensations with the same mode of attention meditation brings to other things—for instance, to inhaling and exhaling the breath. Focus upon the sensation as a sensation, not as *your* sensation, not as a *painful* sensation, but simply upon it as an intense sensation; go inside it with your consciousness, and then surprisingly—at first, unbelievably—the quality of the sensation is altered. No longer a homogeneous lump of pain, it is broken up into parts, with sensations here and there but not everywhere in between. You stay some distance from the sensations; they are observed not so much as *yours,* simply as there. Moreover, the sensations no longer are painful; still felt as intense, sometimes in another sensory mode such as sight, they do not *hurt*. It is as though something's being painful, at least in this one case, depends upon seeing it as your own and in a perspective that projects certain qualities onto the sensation. When the sensations are attended to in themselves, their painful quality is dissolved and they are experienced differently. How far can this "nonpain" phenomenon extend? Perhaps not to sensations that continue for many hours, perhaps not completely to certain intensities. I do not claim that no pain need be involuntarily undergone, but simple meditative techniques are able to reduce or eliminate some pain for some period of time. It seems reasonable to believe that still further reductions would be available with practice and training, and even greater reductions might be available to someone who could utilize enlightenment experiences. Some satisfaction of a pleasure principle—the nonpain principle—therefore will follow in enlightenment's wake.

Ultimately the universe and our place within it are perfect—so holds the enlightenment narrative. It tells us we *can* have everything worth having, to a superlative degree, and be everything worth being; our nature already is congenial to that. The doctrine of enlightenment therefore denies the ultimate reality of tragedy, and the necessity sometimes of really sacrificing or permanently losing some most important good in order to avoid an evil. Does that doctrine thereby contain the deepest wisdom, or is it the very highest and most beautiful foolishness? Shouldn't we suspect that enlightenment, and its whole background theory, is too good to be true? In the absence of hard evidence and proof about its possibility and feasibility, shouldn't one remain skeptical, not putting all one's ego in the enlightenment basket? Isn't the hard and ultimate wisdom rather this: that there is no escaping the human condition, and the belief that one can is, in the last analysis, shallow? Or, rather, is this a case of wisdom's making a virtue of what it once reluctantly and painfully but mistakenly concluded was necessity? Priding itself on hard realism and lack of illusion, does wisdom *cling* to tragedy, like a neurotic to his symptoms, because of the secondary gain?

Sometimes we tend to be dismissive of possibilities, including ones we know very little about, because we do not *want* them to be true, even though they may appear or be quite wonderful. They would require too great a reorganization of our general picture of the world, and of our lives, habits, modes of thought, and goals. We have adapted to the apparent limits of our (personal, intellectual, and cultural) niches and we do not any longer want to believe those limits are malleable. So, quickly we dismiss a possibility with a slick argument and we are comforted and relieved—the necessity of drastic change has been avoided! A wise person, though, would be open to learning new things without being overly credulous. He would pay careful attention to new and surprising possibilities, explore them tentatively, experiment. If a possibility offers some confirmations along the way—whether illuminating and powerful experiences, desirable personal transformations, or encounters with impressive others who have pursued that same possibility further—he will continue more confidently, yet still with some caution. Pascal recommended staking everything in life on the possibility of infinite gain, but we do better to recall the two types of errors statisticians describe—rejecting something when it is true or accepting it when it is false—and to wend our way, sometimes daringly but still with tentativeness, doing our best to avoid, on this important matter, an error in either direction.

22

Giving Everything Its Due

HUMANITY'S GREAT SPIRITUAL TEACHERS— Buddha, Socrates, Jesus, Gandhi, and others—are models, shining personal examples. They make their powerful impact not merely through the propositions and principles they enunciate but also through their own vivid presence. We encounter them, not just their doctrines, and we want to be more like them, to the small extent we can. They seem more real than we, and their vivid reality inspires us. To be more like them is for us to be more real too. The presence and lives of these teachers incarnate their doctrines. We learn what they are saying, we learn what their words mean, by seeing their lives. Their lives— sometimes, their deaths—are their teaching in action; they make their abstractions concrete.

They tell us stories, they relate parables, they give us whatever evocative nodes we can relate to. Not only do they tell stories, nowadays we encounter them in stories: in Plato's early dialogues, in the Pali canon, in the Gospels, in the tales of the Baal Shem Tov. From these tales, we form images of them, of how they act, of what they are. Their lives play a crucial role in convincing us of what they say. It is not that we derive their doctrine, or their being right, from some other body of preformulated statements. If we accept their views upon their authority, still that authority is derived only from what they are and show in their lives, as presented in the stories about them. We do not start out holding principles which assume that what their lives show is the right way. Instead, we look at their lives and find ourselves awed and moved. They teach by shining example.

We can list some features characteristic of spiritual teachers, although not every such figure will have every one. First, they exemplify what they hold important; their values infuse their lives. The things they hold important are in fact good and shining values, admirable ones—for example, inquiry in the case of Socrates, compassion in the case of Buddha, love in the case of Jesus, nonviolence and truth in action in the case of Gandhi. They are marked by certain traits: kindness, nonviolence, love of living beings, simplicity, directness, honesty, purity, focus, intensity, making life a realization of deeper reality, inner calm, relative unconcern for material or worldly goods, radiant energy, great inner strength. These beings speak to, and bring us back to, the best within us. In their presence we are reminded of our own neglected heights, embarrassed to be less than our best selves. We sense in them not just a collection of highly admirable qualities but a different internal organization and structure. They are vessels of light.

The spiritual teachers are exemplars of the full force of their values. Part of their appeal is the appeal of these high values, but another part is the extraordinary reality the spiritual teachers achieve as archetypes and embodiments of these values. It is as if the values as Platonic Forms have been made incarnate here on earth. However, this is possible because spiritual teachers are incarnations of just one value or only a few to the exclusion of many others. Being well-rounded would dilute the radiance of their singular value.

The spiritual teachers adhere completely and totally to what is important to them. They will not compromise these values or deviate from them. They place their whole lives in these values; they stake their whole lives upon them, even unto death. Usually, spiritual teachers stand especially for *single* values, which they are able to do without tradeoffs or compromises. However, there are further values they will share in common; they frequently are devoted to noninjury, putting forth a model of a positive relation to everyone and perhaps even to everything. Under no circumstances, or almost none, will they harm another person. They also live simply; they do not amass material goods—sometimes they give them up—and they present images of great *purity*. Spiritual teachers seem free of the control of external forces—no outside threat would move them—or of inner desires. Nothing pushes them where they do not want to go.

Through a spiritual teacher we see that a life devoted to those values (or to that *one* value) is possible, also that it is remarkable, a good way to be. It strikes us this way, although we might not have thought so had we merely heard the values described, without being presented with a figure who lives them. These spiritual teachers have great effects on many who encounter them, calling them to a higher or deeper purpose, bringing out (what these others feel is) a better self.

We can distinguish three facets in spiritual teachers. First is their ethical and artistic impact: they are striking figures, often paradoxical and artistically interesting ones, sometimes offering hard counsel, and there would be this impact even if the books describing them were works of fiction, explicitly presented as such. Nevertheless, we would find these characters intriguing, inspiring, moving. Second, their existence proves that a certain way of being really is *possible,* for they were that way themselves. Third, above and beyond whatever in our lives follows from these first two facets, there is what follows from those people's *actually* having existed and done what they did, the differences their actions and existence did make—beyond the effects of the narratives describing these and our belief that such things are possible. (Christians, for instance, believe that the life and death of Jesus really did change the relation of man to God.) In treating figures as spiritual teachers I mean to be focusing only upon the first two facets and what follows for us from these; the third is another matter, not my province here, yet I do not mean to offend by leaving that facet in abeyance.

The overall picture of spiritual teachers is striking, even inspiring, yet we may feel some hesitation about some features. Spiritual teachers, who will not compromise what is important to them, sometimes give the impression that they would give up their lives to avoid the *slightest* falling short from their very highest ideals. I, on the other hand, would choose to give up my life to avoid sinking to the very *lowest* level—I certainly hope I would—perhaps also to avoid falling some considerable distance, but I would not, I think, do this simply to avoid the slightest falling from the very highest ideals. This might show how very flawed I am, but I think rather it shows that the uncompromising position of the spiritual teachers is too rigidly perfectionistic to be unreservedly admired, even as an ideal. A wise person, we think, will know when compromise is appropriate, just as he will know when it is not tolerable.

Even if we think spiritual teachers hold to their particular ideals excessively, and even when we do not so admire a particular ideal, still we may wish we had *some* ideal (we may not know which one) that we would stand behind almost as they do. Or more likely, perhaps we believe in the division of labor and are glad that *somebody* is adamantly standing by the highest ideals—somebody else.

Spiritual teachers shine as models *of* their singular value, but do they shine as models *for* us; are they exemplars not just of value but of *living*? For each of the four people we listed—Socrates, Buddha, Jesus, and Gandhi—a continuing life with family and children was nonexistent or lacking, to take one area. I am not saying simply that each of these figures was not perfect or had serious flaws. That may well be, but it would be unseemly to illustrate a rigid perfectionism even as we worry over that of spiritual teachers. In his book *Gandhi's Truth*, Erik Erikson describes how out of human frailties and neuroses of the usual and some unusual sorts, Gandhi was able to shape himself into something extraordinary; W. J. Bate pursues similar themes in his biography of Samuel Johnson. It is carping and unseemly to criticize spiritual teachers for being composed from our common human clay, and ignore the amazing shape and glaze they have managed to give it.

My point was a different one. It is relevant to examine the very positive ideal these teachers put forth and exemplify, to see if *it* is flawed. Was the fact that their lives lacked certain things of value a consequence of their ideals leaving no room for these things? And if some of these things are an important part of normal human life, a part we would not wish to sacrifice or give up, then the spiritual teachers need to be approached with caution as models for *our* lives.

While they are extremely real along *some* of the dimensions of reality, we might wonder whether a balanced life, including its trade-offs, does not have more contact with actuality—and also more reality—than does the spiritual teachers' intense one-sidedness.

George Orwell stated this reservation strongly in an essay on Gandhi: "It is too readily assumed that . . . the ordinary man only rejects [sainthood] because it is too difficult; in other words, that the average human being is a failed saint. It is doubtful whether this is true. Many human beings genuinely do not wish to be saints, and it is probable that some who achieve or aspire to sainthood have never felt much temptation to be human beings." This puts it with too much negative intonation, I think. Don't we feel *both* temptations fully and equally—to sainthood and to humanity?

A concern for the deepest reality, according to the usual conception, seems to remove a person from the ordinary world around us. For example, through focus on the divine, a person often seems removed from the fullest connection to anything lesser, to everyday affairs or to other people, to significant and high values that may not be the very deepest and highest. That cost is not one to be incurred lightly. Suppose, though, that there is no conscious reality with whom a person can connect deepest. Isn't the spiritual quest then vain and quixotic? Yet there would remain the beacons of humanity, having the personal qualities described earlier. It would be remarkable if these people could have become like that *without* having any contact with a deeper reality. This is not an argument for the existence of that deeper reality—remarkable does not mean impossible—and that deeper reality, if it existed, instead of being something external might be a part of themselves. Yet it would be an extraordinary human achievement to simulate contact with a deepest reality, to transparently show forth deeper reality without there actually being any—any, that is, other than that focused reality one has created and imaginatively realized. If there is no conscious deepest reality around with which to connect, still people can do *their* part magnificently. I do not mean to claim that for every kind of desirable situation, people are to act as though it actually exists. It would not be admirable if Robinson Crusoe, alone on an island, decided it would be better if another person were there and thereafter carried on conversations (although alone by himself), stayed away from some spots to give the other "person" privacy, etc. However, to be related to the deepest reality, in the sense we have described, is to embody and exhibit it, something one can do through one's *own* characteristics.

We do want to connect to the very highest and deepest reality—call that the seventh reality principle—but is that the *only* thing we should do? What about the rest of reality? A wider reality principle would call for being connected with and fully responsive to all of reality, not only the deepest or highest—call this the eighth reality principle. The problem is to state it in a plausible form that will avoid objections.

To be fully responsive to reality involves two things: the fullness of the response and the fullness of the reality responded to. And this last encompasses both responding to what is most real (that is, to the deepest and highest reality) and responding to all of reality.

The question is whether all this can be put together. Is it possible to respond with the fullest response to what is most real, the deepest and highest reality, and *also* to respond with the fullest response to the full extent of reality, including that reality which is less than the deepest? Life is short and our capacities are limited; it seems we must forgo something. In his *Ethics,* Aristotle faced an issue with a similar structure: Do we engage in the fullest development and exercise of our very highest capacity, or do we pursue a pattern of well-rounded development? Each seems to involve a significant sacrifice.

What would it be like to respond fully to all of reality, lesser as well as greater? One would not want to respond equally *extensively* to all parts by giving them equal time. That would involve too considerable a neglect of the highest and deepest parts. A better principle would involve responding to things proportionally to their reality. To see the structure of such a principle of proportionality, let us imagine more precision than we have available and suppose that the reality (or importance) of each thing can be measured. The proportionality principle could tell us to respond (in extent of time and attention) to any two things in a ratio that matches the ratio of their (degrees of) reality. This principle leaves us too scattered, however. There are just too many parts of reality that can be responded to for every bit to be given its proportional due. A response to the fullness of reality, though, does not require that every single bit be responded to, only that there be a response to the full *range,* proportional across the range.*

However, some have thought that the highest or deepest reality is infinite, infinitely real, while all other things have a reality that is finite—there is a gulf between the two. But then the ratios of the measures of their reality, infinite over finite, will be infinite as well. Since the infinite swamps the finite, even this principle of proportionality will end up requiring a total and exclusive response to the deepest reality. So it would not differ, although it appeared to, from a principle that explicitly and simply called for focusing only what is *most* real. Does paying due and proportional attention to things require ignoring everything else if some one thing is infinitely real or important? This difficulty can be met if we take account not just of the magnitude of the reality responded to, but also of how real the responses themselves are.

The proportionality principle called for responses that were proportional to the reality of the things responded to. The responses might be proportional to something else, however; that would be a different principle of proportionality. Responses differ not only in how extensive they are, in how much time, attention, and energy they take or are given, but also in how *intensive* they are. Variations in what is responded to will produce variations in the responses also, in how intense and real those responses are themselves. The intensity of attention we can bring to something is (in principle) not in short supply. But differing things might repay that attention differently, due in part to their own nature and in part to ours. Thus, our responses can vary in how much reality *they* have. Responses vary in intensiveness as well as in extensiveness. When principles are allocating our response or attention, what they allocate is the *extent* of it, how much time (and attention and energy) each thing receives. We can make that extent of response proportional not to the reality of the thing responded to (as the first principle did), but to the reality of the

---

* It could work like this: Consider groupings of things based upon rough equivalences in how real they are; a group would have in it things of (roughly) the same reality, differing in reality from what is in other groups. The principle of proportionality applies to the groups; it calls upon us to select at least one thing (but the same number) from each group and then respond to these things in proportion to how real they are. By paying proportional attention to each group, giving each proportional response, it appears that we connect and respond to the *full range* of reality, not to only the highest or deepest parts.

very response to that thing. This new principle of proportionality matches the extensiveness of the response to its intensiveness. The ratio of the extensiveness of two responses to reality is to match the ratio of the reality of these responses themselves, what we have been calling their intensiveness. Roughly put, time is to be given to things in proportion to how intensively they repay that time. (I here ignore the additional complications that ensue if the intensiveness of a response to reality is not uniform throughout but varies internally depending on how extensive it is.)

What this all means in the case of the deepest reality (or of God) is this: Although the deepest reality may be infinitely greater than any other reality—the ratio of the two realities is infinite—our response to it is not infinitely more real than all our other responses. No doubt this is due to our own limitations, regrettable ones but present nevertheless. If we pay attention and respond to things in proportion to how much they repay attention and response—as the second principle of proportionality recommends—then we will not pay exclusive attention to the very deepest reality. Its own nature may swamp all other realities, but our response to it will not swamp all other responses.

Yet the reality and intensiveness of our responses to given things are not rigidly fixed; they can change over time. Perhaps our responding in any degree to the deepest reality enlarges our capacity and so leads to further responding that is still more intensive and real. Under these conditions, the second principle would call for an increase in the extensiveness of response too. Clearly, this cycle (of "positive feedback") can continue. Eventually, then, the very deepest reality *may* receive a total and exclusive response, but only when we are ready.*

The first principle of proportionality says that the extent of responses should be in the same ratio as the reality of those things responded to. The second principle of proportionality says the extent of responses should be in the same ratio as the reality of these very

* The second principle of proportionality may seem too lax, though, in what it recommends for someone who is barely able to respond to the deepest reality. Doesn't it too easily allow him to pay negligible attention to that reality? Perhaps another factor needs to be introduced—not simply for this extreme case but in general—to shade the responses slightly (and somewhat disproportionately) *toward* the greater reality.

responses themselves. We should proportion and calibrate the extent of our responses to match the intensity and reality that those very responses would have. (Since the notion of extent is one of the dimensions of reality, or connected to several, the extent of a response also enters into assessing its total reality.) Each of these two principles is attractive (leaving aside the case of infinite reality), and when a person satisfies both of them together, a third principle also will be satisfied: the ratio of the reality of the responses to two things should be the same as the ratios of the reality of those things—that is, the reality of a response to something should be proportional to that thing's reality. We shall discuss this third principle of proportionality in a moment.*

* The first principle of proportionality was:

$$\frac{\text{extent of attention to A}}{\text{extent of attention to B}} = \frac{\text{reality of A}}{\text{reality of B}}$$

The second principle of proportionality was:

$$\frac{\text{extent of attention to A}}{\text{extent of attention to B}} = \frac{\text{reality of response to A}}{\text{reality of response to B}}$$

From these two principles together, the third follows:

$$\frac{\text{reality of response to A}}{\text{reality of response to B}} = \frac{\text{reality of A}}{\text{reality of B}}$$

If in the second principle the reality of our responses takes center stage and displaces the reality of what the responses are to, then why not maximize the sum total of the reality of these responses, allocating the extent of our responses accordingly? Such a maximization policy is not a principle of proportionality, but it is not necessary here to decide between these. Given the limitations in our capacities of responsiveness, this maximization principle and the second proportionality principle *both* have the consequence of producing responses to varied portions of reality, so either one avoids a focus only upon the deepest reality. How complex the issues are between this second proportionality principle and the maximization principle can be seen in behavioral psychologists' treatment of a structurally similar issue that involves matching or melioration principles versus maximization principles. See R. J. Herrnstein and W. Vaughan, Jr., "Stability, Melioration, and Natural Selection," in L. Green and J. H. Kagel, eds., *Advances in Behavioral Economics,* Vol. 1 (Norwood, N.J.: Ablex, 1987), pp. 185–215; R. J. Herrnstein, "A Behavioral Alternative to Utility Maximization," in S. Maital, ed., *Applied Behavioral Economics,* Vol. 1 (New York: New York University Press, 1988), pp. 3–60. One might keep to the proportionality form in the hope that over time, the intensity (and reality) of responses will thereby become better calibrated to the reality responded to, and so will become proportional to them. This second proportionality principle, then, would grow into the first as your own capacities of due response grew; matching extensiveness of response to intensiveness comes simultaneously to be a matching of extensiveness to the reality responded to.

If life is to be lived so as to be fully responsive to all of reality—this is the eighth reality principle—then the nature of this responding, taking account of our limitations of time, attention, and responsiveness, is specified by the second principle of proportionality. Not all of one's energies will be devoted exclusively to responding to the highest and deepest reality, because, for most of us as we currently are, doing that would not bring proportionally real responses; significant time and attention will be spent responding to varied portions of reality. In some views, however, there is no limit (in principle) to how real our responses can be to *any* portion of reality—recall the transcendentalists, the 613 varied Jewish commandments that are meant to raise and sanctify every portion of life they govern, and the Buddhist tradition, which brings a meditative attitude of complete attention and focus to all activities. It is not merely flaws in our responsiveness, then, that make attractive the second principle of proportionality and a focus upon all of reality.

We may want to be told more, though, than that we temporarily may focus upon less deep parts of reality because of flaws in our responsiveness or because these other things really are somehow deep and significant—namely, we may want to be told that it is perfectly all right to relax and focus upon the trivial and superficial portions of actuality. Yet even here we would want to acknowledge limits on how completely we may focus upon this and for how long. Still, to focus only upon the highest or deepest portion of reality is not to lead a fully *human* life; that involves other things, such as fun, adventure, excitement, relaxation. We prize these, in part, because of the ways they express or satisfy the many sides of our humanity (even though they too have their dimensions of reality).

The third principle of proportionality, formulated above, has the reality of responses proportioned to the reality of what they respond to. Such an overall pattern of proportionality will involve some *factor* of proportionality. A response, for example, can have half the reality of what it responds to, or two thirds or one tenth or five times that reality. The notion of proportionality applies to a group of responses together. Any one response, isolated all by itself, cannot fail to be proportional—that is, it will show *some* factor of proportionality or other. A group of responses, however, is proportional only if it exhibits (or to the extent that it exhibits) the very *same* factor of proportionality across the board, all of the responses, for example, having one third the reality of what they respond to. The only way for a factor of proportionality for an isolated response to be wrong, I think, is by being greater than 1. Responding to something with a greater reality than it has will be an overresponse, excessive, unless that response also can increase that thing's reality. (J. D. Salinger has described sentimentality as loving something more than God does.) That the world is abundantly rich means we cannot run out of things to respond to, even when the factor of proportionality stays below or equal to 1.

A pattern of proportionality has great abstract appeal, but when I think about details I worry about its adequacy. Disproportion occurs when one response's factor differs from the rest; all of the other responses have half the reality of what is responded to, for example, while this one response has two thirds. This does not mean, though, that one is to diminish that exceptional response next time rather than (to try) to increase the others. Perhaps the ideal pattern is to respond with a factor of 1 uniformly, bringing all one's responses up to that level; but while we cannot enlarge our own capacities to *that* great an extent, we can move to higher and higher proportions. Yet must that movement be in lockstep? Spurting ahead in one response's proportionality factor might increase our ability later to raise the other responses' factors too.

Even while granting that overall proportionality is desirable, still we sometimes might want to move vastly ahead in some responses by bringing their factor closer to 1 (even when that will not serve to raise other responses). This will be especially so in two cases: first, where something's reality is particularly high—another person or a work of art or divinity—and so therefore can our response be in its magnitude, and second, where the reality of something is extremely low, so that without any great effort one can match its reality completely (with a factor of 1). The especially unseemly disproportions are different; they involve responding with a very high factor of proportionality (yet still considerably less than 1) to things whose degree of reality lies in the middle range, while also responding with a much lower factor to things having much greater reality.

This seems most objectionable when the proportionality factors differ so greatly that the less real thing is responded to with a greater absolute amount (and not merely proportion) than the more real, something that may be especially clear when both things are of the same kind or genre. Yet nevertheless we do not find objectionable the extremely intense response of the artist to the apparently small—the meditation of Wallace Stevens on a glass jar, the still lifes of Chardin—although it is perhaps important that the scale of these works also is kept small. Here we think the artist is responding to almost *all* the reality there is in his subject, with a factor close to 1; from this we learn about its immense and unsuspected reality, and also perhaps, therefore, by extrapolation, we conclude that further things, heretofore responded to less fully, have a vastly greater reality also. (By the depth of reality they can find in the apparently insignificant, do these works show instead that the reality of everything is equal? This would fit our earlier observation of each thing in its own patient entityhood, waiting there.) Since it is important to respond fully (with factor 1) to *something* of some significant degree of reality—Rilke tells us in the seventh Duino Elegy that "one earthly thing, truly experienced, even once, is enough for a lifetime"—the only disproportion that is objectionable, then, may simply be one that stems from a mistaken estimate of the relative realities, one that purports (falsely) to be proportionate. What would be important then would be knowing the truth; an individual disproportional response would be all right if accompanied by the right estimate. However, this discordance cannot be too general, for we must live the right estimates too, not just say them. Still, there is leeway for people to exercise their own judgment about the respective weights to be given to proportionality and to increasing the fullness of some particular responses.

In writing about proportionality in these pages, I sometimes have felt myself *forcing* things into that structure.* To say we should

---

* *Some* of the earlier difficulties are avoided by a technical expedient that I recommend most readers skip over. Instead of proportioning our responses to their reality, we can maximize the *primary bulk* of the reality of our responses. (This notion of the bulk of a curve was explained in the meditation on Being More Real.) In a bar graph of responses, the height (along the y-axis) represents the reality of the response, the width along the x-axis the weight assigned to the response. One procedure would be to assign equal weight (hence equal width) to each response—all responses are created equal. Maximizing the bulk of the responses' reality, as defined by this procedure, would allow varied responses, not necessarily propor-

live proportionally and give everything its due *seems* like an acceptable principle—indeed, it sounds as though wisdom would require that. Wisdom itself is supposed to give everything its due, to appreciate it, understand it, know its value, meaning, and more generally, its contour along each of the dimensions of reality. Does that mean our *lives* are supposed to do that also? This question sounds as though it asks whether we are supposed to live wisely, so it seems the answer *must* be yes. Yet suppose that it would be better to live disproportionally, putting most of our attention into only a few activities and channels. Wisdom then would give *that* mode of living its due, and would recommend living that way. Wisdom would not, however, follow that advice itself and thereupon give some things less than their due, for wisdom's task is something different than to live a life. To be sure, wisdom *is* supposed to guide a life, but a life so guided need not necessarily duplicate the wisdom's full panoply. A life can do what wisdom says without saying everything wisdom does.

It is so difficult to give *anything* its due; how can we be expected to give this to everything? Perhaps what something is due is a full response from our full being, one whose reality fully matches the reality of that thing, so the proportionality factor is 1. We cannot do this for everything, and it is not obviously better to hold back any

---

tional, while avoiding our having to respond only to the deepest or highest reality—the original difficulty that launched us upon the proportionality path. Another procedure would give different weights to different responses—the bar graphs would differ in width. One appealing thought is to weight the responses exactly according to the reality of what they are responses to. The height of the bar would represent the reality of the response, its width the reality of what it responds to, and the total area this response is graphed as encompassing would be the product of these two. Our very first principle of proportionality, we recall, sought to proportion responses to the reality to which they respond. However, this reintroduced the original difficulty; if any one thing had infinite reality, then *all* responses would have to be directed toward it. The current proposal too faces a difficulty if something has infinite reality. The graph of a response to it will be infinitely wide, hence (when the height of the response is greater than infinitesimal) include an infinite area, hence no responses to other things (and even no larger response to it) could count positively since they could not add to the total of the area under the curve or to its bulk. This particular differential weighting still is worth investigating, though, for the finite cases. Meanwhile, notice that the first procedure, where each response gets equal weight and width, does not fall before the infinite case, for the height of the response along the y-axis will be *its* reality, not the reality of what it responds to; the total area of that bar therefore will remain finite.

response, already inadequate, in order to make other inadequate ones somewhat less so.

I think that what is important is to offer responses as something *due*, to respond to things as homages to their reality. What would matter, then, would be not the quantity of our response, even the quantity (or bulk) of the response's reality, but the manner of the response, the spirit in which it is done. Speaking of what is "due" may make it seem like a debt owed, though, or an obligation, whereas I mean something more like applause. Or an offering. Or, perhaps, more like love. To love the world and to live within it in the mode this involves gives the world our fullest response in a spirit that joins it.* The fullness of *this* response enlarges us, too; people encompass what they love—it becomes part of them as its well-being becomes partly theirs. The size of a soul, the magnitude of a person, is measured in part by the extent of what that person can appreciate and love.

To give the world this response, and live in it this way, would not require proportional attention, however. The person who does lead a fully balanced life might therefore be seen as doing this: giving the *relative proportions* of reality among all things *their* due. That, though, is just one thing to which due can be given. Yet I also want to say that over a lifetime everything important should receive some significant weight and attention, even if not in any exact proportion, and even if some receive it only in vicarious activity. But perhaps my wanting to say this is simply my own way of offering what is due.

---

* In principle, can the degree to which a response embodies a particular manner or spirit itself be measured, so that another quantitative criterion emerges? But a focus upon maximizing that total quantity will detract from the manner and spirit of the particular action, and adhering to such a policy oneself also might not show that spirit toward one's own reality.

23

What Is Wisdom and Why Do Philosophers Love It So?

PHILOSOPHY means the love of wisdom. What is wisdom? How shall it be loved? Wisdom is an understanding of what is important, where this understanding informs a (wise) person's thought and action. Things of lesser importance are kept in proper perspective. Wisdom's understanding is a special one, special in three ways: in the topics it concerns—the issues of life; in its special value for living; and in its not being universally shared. Something that everyone knew might be important but would not count as wisdom.

Wisdom is practical; it helps. *Wisdom is what you need to understand in order to live well and cope with the central problems and avoid the dangers in the predicament(s) human beings find themselves in.**

---

* Complications could be added to this rough general description by ringing variations on each of its component notions. Is wisdom what you need to know or understand, or what it is important or necessary or very useful to understand? Does wisdom also include knowing how to come to know or understand it? Is it needed in order to live well, or best, or successfully, or happily, or satisfactorily, or as we are supposed to, or whatever the most important goal is, including

This general account is designed to fit different particular conceptions of wisdom. These conceptions may differ in the goals (or dangers) they list or how they rank them, the coping devices they recommend, and so on, but what makes them all conceptions of wisdom, even when they differ in their content, is that all fit this general form. They fill in the schema: what you need to know in order to live well and cope. . . . Yet while this schema encompasses differing conceptions of wisdom, it is not empty. Not everything in the world fits it. (Sour cream does not.) Indeed, it might be thought that in specifying that wisdom is a kind of understanding or knowledge, the schema is unduly narrow. Couldn't some imaginable view hold that the best life is one lived without any knowledge or understanding at all? Perhaps so, but though that *view* might (if it were correct) itself contain wisdom, it would not be recommending a *life* that contained wisdom, whatever its other virtues. The point can be generalized. If wisdom is something specific that a person can have, we can imagine a view that maintains that the best life is one without that specific thing. So someone might object to any account of wisdom as arbitrarily excluding certain lives as best, those without that thing that has gotten specified as wisdom. This objection would be mistaken, however; the account itself will not exclude certain lives as best, only as being wise. It is theoretically possible, of course, for wisdom to describe the best or highest life without itself being any part of it. However, it is my assumption here that wisdom will be conducive to the best life as a means and also be some integral part of it. Any account of wisdom that was incompatible with its having this double role would be defective, I think. If wisdom is a certain kind of knowledge or understanding, we are committed then to valuing that kind of knowledge and to saying the best or highest life itself contains at least some of it. To what extent, and

---

perhaps achieving *satori* or the best existence in an afterlife? Is it the central problems that are to be coped with or also the dilemmas or issues or tragedies of life? Does it avoid the dangers or sometimes only diminish them? Does it sometimes tell how to escape from the human predicament completely? And so on. The simple description in the text will serve us well enough, though. An even fuller discussion would take account of the fact that wisdom comes in degrees; a person can be more or less wise. It is not a question simply of being wise or not.

in what form, that knowledge is held is not decided by wisdom's general description.

Wisdom is not just knowing fundamental truths, if these are unconnected with the guidance of life or with a perspective on its meaning. If the deep truths physicists describe about the origin and functioning of the universe have little practical import and do not change our picture of the meaning of the universe and our place within it, then knowing them would not count as wisdom. (However, a view that traced the origin and continuance of the universe to a divine being's plans could count that knowledge as wisdom if it yielded conclusions about the purpose and most appropriate mode of human life.)

Wisdom is not just one type of knowledge, but diverse. What a wise person needs to know and understand constitutes a varied list: the most important goals and values of life—the ultimate goal, if there is one; what means will reach these goals without too great a cost; what kinds of dangers threaten the achieving of these goals; how to recognize and avoid or minimize these dangers; what different types of human beings are like in their actions and motives (as this presents dangers or opportunities); what is not possible or feasible to achieve (or avoid); how to tell what is appropriate when; knowing when certain goals are sufficiently achieved; what limitations are unavoidable and how to accept them; how to improve oneself and one's relationships with others or society; knowing what the true and unapparent value of various things is; when to take a long-term view; knowing the variety and obduracy of facts, institutions, and human nature; understanding what one's own real motives are; how to cope and deal with the major tragedies and dilemmas of life, and with the major good things too. There also will be bits of negative wisdom: certain things are *not* important, other things not effective means, etc. Any good collection of aphorisms will contain this and more, mixed among its witty cynicisms.

Perhaps the diversity of wisdom is only apparent and it all can flow from some one central understanding, but this should not be assumed or stipulated at the outset. Would someone who understood the one truth from which all of wisdom flowed be wiser than someone who lived and advised similarly yet grasped only the diversity? The first would see more deeply, but, if the theoretical unification could make no practical difference, it is not clear he would be wiser.*

A wise person knows these diverse things and lives them. Someone who only knew them, who offered good advice to others yet who lived foolishly himself, would not be termed wise. We might voice the suspicion that this person would not know at least one thing—namely, how to apply the rest of what he knew. Is it strictly impossible, though, that he did know how to apply the rest of his knowledge, he just did not *do* so? One can know how to swim without going swimming. However we answer this question, to *be* wise, a person not only must *have* knowledge and understanding—have wisdom, if you will—but also use it and live it. That does not mean, though, that in addition to her understanding and know-how the wise person must possess something else that in combination with these then applies the understanding to produce a life in accordance with it. Perhaps being wise just is living a certain way *because* of the understanding and know-how one has; there need be no additional *third* factor that both is part of wisdom and gets from the understanding and know-how to the living of it.

Wisdom does not guarantee success in achieving life's important goals, however, just as a high probability does not guarantee truth. The world must cooperate, too. A wise person will have gone in the right direction, and, if the world thwarts his journey, he will have known how to respond to that too.

For no very good reason, the notion of wisdom seems to find a more congenial place for constraints on feasibility than it does for expansion. Attending to the limits of what is feasible includes knowing three things: first, the negative aspects of the best alternative that is available; second, the value of the next best alternative which has to be forgone or given up in order to do the best—economists

* Whether or not the different components of wisdom are derivable from one single truth, one might try to see them as aspects of one coherent intellectual structure: for example, something analogous to the economists' diagram wherein a person moves to the highest indifference curve bounded by the budget constraints, which contains an ordering of preference or value, including tradeoffs, a knowledge of the limits of what is feasible, and a principle of choice. Other of wisdom's components too might be congenial to structuring within an economic mode of thought (such as the costs of action, level of aspiration, knowledge of alternative actions). However, I do not know of any one integrated structure that illuminatingly includes all the pieces of wisdom.

call this "the opportunity cost"; and third, the limits on possibility themselves, which exclude certain alternatives as possible or feasible objects of choice. In *Civilization and Its Discontents,* for example, Freud lists among the negative aspects of civilization the suppression of the free exercise of sexual and aggressive instincts, holding that this is the unavoidable price for civilization's benefits. The combination of the benefits of civilization without the negative aspects is *not* within the feasibility space.

Wisdom's special penchant for limits seems arbitrarily to favor conservatives over radicals. Pointing to an important and unappreciated constraint can constitute an important piece of wisdom, but why more so than pointing to an important possibility that had mistakenly been thought not to be possible? Why is contracting the domain of feasibility any wiser than expanding it? Those who speak of the limits to economic growth, if they are right, speak wisdom. Another author, Julian Simon, in his book *The Ultimate Resource,* argues that the actual limits are much farther back: the amount of each resource within the physical ball we inhabit, the earth, is vastly greater than the quantities others list as absolute limits, and new technologies can be developed to extract these; exhaustion would come many many centuries hence, long after space flight would make massive migration possible. (I myself am *not* recommending pillaging the earth and then abandoning it! Nor, I assume—except for his thought experiment to show how far back are the physical limits of feasibility—is Simon.) If Simon is right, this too should count as a piece of wisdom, saving us from much unnecessary constriction. If utopian theorists of society are right about how very harmoniously we could live together, that too would be wisdom. There is no reason why wisdom should asymmetrically favor the dour view. Even if some general argument showed that there had been more cost to humanity from mistaken attempts to do the impossible than from mistaken neglecting of what was possible, this would recommend paying special attention to cautions, but not stopping our welcoming of new possibilities.

The notion of wisdom I have described is human-centered; it focuses on what is important in human living. Yet things other than people can have well-being; this includes animals, extraterrestrial rational beings, and perhaps such things as economies, ecological systems, societies and civilizations, plants, and some inanimate physical objects too—books, records, clothing, chairs, rivers . . . A more general and generous view of wisdom might therefore see it as knowing each and every thing's well-being, what the dangers are to each thing's well-being, and how these can and should be coped with. (Since portions of ethics are concerned with conflicts among different people's well-being, or people's versus other kinds of well-being, in knowing how these conflicts are to be coped with or resolved, wisdom would encompass those portions of ethics.) A more limited wisdom would be about a particular thing or kind; it would involve knowing *its* well-being, the dangers to it, etc., and such wisdom sometimes is found in particular roles or occupations. Yet a person would not be wise in general who did not know how extensively the notion of well-being applied; he might mistakenly think some particular things did not have any well-being at all, and therefore that there could not be any wisdom about that kind of thing. He would be wise only about people, and even here his wisdom would be limited. In not being able to specify how people should respond to the other things' well-being, he would not be able to specify an appropriate part of human relation to reality—and *that* is part of *human* well-being. Even his wisdom about humans, therefore, would be only partial.

Wisdom can be partial also in the part of human life it is concerned with, as when people are (said to be) wise about specialized areas, one about economic matters, another about foreign affairs, another about raising children, another about waging warfare, another about pursuing an occupation successfully. Common to all these would be their fitting the general notion of *wisdom about* something, in the sense of knowing what is important about it, how to avoid dangers concerning it, etc.; the differences would be in what somethings the wisdom was about. In different social situations or emergencies, we might especially need different portions of wisdom, hence give these portions differing weights. Is there any one kind of thing, then, that constitutes wisdom about life? That last wisdom is not simply a weighting of all the different particular specialized kinds of wisdom. Rather, it is a wisdom about what is common to all of our lives, about what (we judge) it is important for any normal human life to be concerned with. And it is that which we mean when we speak (simply) of wisdom (period), without specifying any special area the wisdom is about; it is that sense which enables us to say of someone, for instance, that although he may have been wise about business matters he was not a wise person.

Socrates, reputed by the oracle to be the only wise person in Athens, explained this surprising pronouncement by saying that unlike all the others who thought they were wise, he knew he was *not*. He also tried to spread this kind of knowledge to others! Frequently engaging them in conversations about some important notion of common human concern, such as piety or friendship or justice or the good, he led them to contradict themselves or to confess confusion finally. They were unable to define these important notions, to offer an explicit account that applied to all the cases where the intuitive notion applied correctly, and only to those cases, delineating that notion from other ones close by. Socrates concluded from this that they didn't know what piety or justice or friendship was. But does this follow simply from the inability to define or explain the notion? We know what grammatical sentences are without being able, unless we are linguistic theorists, to define the notion of "a grammatical sentence" and correctly delineate the full set of grammatical rules that specify this. We can recognize and reliably produce grammatical sentences and distinguish ungrammatical ones, all by "ear." Similarly, a companion of Socrates could know what friendships were, maintain them, recognize a betrayal of one when he came across it, offer advice to someone about difficulties in friendship, all without being able to define correctly the general notion of friendship.

The knowledge wisdom involves also may be something one can possess without being able to expound explicitly. To be wise, it is not necessary to be able to pass the severe test of being grilled by Socrates, either on the general notion of wisdom or on the particular things one is wise about. This is not to deny that such explicit knowledge and understanding can be valuable and satisfying. Explicit knowledge also might be of help in coping with difficult situations or in teaching someone else some wisdom, yet a particular wise person also might teach by his or her own example or by invoking an appropriate proverb or platitude—knowing which one to invoke when. (The philosopher, however, is someone who is beset by the temptation to say everything explicitly.)

What thing is it, then, that a wise person will deem *most* important? It is tempting to answer (or to sidestep the issue by saying) that what matters most, the supreme good, is wisdom itself. Its importance as a means is clear; you are far more likely to live rightly if you know what is important and valuable, and also know the dangers and hazards of life and how to cope with them. But even as a means to other good things, wisdom is not strictly necessary. Someone might happen luckily to be pointed toward the important goals, perhaps by social conditioning, without fully understanding their nature and importance; and his own circumstances might be so fortunate that these goals are attained easily without any navigating through dangerous shoals. That lucky person would, through no virtue of his own, gain many particular goods. He would not, however, be living wisely; he would not be exercising his own knowledge and intelligence to shape his life and himself.

What is involved in philosophy's loving wisdom? Of course, it recommends living wisely, seeking more wisdom, esteeming it in others; it holds that wisdom has intrinsic, not merely instrumental, value, and it ranks wisdom highly. But when philosophy loves wisdom, does it love it above all else? Above happiness and above enlightenment? Philosophers frequently have wanted to say that it is wisdom that can bring the greatest happiness, and even that wisdom guarantees this. (Hence the ancients' frequent discussions of the difficult situation of the wise person who is being tortured; see, for example, Cicero's Fifth Tusculan Disputation.) Perhaps they insist wisdom must bring the greatest happiness because they worry that wisdom will be neglected if the two diverge. This neglect would not occur, however, if the goods were ranked in the following order: first, wisdom conjoined with happiness; second, wisdom without happiness; third, happiness without wisdom; and fourth, neither happiness nor wisdom. Add to that the strong tendency of wisdom to produce happiness, and the first becomes more likely than the second. (And since the lack of wisdom often leads eventually to great unhappiness, the third is less likely than may appear.) Wisdom's tendency to produce happiness is due to two things. First, and most obviously, one of its concerns may be how to gain happiness. Second, since wisdom is extremely valuable in itself, possessing it and recognizing that fact will by itself produce deep happiness (unless this is overridden by torture or other such factors).

When the philosopher loves wisdom, like other lovers, does he too magnify the virtues of his loved one? (And which does a philosopher really love more, wisdom or the loving of wisdom?) When he sings the praises of wisdom and his love of it, is the proper response—as with all happy lovers who pronounce their love fairest of them all—to smile indulgently?

In any case, will not a wisdom which knows the limits of everything also know its own; won't a wisdom which sees everything in proper perspective see itself in perspective too; won't a wisdom which lauds self-knowledge know itself? If something else is more important than wisdom, then wisdom, knowing what is important, should be able to tell us that. There is nothing inconsistent in wisdom's concluding that something else is more important. Nor would the ability to discern that thereby make wisdom most important; a road sign that points to a city is not more important than the city. (Plato used to ask how the lesser could judge the greater; however, it certainly can know enough to recognize the greater as greater.) If wisdom sees something else as more important, to gain more of that thing it may even recommend sacrificing some wisdom or opportunities for it. One level up, then, wisdom would rule supreme. However, even that act of ruling does not make it most important. The Supreme Court ultimately has the power to judge everything else, but this does not make it the most important organ in government; and if political officials hold (legitimate) power over all other activities in the society, this does not make holding and exercising power the society's most important and valuable activity.

It is part of wisdom to understand what things are most important in life and to guide one's life by that; we cannot short-circuit that understanding by announcing simply that the very most important thing is wisdom itself. Yet we can produce reasons for valuing wisdom greatly. One of the most important goods of life, Aristotle held, is internal to living life: being someone with the capacity and tendency to live rightly in a wide range of circumstances, and living by the skillful and wise exercise of that capacity. Wisdom and its exercise also can be an important component of the self, which gains articulation in applying and developing wisdom. Hence, wisdom is not simply an important means to *other* ends but itself is one important end, an intrinsic component of one's life and self.

Moreover, the process of living wisely, pursuing or opening

oneself to what is important, taking account of a range of circumstances and utilizing one's fullest capacities to steer skillfully through them, is itself a way of being deeply connected to reality. The person who lives wisely connects to reality more thoroughly than someone who moves through life spoon-fed by circumstances, even if what these try to feed is reality. Whether or not he proportionally pursues the full range of reality, he is aware of that range; he knows and appreciates reality's many dimensions and sees the life he is living in that widest context. Such seeing itself is a mode of connection. Living wisely, then, is not just our means of connecting most closely to reality, it also is our way. (This is the central thing I want to say about wisdom.)

Wisdom is not simply knowing how to steer one's way through life, cope with difficulties etc. It also is knowing the *deepest* story, being able to see and appreciate the deepest significance of whatever occurs; this includes appreciating the ramifications of each thing or event for the various dimensions of reality, knowing and understanding not merely the proximate goods but the ultimate ones, and seeing the world in this light. This it is that the philosopher loves, and *its* claim to preeminence is less easily dismissed.

Nevertheless, the principles of wisdom that have been explicitly formulated within the Western tradition, when they are general enough to be widely applicable, are not precise enough to decide by themselves difficult life choices or resolve particular dilemmas. This includes Aristotle's principle of choosing the mean between extremes (which one interpretation sees as recommending responses and emotions that are proportional to the situation—that is, *fitting* ones), Socrates's dictum that the unexamined life is not worth living, and Hillel's statement "If I am not for myself, who will be? And if I am only for myself, what am I? And if not now, when?" When principles of wisdom do specify general types of goals and goods (and recommend general ways of combining them), the guidance they offer is no substitute for judgment and maturity. Nevertheless, such principles can be illuminating; even a simple list of what to take account of in life can be helpful, even when *how* to take account of them is not specified.

Yet why cannot general principles be formulated to apply to each and every situation that yet are precise enough to specify particular courses of action to be followed in them? It is not enough here to quote Aristotle's dictum that we should not expect more precision than the subject matter admits. (Many writers on many topics since Aristotle have comforted themselves by citing these words, but perhaps only his extraordinarily powerful mind was entitled to confidence about where the limits of precision are located.) Why doesn't the subject of life admit of a more exact understanding? To reply that life itself is fuzzy or vague is no explanation, for, insofar as we can understand that statement, it seems merely to restate the fact to be explained.

I'm not sure of the answer, but there is an analogy to scientific knowledge that seems helpful. One might think that in science a hypothesis can be established or refuted by isolated data (for the time being, at any rate, until new data comes along). However, recent theorists, following Pierre Duhem and W. V. Quine, have emphasized the extent to which the body of scientific knowledge forms an interconnected web, where particular data can be accommodated or discounted depending upon what particular other hypotheses or theories one is willing to adopt or modify. Whether to reject a particular hypothesis, or instead to accept it but make theoretical modifications elsewhere to accommodate apparently conflicting data, depends upon how good the resulting overall theories would be. This would be determined by some measure of the overall goodness of a theory, compared to that of competing theories, taking account of its fit to the data and to the ongoing problem situation, its explanatory power, simplicity, theoretical fruitfulness, and coherence with an existing body of accepted knowledge. Thus far no adequate overall rule has been formulated to incorporate and balance each of the partial evaluative factors thought relevant: In making the overall scientific assessment we must use our intuitive judgment in balancing the diverse subcriteria. (Have we simply not yet found the adequate rule, or is it impossible in principle or beyond our limited intelligence?) But even if one could be formulated, it would assess the overall character of a large theory and therefore would apply only indirectly to a decision about a particular hypothesis, and then only after a long chain of reasoning had taken account of the different possibilities for all the other parts too. That a painting is to be of a horse does not determine what color pigment is to be applied at a particular point on the canvas. Moreover, even if an overall criterion in fact determined some particular result—in that no other result actually would be compatible with the criterion—there need be no guarantee that in a given fixed number of steps or amount of time we could apply the criterion to find out which result that was.

About a life too, with its many aspects, domains, portions, and interconnections, perhaps only an overall criterion can be offered—for example, that it is to be contoured somehow to enhance its, and our, relating to reality. There are diverse subcriteria (the various dimensions of reality) that an overall assessment must balance and in this we must use our intuitive judgment; no explicit rule exists to perform that task. The individual is to adapt her life to the overall criterion, but how that is best done will depend upon her characteristics, her current and future opportunities, how she has lived thus far, and the situation of others, as well as on her overall balancing of the subcriteria. Wisdom about life too, as does scientific knowledge, takes a holistic form. There is no formula to learn and apply.

Completely balanced and proportional judgment might inhibit youth's forceful pursuit of partial enthusiasms and great ambitions, through which they are led to intense experiences and large accomplishments. Even an older person with balance need not stay always on the Aristotelian mean; she may follow a zigzag path, now moving with an excessive enthusiasm in this direction, later counterbalancing it with another in the opposite. Her balance may be shown in the direction of the central tendency, and also by the fact that the deviations are not too great for too long and leave no lasting ill effects. Her ability to soon right herself gives the ongoing pattern over time balance, yet in a way that allows and expresses some of youth's romance and passionate excess. Wisdom need not be geriatric.

24

The Ideal and the Actual

A WISE IDEAL will take account of the way it will get followed. Often an actual situation is described as a *corruption* of the ideal it purports to follow, and different people have said of communism, capitalism, and Christianity each that "it is a good idea that never has been tried." (Couldn't one say, instead, "It's a good idea; too bad it's been tried"? Each of these systems has its critics also, who hold that it is not desirable even as an ideal.) Yet if time after time an ideal gets institutionalized and operates in the world a certain way, then *that* is what it comes to in the world. It is not allowed then simply to disclaim responsibility for what repeatedly occurs under its banner.

I recall reading about the testing of a new antiaircraft gun during the Second World War. It worked very well in tests, hitting many planes, yet when it was manufactured and distributed to troops, it failed to perform successfully. The unit that had operated it in the tests was extremely skilled, alert, dexterous, intelligent, cooperative, motivated. The weapon was complex, highly delicate, its accuracy sensitive to precise details about its firing. When ordinary gun crews used it under the usual field conditions, *they* could not get it to do its job. In some sense, perhaps, it was an ideal gun, but what it came to in this world, operated in significant numbers by the people here, was an inefficient weapon, a disaster.

The capitalist ideal of free and voluntary exchange, producers competing to serve consumer needs in the market, individuals following their own bent without outside coercive interference, nations relating as cooperating parties in trade, each individual receiving what others who have earned it choose to bestow for service, no sacrifice imposed on some by others, has been coupled with and provided a cover for other things: international predation, companies bribing governments abroad or at home for special privileges which enable them to avoid competition and exploit their specially granted position, the propping up of autocratic regimes—ones often based upon torture—that countenance this delimited private market, wars for the gaining of resources or market territories, the domination of workers by supervisors or employers, companies keeping secret some injurious effects of their products or manufacturing processes, etc. This is the underside of the capitalist ideal as it actually operates. It is not the *whole* of the story about this ideal; there also is very extensive free and voluntary production and trade, individual earning, and so on. But it *is* part of that story.

The communist ideal of freely cooperating people living equally in a society without class distinctions or special privileges, jointly controlling the conditions of their labor and social life together, no one left in need, none able to live well without laboring productively, has been coupled with and provided a cover for other things: great inequalities of income and privilege for political functionaries, coercive threats to maintain labor discipline, the absence of labor organizations independent of the government, the absence of a political system with parties competing for power, no rights of free speech maintained, extensive censorship, control of the arts, slave labor camps, organized systems of informers, brutal and autocratic rule, a state that sees no part of the society as private or immune to its actions. This is not the *whole* story about the communist ideal as it actually operates in the world, but it *is* part of that story.

The Christian ideal of loving one's neighbor and loving one's enemy, nonviolence, serving the poor and suffering, redemption and salvation through the descent of God to earth, sharing together in a community of faith, has been coupled with inquisitions to root out those whose faith deviates or to impose the faith on those who do not choose it, averting the gaze from (when not blessing) the monstrous crimes of those in power, conquest in the name of bringing the doctrine to the benighted, following in the wake of colonial influence, opulent and satisfied status as an official and dominant ceremonial religion in the West. This is not the *whole* story about the Christian ideal as it actually operates in the world, but it *is* part of that story.

Nationalism, too, has its ideal of love of country and its traditions and possibilities: attachment to one's fellows, pride in the country's accomplishments, helping to make it especially good, preserving it against aggressive threats. Perhaps these attachments could be quite harmless—a beneficial kind of family feeling writ large—yet in practice nationalism in power is strident, antagonistic to other nationalisms, territorily expansive, willing to believe the worst of others or to transform them into "enemies," bellicose, aggressive, inuring its citizens to the committing of atrocities, justifying the most fervent pursuit of warfare. This is not the whole story about how the nationalistic ideal operates in the world, but it *is* part of that story.

Is it our own human nature that renders us incapable of realizing these ideals? Issues about innate human nature have tended to be discussed in terms of what traits or features are *unalterable*—for example, are people ineradicably possessive and self- and family-centered or (this seems to be the implicit alternative) is socialism possible? It seems more fruitful to consider how much energy society would have to expend to alter or diminish certain traits and how much energy to maintain modes of cultural socialization that would avoid these traits. Innate human nature is best conceived not as a set of fixed outcomes but as a gradient of difficulty: here is how steep the price is for avoiding certain traits. So while human nature may not render certain social arrangements impossible, it may make them difficult to achieve and maintain.

The temptation is to say simply that none of the actual results listed was intended by the originators or founders of these ideals, that capitalism's underside is not true capitalism at all but government intervention or private abuses, that communism's underside is not true communism but primitive power lust, that Christianity's underside is not true Christianity but institutionalized hypocrisy, that nationalism's underside is chauvinism and jingoism instead. But this reply will not do. That is how those ideals operate, over and over again, in this world, on this planet, when we are the ones who do the operating. That is what they come to, what we make them come to.

It is not all they come to, however. Aspects of the ideals sometimes are realized; institutionalization does not undercut them completely. And the ideals encompass more than what actually occurs. When we consider them, we tend to think of how they would work out if operated on a large scale as intended, and *that* picture may be attractive and alluring. The content of an ideal is not exhausted by how we actually manage to work it; it also includes its realization by better people than we are. We can think of each ideal as a group of situations: first, the actual situation regularly produced by those who operate it, second, the situation where it is operated as intended by people suitable for operating it—call that "the ideal situation"—and third and afterward, the various situations in between. (Should we also include in the range encompassed by the ideal some situations that are worse even than the actual one?)

In thinking of the ideal *qua* ideal, we tend to think only of the second situation, the "ideal one." This is a mistake. Yet it would be misleading to think instead only of the first situation, the actual way the ideal continues to operate. That also is one-sided. However, thinking neutrally of the ideal just as all the ways together is too undiscriminating. (It is in this way that semantic theory thinks of a concept, specifying it by its reference in all possible worlds, a mapping from each of the possible worlds to objects.) The situations have different importance in the total concept, so in our conception of the ideal we can give these situations different weights. It seems appropriate that the actual situation count at least for half, for this is the long-term way the institutionalized ideal operates time and again. What always actually happens is at least half of what the ideal comes to.

It is not the whole of it, though, as I have already said. For ideals will pull us in a certain direction, thereby affecting the future actuality. And it is inspiring to have an admirable ideal, even when we are falling short of it. It can be illuminating to see the world in its light, and we might even be willing to be in a slightly worse actual situation when that situation basks in the glow of a considerably better ideal one. So I do not say we would be better off without these ideals. The counterfactual is unclear, anyway; would we instead have different ideals or no ideals at all? In either case, it is doubtful that we would behave better, or that we would feel any better about ourselves. Should the fact that we can formulate ideals better than we together are able consistently to behave occasion shame or pride? Both I think. (But in which proportions?)

When we attempt to follow a philosophical ideal, we associate our lives with how that ideal would have worked out in other and better worlds. As integrated philosophy is not simply some arbitrary mapping of possible worlds onto lives; and through its integration it can associate those other possible lives that would fit it perfectly with our own lives here, in a way that adds richness of reverberation to ours. Due to similar considerations, a person can wish to be rational or wise even if the actual world might thwart its intended results, because of that ideal's associations and spread in other possible worlds. Exemplifying an ideal here, we overflow elsewhere. Thus, following an ideal performs some of the functions of immortality, not in time but through possibility, enlarging our lives so that they are not wholly contained in the actual world.

We can think of an ideal, for most purposes, as consisting of the ideal and the actual in equal measure: how it actually does work out, consistently and repeatedly, when operated by human beings as we are; and how it works out "ideally" when operated by beings (better than we) who are best suited for carrying it through. This balanced view of ideals as including both components equally will seem deflationary to those who tend to ignore how an ideal actually gets implemented, and inflationary to those who notice only that. I mean it to be both.

In comparing two ideals, we have to judge the first's actual situation against the second's, and the first's "ideal situation" against the other's. It would be unfair to judge another actuality against your ideal—that is, to judge how another ideal actually works out against how your ideal *ideally* does. It would be nice if one ideal topped all others on all counts, if its ideal situation looked most attractive and its actual one worked out best. The situation is more difficult and more interesting if there is no such victory across the board, and in particular, if one ideal has a superior "ideal situation" to a second, while the second one actually and constantly works out better. Perhaps we live at a historical time when communism's "ideal situation" has very great appeal to many around the world, while how capitalism actually works out, flaws included, is greatly better. That is an unstable situation, one of great "cognitive dissonance," and the temptation to certain denials will be very great. It is quite difficult to resist the allure of the "ideal situation," to avoid hoping and believing that things will manage to work out better this next time. If different people consistently gave these two of the concept's factors, the ideal and the actual, differing weights—for example, one person weighting them equally while another weighted the ideal factor as three times the actual—it would not be surprising if their disagreements were fervent.

Is it a defect of an ideal that its ideal situation and actual implementation diverge greatly? But although a modified or different ideal might get carried out more faithfully, that might not move people as far from their previous situation as the first one, in whose fitful pursuit they fall far short. A theory of the optimal formulation of ideals would consider ideals as practical tools for maximum movement, and specify the features they should possess, given human beings as they are (and as they would be changed in operating that ideal). An ideal (whose envisioned end is desirable) is defective not if we always fall short of it but if another ideal actually would move us further in that direction (though that second ideal might be one we would fall even more short of).

Freudianism and Marxism often are described as having been vulgarized, but their formulators, acute social theorists, might have been expected to realize that and how such a process would take place and to design their doctrines specifically for such vulgarization. Of all the doctrines in an area, shouldn't they present the one which, after being vulgarized, turned out best or most nearly true? At the very least they should have taken significant precautions against distortion and misuse of their views, we now can say with hindsight. Lesser thinkers too might appropriately concern themselves with the nature of their possible effects. Since wide-scale distortions get based upon secondary descriptions, there is one precaution I can take: to ask that no reader summarize this book's contents or present slogans or catchwords from it, no school give examinations on the material it contains.* The trickled-down philosophy is not worth following.

* Some earlier writers, Leo Strauss tells us, followed another course, disguising their doctrines under a plausible surface so that only the most diligent and intelligent readers could discover what they actually meant. However, while that might prevent distortions of their "true" doctrine, it could not prevent misuses of the readily available one on the surface. In any case, that method could not do as a way of presenting a philosophy that prized transparency of expression and response to reality. Of course—it would be clever to notice—if *that* were only the *surface* doctrine of this book, then there could consistently be another one presented underneath. But there isn't.

25

The Zigzag of Politics

WE WANT our individual lives to express our conceptions of reality (and of responsiveness to that); so too we want the institutions demarcating our lives together to express and saliently symbolize our desired mutual relations. Democratic institutions and the liberties coordinate with them are not simply effective means toward controlling the powers of government and directing these toward matters of joint concern; they themselves express and symbolize, in a pointed and official way, our equal human dignity, our autonomy and powers of self-direction. We vote, although we are cognizant of the minuscule probability that our own actual vote will have some decisive effect on the outcome, in part as an expression and symbolic affirmation of our status as autonomous and self-governing beings whose considered judgments or even opinions have to be given weight equal to those of others. That symbolism is important to us. Within the operation of democratic institutions, too, we want expressions of the values that concern us and bind us together. The libertarian position I once propounded now seems to me seriously

inadequate, in part because it did not fully knit the humane considerations and joint cooperative activities it left room for more closely
into its fabric. It neglected the symbolic importance of an official
political concern with issues or problems, as a way of marking their
importance or urgency, and hence of expressing, intensifying, channeling, encouraging, and validating our private actions and concerns
toward them. Joint goals that the government ignores completely—it
is different with private or family goals—tend to appear unworthy of
our joint attention and hence to receive little. There are some things
we choose to do together through government in solemn marking of
our human solidarity, served by the fact that we do them together in
this official fashion and often also by the content of the action itself.*

"It is all very well," someone might say, "to mark human solidarity through official action, but we do that through respecting the
rights of individuals not to have their peaceful lives interfered with,
not to be murdered, etc., and this is sufficient expression of our
human respect for our fellow citizens; not only is there no need to
interfere any more greatly in citizens' lives in order to bind them more
closely to their fellows, that interference with individual autonomy
itself denotes a lack of respect for it." Yet our concern for individual
autonomy and liberty too is itself in part an expressive concern. We
believe these valuable not simply because of the particular actions
they enable someone to choose to perform, or the goods they enable
him to acquire, but because of the ways they enable him to engage
in pointed and elaborate self-expressive and self-symbolizing activities that further elaborate and develop the person. A concern for the
expression and symbolization of values that can best and most pointedly, not to mention most efficiently, be expressed jointly and
officially—that is, politically—is continuous with a concern for individual self-expression. There are many sides of ourselves that seek
symbolic self-expression, and even if the personal side were to be
given priority, there is no reason to grant it sole sway. If symbolically
expressing something is a way of intensifying its reality, we will not
want to truncate the political realm so as to truncate the reality of our

---

* In these remarks I do not mean to be working out an alternative theory to the one
in *Anarchy, State, and Utopia,* or to be maintaining as much of that theory as
possible consistent with the current material either; I am just indicating one major
area—there may be others—where that theory went wrong.

social solidarity and humane concern for others. I do not mean to imply that the public realm is only a matter of joint self-expression; we wish also by this actually to accomplish something and make things different, and we would not find some policies adequately expressive of solidarity with others if we believed they would not serve to help or sustain them. The libertarian view looked solely at the purpose of government, not at its *meaning*; hence, it took an unduly narrow view of purpose, too.

Joint political action does not merely symbolically express our ties of concern, it also *constitutes* a relational tie itself. The relational stance, in the political realm, leads us to want to express and instantiate ties of concern to our fellows. And if helping those in *need*, as compared to further bettering the situation of those already well off, counts as relationally more intense and enduring from *our* side and from the side of the receivers also, then the relational stance can explain what puzzles utilitarianism, *viz.*, why a concern for bettering others' situation concentrates especially upon the needy. If manna descended from heaven to improve the situation of the needy, all without our aid, we would have to find another way to jointly express and intensify our relational ties.

But don't people have a right not to feel ties of solidarity and concern, and if so, how can the political society take seriously its symbolic expression of what may not be there? By what right does it express for others what they themselves choose not to? These others should feel—they would be better human beings if they felt—ties of solidarity and concern for fellow citizens (and for fellow human beings, perhaps also for fellow living things), although they do have a right not to feel this. (People sometimes have a right not to do or feel something even though they should; they have the right to choose.) Their fellow citizens, though, may choose to speak for them to cover up that lack of concern and solidarity—whether or not the people themselves realize they are *lacking* something. This covering up for them may be done out of politeness, or because of the importance to the others of a joint public affirmation of concern and solidarity, if only so they won't be forced to notice how uncaring and inhumane some of their compatriots are.

To be sure, this joint public affirmation is not simply verbal; those spoken for may have to pay taxes to help support the programs it involves. (That a fig leaf was created to cover the shame of their unconcern does not mean they do not have to help pay for it.) The complete absence of any symbolic public expression and marking of caring and solidarity would leave the rest of us bereft of a society validating human relatedness. "Well, why don't those who want and need such a society voluntarily contribute to pay for its public programs rather than taxing the others, who don't care anything about it?" But a program thus supported by many people's voluntary contributions, worthy though it might be, would not constitute the society's solemn marking and symbolic validation of the importance and centrality of those ties of concern and solidarity. That can occur only through its official joint action, speaking in the name of the whole. The point is not simply to accomplish the particular purpose—that might be done through private contributions alone—or to get the others to pay too—that could occur through stealing the necessary funds from them—but also to speak solemnly in everyone's name, in the name of the society, about what it holds dear.

A particular individual might prefer to speak only for himself. But to live in a society and to identify with it necessarily lays you open to being ashamed of things for which you are not personally responsible—wars of oppression or subverting of foreign governments—and to being proud of things you yourself have not done. A society sometimes speaks in our names. We could satisfy the people who object to the joint public expression of caring and solidarity and their attendant programs by eliminating such expressions, but this would leave the rest of us ashamed of our society, whose public voice of concern is silent. That silence would then speak for us.

"Just stop identifying with the society, then! You then won't have to be ashamed of what it does or doesn't do or say." To accommodate the objector to the public program, then, not only must we thwart our desire and need to jointly mark what we hold to be most central about our interrelations—a desire and need that are continuous with those for personal self-expression—we must stop identifying with our society despite all this means for our emotional life and sense of ourselves. This cost is too great.

If a democratic majority desires to jointly and symbolically express its most solemn ties of concern and solidarity, the minority who prefer differently will have to participate sufficiently to be spoken for. That majority too, though, might express its ties of concern and solidarity also toward this minority by not pressing it to go quite as far as the majority itself alone would wish.

More pointedly, I think someone who conscientiously objects on moral grounds to the *goals* of a public policy should be allowed by the society to opt out of that policy insofar as this is possible, even though the rest would wish to include that person in their joint symbolic affirmation. A recent example in the United States is a war to which much of the population morally objected; a current example is the aborting of fetuses, which some portion of the population finds akin to murder. When such things are done or funded through the political system, everyone is willy-nilly an accomplice. Some propose removing anything morally controversial from the political realm, leaving it for private endeavor, but this would prevent the majority from jointly and publicly affirming its values. A more discriminate alternative is to allow those who morally object to such programs to opt out of participating in them. We do not want to allow objections that are frivolous, and if we allowed people merely to hold back tax payments toward such programs, there would be a large problem of assessing the sincerity of such objections. So a system might be instituted in which a person could opt out of paying taxes for some programs he found morally objectionable if he substituted somewhat more than that (perhaps 5 percent more) in tax payments toward some other public program. Even given this financial assurance of seriousness, we might worry about allowing conscientious objectors to opt out, for the political process is served when they work seriously to change the policy they object to, and their incentive might be diminished if they were no longer personally implicated. However, this consideration should be subsidiary, I think, to the general principle that if we at all can, we should avoid compelling people to participate in aims they find morally objectionable or heinous. (If some anarchists morally objected to participating in the state at all, we might allow them to contribute 5 percent above the tax they otherwise would have to pay to some from a list of specified private charities—and perhaps we can ignore their complaints about having to file with the state proof that they have done this.) All this may seem like merely symbolic bookkeeping—does someone who earmarks a contribution to a joint charity affect the resultant allocation?—yet even such symbolism can be extremely important to us.

The bonds of concern for others may involve not simply symbolically expressive and (it is hoped) effective policies through the general tax system, but also particular limitations of liberty concerning kinds of action. To take one example, consider the case of discrimination. What might be tolerable if done by some idiosyncratic crank—someone who discriminates against redheads, say—becomes intolerable when a large portion of the society discriminates to the considerable detriment of the very same group, especially when some significant portion of their self-identity resides in that trait or group membership. Hence—concerning blacks, women, or homosexuals, for instance—there is justification for antidiscrimination laws in employment, public accommodations, rental or sale of dwelling units, etc. A concern for generality and neutrality then transforms these into laws against discrimination on the basis of race, sex, sexual preference, national origins, etc., even though the rare discrimination against others does not cause them any great burden. It is not necessary to decide whether there is a right to discriminate that gets overridden when such discrimination is prevelant enough to constitute a significant burden to a group, or whether there is no such right yet some rare discriminations are too trivial in their effects to warrant systematic legal interventions which too have their costs and effects.*

* We might be led, even, to weigh limits on a liberty as important as freedom of speech and assembly. Consider KKK members in white costume marching through neighborhoods largely populated by blacks, people in Nazi uniforms with swastika banners marching through largely Jewish neighborhoods, and marchers through Native American Indian reservations, Asian-American communities, Armenian neighborhoods, or significantly gay neighborhoods, with similarly pointed and offensive banners. Must the residents in their home neighborhoods be asked to endure such declaiming and flaunting of support for previously widespread evil (and illegal) actions—murderous, enslaving, genocidal, persecutory—directed at a group membership that is part of their very self-conception? Must we simply hope that other peaceful citizens from outside will express solidarity with these victimized groups by sitting athwart the path of those marchers to bar their way, showing a concern great enough to incur arrest and jail sentences for obstructing that march? Or can we formulate specific principles whose scope is "tailored" to this very kind of situation, in order to legally bar such incursions, while mindful still of our general and strong commitment to the free interplay of opinion within the society?

Since ties of concern and solidarity can range from caring for the destitute all the way to love of one's neighbor, how extensive and intense will be the ties that get expressed in the public political realm? No principle draws that line. It will depend upon the extent and range of the general population's actual feelings of solidarity and concern, and their felt need to give these symbolic political expression. Ties of solidarity and concern, however, are not the only things which we might wish to see solemnly marked and expressed in the joint political realm. Which values is it most important to express and pursue and symbolize in that realm?

Political theorists often are attracted to "positions" in politics, and they bemoan the lack of theoretical consistency in democratic electorates, who first place one party in power and then, after some years, place another. American writers sometimes look wistfully to the greater ideological purity of European parties, but there too we find the voters alternating in power social-democratic and conservative parties. The voters know what they are doing.

Let us suppose that there are multiple competing values that can be fostered, encouraged, and realized in the political realm: liberty, equality for previously unequal groups, communal solidarity, individuality, self-reliance, compassion, cultural flowering, national power, aiding extremely disadvantaged groups, righting past wrongs, charting bold new goals (space exploration, conquering disease), mitigating economic inequalities, the fullest education for all, eliminating discrimination and racism, protecting the powerless, privacy and autonomy for its citizens, aid to foreign countries, etc. (Justice, too, might simply be one further important value—perhaps adequately captured by the "entitlement theory" I presented some years ago,* perhaps not—but in any case one that sometimes could be overridden or diminished in trade-offs.) Not all of these worthy goals can be pursued with full energy and means, and perhaps these goals are theoretically unreconcilable also, in that not all good things can be adjusted together into a harmonious package. (This latter point has been stressed especially in the writings of Isaiah Berlin.)

Each political party, then, will have a package of proposals that includes, with rough consistency, some but not all of these goals; they

---

* *Anarchy, State, and Utopia*, Chapter 7.

will differ in which goals they select and also in how highly they rank some of the ones they hold in common. A "principled" position in politics will involve such a selection and ranking of some of the goals, along with a theoretical rationale for this selection and a criticism of other selections.

It is *impossible* to include all of the goals in some consistent manner, and even if one could give the appearance of this—by ranking some goal 93rd, for example—nevertheless, some goals would not be salient enough to be seen (or acted upon) as part of the position. However, many goals that cannot be pursued together at the same time can be reconciled over time or at least combined, first by pursuing one for some years, then another some years later. Yet no party platform says that such and such goals will be pursued for four years, then other ones afterward. The term of office is not long enough to make this appropriate; there is time enough in the next electoral period to announce those other goals.

In fact, however, the party in power will not be able to shift significantly to other goals when that time comes. It will have mobilized constituencies to support the very goals it has been pursuing, constituencies whose self-interest may well lie in the further pursuit of those goals. To renounce these goals during the coming period or to significantly downplay them would require building a very different electoral constituency—a difficult task. Moreover, some of the programs undertaken in good faith in pursuit of goals will not have worked out very well; there will be unanticipated unpleasant side effects, unforeseen difficulties in achieving the goals, etc. The response of the party will be to pursue those programs all the more intensively; it will have mobilized constituencies for those very programs; some part of the party's apparatus will have careers involved in those programs or in maintaining a high public estimation of them—that is part of their "record of accomplishment," after all. For this reason, it would even be extremely difficult for the party to now use very different means to (continue to) pursue those very goals, drastically curtailing or transforming the programs it has instituted.

On the other hand, the programs may have worked quite well; the goals they were designed to achieve may have been advanced appreciably. How much will count as "enough"? When will it be time to turn to other goals, ones which are now more urgent either because of changed circumstances or because of the recent progress made on the first goals? With broad political goals, it is safe to say that always there will remain some people who think it important to pursue them still further, perhaps in a way that involves significant "structural" changes in the society, while others will think enough has already been done, either because different goals now seem more pressing to them or because, in any case, they do not want those previous goals pursued to any greater extent.

The most active participants in the political party, however, will come late to turning to other goals; they may be among the very last. For it may be the fact that these participants give these goals such great priority, greater than most other people do, that attracted them to the party in the first place or made them devote sufficient energy to become politically active, and many of them will have become even more committed to the goals in the course of years of campaigning and working for them, building expertise about them, making careers on them. It is not impossible for them to shift, perhaps, but they will be reluctant to do so, and will see no great need to until emphatically told to do that by the electorate. The party in power will not yet have heard this message.

The electorate I see as being in the following situation: Goals and programs have been pursued for some time by the party in power, and the electorate comes to think that's far enough, perhaps even too far. It's now time to right the balance, to include other goals that have been, recently at least, neglected or given too low a priority, and it's time to cut back on some of the newly instituted programs, to reform or curtail them.

A new party now comes into power with its own new programs, and with a weak enough commitment to the ones recently introduced by the opposition to do some needed alteration of them—perhaps too much, but then there will be an opportunity to redress that, too, sometime later. The party out of power bides its time, revises its programs somewhat, adds some new goals it had not previously pursued which also are not being pursued by the current party in power, and waits for the pendulum to return to its (modified) side. One temptation will be to adhere even more strongly and purely to its old goals, arguing that the party has lost power because they have not pursued these goals thoroughly enough—the British Labour

Party is an example of this—but this misconstrues what the electorate wants.

The electorate wants the zigzag. Sensible folk, they realize that *no* political position will adequately include all of the values and goals one wants pursued in the political realm, so these will have to take turns. The electorate as a whole behaves in this sensible fashion, even if significant numbers of people stay committed to their previous goals and favorite programs come what may. For there may be a significant swing bloc of voters that will shift to new goals and make the difference—that the least ideologically committed voters may determine an election is abhorrent to the view that wishes politics to institute one particular set of principles, yet desirable otherwise—and in any case, a new generation of voters will appear on the scene ready to seek a different balance, eager even to try something new.

This is not a theory that enables us to predict when the next shift will take place. Have things gone far enough, too far? Is it time to turn to neglected tasks and goals? Should we pursue more vigorously what we already have made some progress on? That is for the electorate to decide, and what it decides may well depend in part upon what it hears articulated during a political campaign, and by whom. (It would be desirable to think of ways to help it decide more thoughtfully.) The task for a party that leaves power and moves into opposition is not to repeat its previous position unchanged but to observe with some understanding and even sympathy the pursuit of other goals worthy enough to move a considerable portion of the electorate, and meanwhile to articulate its own vision, building upon old or even new goals it feels a special kinship with, in time helping the public to formulate its vision too of the next zag.

As individuals we might choose to shift at a different time, earlier or later, than a voting majority has. However, we each should be unfanatical enough to admit that after *some* time it would be appropriate for society to shift to energetically pursuing goals other than the ones we currently most favor, and we should be modest enough to think that deciding when that time has come, and what the balance currently should be among worthy goals that cannot all be combined or pursued energetically together, is not something that should be decided by any one person alone, ourselves included. Is it simply that a democratic electorate, living through one period's pursuit of goals and hearing other visions articulated, knowing personally a fuller range of consequences of policies, is a better judge of the appropriate current balance than any one person alone? Or is it that what balance *is* appropriate for them then depends in part upon where they want to go next? In any case, given a choice between permanently institutionalizing the particular content of any group of political principles thus far articulated—I mean the types of principles meant to specify what goals should be pursued *within* a democracy, not the ones that underlie a democracy itself by providing its rationale and justification—and the zigzag process of democratic politics, one where the electorate can have been presented with those same principles too among others, I'll vote for the zigzag every time.

26

Philosophy's Life

IT IS often thought that there are only two rational ways to arrive at new ends and goals that we do not already accept: first, by discovering they are effective means to existing ends of ours—deliberation is always about means, Aristotle said, never about ends—and second, by refining and recontouring some existing ends to fit better with still other existing ends that similarly get recontoured to fit—what some philosophers have called "cospecification." However, there is another rational way to arrive at new ends, this time at a deeper level. We can examine the diverse ends and goals we already have to discover what further ends and values might underlie and justify them or provide them with a unified grounding. In this way we can be led to quite new and unsuspected ends, surprising in their implications. We also can be led to modify or even reject some of the ends and goals we began with, including some we had been attempting to understand and ground. Compare the way adopting an explanatory scientific theory can lead one to modify or even reject some of the data or lower-level theories this theory initially was introduced to explain. (For example, it is not exactly Kepler's laws of planetary motion—but modifications instead—that Newton's laws yield and explain, although that was one place his task began.) Investigating our goals and ends philosophically, then, provides a powerful tool for advancing to new ones rationally, and at a new or deeper level.

Somebody "has a philosophy"—we ordinarily say—when she has a thoughtful view of what is important, a view of her major ends and goals and of the means appropriate to reaching these. A coherent view of aims and goals can help to guide someone's life without being invoked explicitly. Most often, it will not be. Rather, a person will devote some of her general alertness to monitoring how her life is proceeding. Only when she is deviating significantly from what her philosophy calls for will it be brought to conscious attention. A philosophy of life need not make life overintellectualized.

A person may feel that she and her life are richer than any theory. She might formulate a philosophy that leaves room for this feeling too, one that holds it is important sometimes to be spontaneous and not apply any maxim, including that very one. Later, a time she lives spontaneously would fall under the maxim without being any ap-plying of it. She could then well feel she encompasses multitudes beyond any theory. This might not take the point seriously enough, however. Perhaps life itself defies formulating any general theory to cover it all. Having a philosophy of life is not the same, of course, as having a general and complete theory of what is important in life. Would such an encompassing theory be possible? Even an elaborate theory will mention at most—let us be hyperbolic here—a thousand factors, but perhaps complete accuracy will require many times that. Don't the size, scope, and multifariousness of the major Russian novels, and of the body of Shakespeare's plays, show how inadequate any particular theory will have to be? Here I have been thinking of the sheer number of life's aspects and factors as thwarting a com-pletely general theory; there also is the possibility—I do not know of reasons to accept this—that there are particular factors too complex (or too simple?) to be adequately treated by any theory. But recall the earlier point about how the absence of prefixed determinate weights for the dimensions of reality leaves room for free choice.

A philosophy of life might seem insignificant before the phenomenon of life in another way, because the fact of life itself might seem more important than any particular way a life can be. If we imagine scores or points given for the components of a person's existence, where the maximum possible score is 100, being alive might bring fifty points, being human might bring thirty points, being at some reasonable threshold of competence and functioning might bring ten more points, adding up to a total of ninety points thus far. The question of how to live, according to what particular philosophy, would then concern or determine only how many of the remaining ten possible points one would achieve or gain. These remaining ten points would be the ones we could control by our actions, but whether we managed to get six or seven points would be less important than the fact that we already had ninety points, willy-nilly. (Behind these ninety, there might be still other points that are guaranteed, ones for existing or even for being a possible entity.) Any particular choices we made would pale in significance alongside the fact that we are alive and make choices. Thus, it might be important in life not to focus solely upon the discretionary ten points but always to keep in consciousness the major thresholds we and all other persons already have passed without any action on our part at all. (In a dark and cold corner of the universe, wouldn't we feel companionship with *anything* that was alive— provided that it didn't threaten us?) A part, then, of philosophy's advice about the discretionary part of life, the possible 10 percent left, would be to spend some of it focusing upon and appreciating the 90 percent that is already present. Such advice evidences a grasp of life's magnitude and helps with the remaining 10 percent too.

We may feel a need for some further purpose, an ultimate one beyond those we have sketched thus far. It is tempting to imagine this as some further external purpose, another realm our lives are designed to reach afterward, another task we are to perform. Some traditional religious doctrines have hoped for an afterlife, a time and realm in which believers would sit at God's right hand and gaze at his face. Others have complained, with some glee and justification, that these visions, as described, are *boring*. If there *were* another realm, an afterlife, what we would want to do in it would be to explore it, respond to it, relate within it, create, utilizing whatever we had gained thereby, and then perhaps transform ourselves still further, beginning again. Any further realm would be another arena for the spiral of activities. To be sure, it might be a more conducive arena for that spiral, more richly rewarding—the *perfection* of that realm might consist just in its being amenable to the most intense exploring, responding, etc., alone or together—but then it is relevant to point out how far we are from having exhausted this present arena.

My reflections here have not been directed toward some further realm that comes next. But if earthly life *is* followed by a next realm, what we are to do there is the very same type of thing as here—encounter reality and become more real ourselves through a spiral of activities, and together enhance our-relating-to-reality—in the ways that are possible there. (If union with God *were* the goal, that continued existence would be a state for us to explore, respond to, etc., and within it these activities would be exceedingly real.) That further realm might allow a different level of magnitude of these activities, and display novel dimensions of reality, but it would be judged by the very same criterion: the nature of the spiral of activities there and how real we can be. (If further appropriate activities were possible there, these too would be added to the spiral.) Perhaps there *is* a further realm, but its purpose will not be found in a still further one, or if it is, then sooner or later there must be a realm whose purpose is not found in another, further one. And in that realm, wherever it is, it is *this* philosophy that holds.

That would not necessarily mean that this philosophy is to be followed now as well. It is theoretically possible that this present realm is simply a means to acquiring some trait, rather like a trip to the dentist, a realm where now to apply the appropriate final philosophy would curtail the extent of its later application. That philosophy would be right for us sometime—just not now. However, the holiness of everyday life we discussed earlier is a holiness of the present realm. Whether or not there is any further realm in the future, the realm that is present and current is an appropriate arena for living one's final philosophy, for the fullest engagement within the spiral of activities and the pursuit of reality. Some who prize reality have been led by this world's defects to seek reality elsewhere—the Gnostics and some Platonists are examples—but reality here is reality enough. That is what the very greatest works of art, by their own reality, *show* us, even when this is not what some say. The philosophy developed here is not for the final realm alone, though this present realm may well be exactly that. It is to be followed and lived in any realm that is holy.

In our meditation on Giving Everything Its Due, that turned out to mean offering responses *as* something due, or rather offering the acts of responding, exploring, and creating as a celebration of reality, as a love of it. Love of this world is coordinate with love of life. Life is our being in this world. And love of life is our fullest response to being alive, our fullest way of exploring what it is to be alive.

This love of life is continuous with an appreciation of life's energy in its various forms, with the variety and balance and interplay of life in nature. Appreciating this, we will not wantonly exploit animal or plant life; we will take some care to minimize the damage we do. Would an appreciation of the complicated developmental history of the living things we encounter prevent us from making any use of them at all? We cannot survive without doing so—we are part of nature too—but it would be too glib simply to say we also appreciate our lives and their imperatives, and this warrants our using and killing other life forms as a means. Yet as part of nature and its cycles, we can repay our debt for what we take, nourishing and strengthening life, fertilizing the soil with the products of our eating, eventually having the material of our own body, after death, recirculated. What constitutes us is had on loan.

It calms the spirit to see ourselves as part of a vast and continuing natural process. (Recall, for example, sitting beside the ocean, seeing and listening to wave after wave never ending, knowing the ocean's immensity.) To see yourself as a small part of a vast process makes your own death seem not so very significant, unworrisome even. When we identify ourselves with the totality of the vast (apparently) never-ending processes of existence through time, we can find our significance in (being part of) that, and our own particular passing comes to seem to us of passing importance.

But can such significance accrue to us through being part of a vast process, unless we are a necessary or irreplaceable part? How can the significance of that process help us if we are superfluous to it? However, if you take away from the vastness of existence everything that is unnecessary or replaceable, the truncated existence that remains is not nearly as wonderful. The totality of existence and its processes over time is wonderful in part because of its great super-fluity, and so our existence, the existence of kinds of things like us, is a characteristic and valuable part. This existence of ours, moreover, is permeated by the very same scientific laws and ultimate physical material that constitute all the rest of nature; a representative piece of nature, we encapsulate its sweep.

I see people descended from a long sequence of human and animal forebears in an unnumbered train of chance events, accidental encounters, brutal takings, lucky escapes, sustained efforts, migra-tions, survivings of wars and disease. An intricate and improbable concatenation of events was needed to yield each of us, an immense history that gives each person the sacredness of a redwood, each child the whimsy of a secret.

It is a privilege to be a part of the ongoing realm of existing things and processes. When we see and conceive of ourselves *as* a part of those ongoing processes, we identify with the totality and, in the calmness this brings, feel solidarity with all our comrades in existing.

We want nothing other than to live in a spiral of activities and enhance others' doing so, deepening our own reality as we come into contact and relation with the rest, exploring the dimensions of reality, embodying them in ourselves, creating, responding to the full range of the reality we can discern with the fullest reality we possess, becoming a vehicle for truth, beauty, goodness, and holiness, adding our own characteristic bit to reality's eternal processes. And that wanting of nothing else, along with its attendant emotion, is—by the way—what constitutes happiness and joy.

27

A Portrait of the Philosopher as a Young Man

WHEN I was fifteen years old or sixteen I carried around in the streets of Brooklyn a paperback copy of Plato's *Republic,* front cover facing outward. I had read only some of it and understood less, but I was excited by it and knew it was something wonderful. How much I wanted an older person to notice me carrying it and be impressed, to pat me on the shoulder and say . . . I didn't know what exactly.

I sometimes wonder, not without uneasiness, what that young man of fifteen or sixteen would think of what he has grown up to do. I would like to think that with this book he would be pleased.

It now occurs to me to wonder also whether that older person whose recognition and love he sought then might not turn out to be the person he would grow up to become. If we reach adulthood by becoming the parent of our parents, and we reach maturity by finding a fit substitute for parents' love, then by becoming our ideal parent ourselves finally the circle is closed and we reach completeness.

INDEX OF NAMES

About the Author

Robert Nozick, Arthur Kingsley Porter Professor of Philosophy at Harvard University, is the author of *Anarchy, State, and Utopia* (which received a National Book Award) and of *Philosophical Explanations*.